TO MOM AND DAD

Thank you for always supporting me and
not shipping me off to boarding school
when I was a terror in high school.

TO MY SISTER, MEISHA

Thanks for always keeping me grounded by
reminding me that no matter how hard I try,
you'll always be the cooler Chiera.

TO MY INCREDIBLE WIFE, JACKIE

Thank you for relentlessly supporting
my businesses and ideas, especially the
harebrained ones that I wake you up in the
middle of the night to tell you about.

WITH SPECIAL THANKS TO OUR CONTRIBUTORS

Jason Abrahams

Ilona Abramova

Marisa Amorasak

Geoff Anderson

Paul Baguley

Shaun Bond

Nicole Brashear

Kaspars Brencans

Alexandra Brown

Meg Brunson

Craig Campbell

David Chapman

Michelle Chiera

Austin Chu

Maeve Cloherty

Julian Scott Connors

Cate Conroy

Stephanie Crededio

Ron Culp

Ryan D'Souza

Ben Dahl

Chantal Dalton

Jon Davis

Valerie Del Toro

Sydney DeLoach

Robert Drew

Anthony Dulieux

Amanda Elliott

Vladimir Fefer

Jessie Fenton

Tucker Ferwerda

Mark Fitzsimmons

Kenneth Fong

Carolyn S. Fraser

Kristi George

David Ginsburg

Bob Girolamo

Erin Gleason

Kyle Henderick

Julia Hockstein

Michael Hodgdon

Josh Hoffman

Jeff Hogard

Holly Johnson

Ryan Johnson

Matthew Jonas

Lina Khalil

Phoebe King

Arnie Kuenn

George Landes III

Rina Liddle

Andrew Liwanag

Chris Madden

Adam Mankoff

Megan Martin

Ben Meyer

Dirk Mieth

Leah Miranda

Greg Mischio

Dorine Mooney

Robert Lee Mullowney III

Nikki Nardick

Jay Nash

Jonathan Ng

Andrew Nuno

Wilhelm Ong

Igor Onyshchenko

Ben Oren

Maddy Osman

Nick Oswald

Dan Paloma

Kaylyn Parker

Rachel Pedersen

Charlene Peters

Daniella Peting

Ashley Poynter

Brad Putney

Meg Raiano

Terry Reeves

Megan Robinson

Scott A. Rogerson

Chris Romero

Mindi Rosser

Barbara Rozgonyi

Scott Salwolke

Allison Schaffer

Marly Schuman

Bill Slawski

Joe Slepski

Brian Sly

Bob Spoerl

Sam Sprague

Brett Swensen

Sabrina Torres

Kyle J. Volenik

Rob Watts

Todd Weitzman

Christine Pietryla Wetzler

Brian Yaro

Aaron Zakowski

TABLE OF CONTENTS

INTRODUCTION

This book is a compilation of first-hand insights from 101 digital marketing specialists who are "in the trenches" executing campaigns.

I put this collection of marketing wisdom together because I couldn't find a resource like this one for myself. There are plenty of books out there that share only *one* person's insights about digital marketing. This is a book where you'll find **101** digital marketing specialists sharing their favorite tools, tips, tactics, and predictions for the future.

This book contains advice on diverse digital marketing specializations: Search Engine Optimization, Google AdWords, Facebook Ads, Social Media Marketing, Content Marketing, PR, Email Marketing, and Affiliate Marketing. You'll gain a comprehensive overview of digital marketing and how to be successful running various types of digital marketing campaigns.

The specialists featured in this book represent a broad range of roles. You'll find insights from Fortune 500 in-house marketers, B2B marketers, B2C marketers, small business freelancers, agency owners, and consultants who work with some of the largest brands in the world.

All the contributors in this book took the time to share valuable insights about their successes and mistakes in digital marketing, including their favorite tactics and tools. They've also included information about how to best contact them, which I highly recommend you take advantage of.

There isn't a wrong way to read this book. Feel free to skip around the book to the digital marketing specializations that apply most to you or read the book cover to cover for a comprehensive look into what expert digital marketers are doing across a broad spectrum of digital marketing specializations.

I recommend reading the "simple explanation" section at the beginning of each chapter. This section will explain key concepts and terminology that will provide important reference points for the contributors' responses.

As you're reading, keep in mind that although each of the digital marketers in this book are speaking to a single specialization, effective digital marketing often requires the use of multiple channels to achieve a goal. Think about how a tactic in one channel might support a digital marketing campaign in another. For example, a Social Media Marketing tactic might help to improve your Email Marketing. Or a Google AdWords tip may be applicable to Facebook Ads as well. Also, think about how channels can work together, for example, how Content Marketing and Search Engine Optimization can be used in tandem for maximum effect.

A note on marketing funnels: throughout this book, you'll see contributors mentioning marketing "funnels." A marketing funnel is the set of steps that a prospective customer goes through before reaching a desired "conversion" such as completing a lead-generation form or purchasing a product from a company. At the beginning of the process (the top of the funnel) a lot of people will take a first step in interacting with a company. Then, as people continue along and more interactions with the company are taken, some will drop out, and the funnel narrows. Eventually, a small number of people will perform the desired action (conversion) at the bottom of the funnel. This is an important marketing concept that is referenced in various contexts in this book.

If you've never set up a digital marketing campaign, this book will give you the information to set yourself up for success. If you're an expert marketer, you'll obtain fresh insights and recommendations to improve your day-to-day work. If you're somewhere in the middle, you'll get the best of both worlds.

Happy marketing!

MATT CHIERA

CHAPTER 1
SEARCH ENGINE OPTIMIZATION (SEO)

A SIMPLE EXPLANATION OF SEO

Search Engine Optimization (SEO) is the process of affecting the online visibility of a website or online property in a search engine's organic (free) listings.

It's important to note that SEO can stand for Search Engine Optimization *as well as* Search Engine Optimizer—often marketers will refer to Search Engine Optimization specialists as "SEOs."

The goal of SEO is often to drive people in a company's or organization's target market from a search engine into the company's website so that the customers will perform a conversion—a desired action like purchasing a product or filling out a contact form.

Companies and organizations typically want their website to appear in top listings in search engines for keywords (search terms) related to their products or services. For example, a company that sells black denim jeans would benefit from being at the top of the search results for people searching for "black denim jeans" in Google. The searcher is looking for the company's product and may purchase from the company if their website is found on Google for that search term.

There's an old SEO joke that "the best place to hide a dead body is in page two of Google's search results...because no one ever looks there." As far as rankings are concerned, SEOs are primarily concerned with getting their company on the *first* page of Google's search results.

Primarily, SEO is geared toward getting traffic from Google, since Google is the most popular search engine. However, SEO experts may also work to get traffic from Bing, Yahoo, and other lesser-used search engines.

How do search engines work? Search engines send out programs called "crawlers" (sometimes called "spiders" or "bots") that gather information about all the content they can find on the Internet. The crawlers bring this data back to the search engine to update their "index" of Internet content. That index is then fed through an algorithm that tries to match all that data with the searcher's query. The search engine's goal is to show the highest-quality and most relevant information possible for the query.

There are many factors that determine whether or not a website will rank for a given keyword and therefore show up in the search engine results page (SERP).

Often, SEOs employ a combination of tools and tactics to drive organic traffic. For example, they may improve a website to be more SEO friendly, publish blog posts and high-quality content, or accrue links to a website from third-party sources.

Increasingly, SEO also refers to optimizing an organization's information in the SERP itself. Google and other popular search engines allow companies to display information like their address, hours of operation, images, contact information, and reviews on the search engine results page. This allows people to view important company information in the search engine without the need to visit the company's website or other online properties like social media pages. Modern SEOs now need to ensure that a company is not only gaining organic traffic from search engines to their website and online properties, but also that the company displays up-to-date and relevant information on the search engine results page as well.

The leading search engines are always working to improve their technology to crawl the web more deeply and return better results to users. Therefore, SEOs must constantly be observant of search engine updates and change their tactics accordingly.

SEO SPECIALISTS
SOUND OFF

RYAN JOHNSON

SEO PROGRAM MANAGER, RICOH USA

HOW DO YOU DETERMINE THE EFFECTIVENESS OF AN SEO CAMPAIGN?

A quality SEO campaign has to have established and measurable business objectives in service of a larger goal. "Thought leadership" is not a measurable objective, nor is "awareness." Objectives may include an increase in revenue from organic search (and the ROI of your SEO program), increases in organic search traffic to specific pages, increases in non-branded organic traffic, or a larger share of voice in organic keyword rankings versus competitors. Start by establishing a time frame for the project and an overarching goal, and then apply measurable objectives to that goal. Follow this by developing tactics to reach that goal. As the project proceeds, measure progress toward objectives (and the goal) rather than comparing this month to last month. Thinking long term helps manage expectations and keeps everyone focused on the big picture rather than panicking because August had less traffic than July.

WHAT IS THE SINGLE MOST EFFECTIVE SEO TACTIC YOU'VE LEARNED?

The single most effective SEO tactic is research. Research the topics in your industry that are trending. What topics are oversaturated? What questions are customers asking on sites like Quora? What keywords are your customers using to describe your products and services? Are they the same words you would use? Too much web development and content creation is still ego-driven: "I like this, therefore it is good." A data-driven approach to your site design and content creation will result in quality traffic.

IF YOU COULD CARRY ONLY FIVE TOOLS IN YOUR SEO TOOLKIT, WHAT WOULD THEY BE?

Screaming Frog, SEMrush, Moz, BrightEdge, and Google Search Console.

WHAT'S THE SINGLE BIGGEST MISTAKE YOU SEE PEOPLE MAKE IN SEO?

The number-one mistake in SEO is that brands use too much vague or branded language on their websites. It is important to remember that a robot has to read the website, understand it, and deliver results to people looking for whatever it is that you sell. Stop focusing so much on the branded terms you came up with on your corporate retreat. Ask yourself, *How would I describe this product/service/business to someone at a barbeque? What words would I use?* Those are the words that need to be on your website. SEO rule number one: think like a human, not a corporation.

WHAT ADVICE WOULD YOU GIVE TO PEOPLE WHO ARE LOOKING TO RUN SUCCESSFUL SEO CAMPAIGNS?

Start by thinking about what success looks like. Why do you want SEO for your site? What would you like to see happen? Successful SEO campaigns ask these questions up front and then establish specific and measurable goals over an extended time period. SEO is slow growing—like an interest bearing account—so don't expect results overnight. Smart campaigns start like this: At the end of (one month/six months/one year), we are going to be improved in (thought leadership/awareness/conversions). We are going to prove it by measuring an X percent increase in X, Y and Z. To get to those goals, these are the tactics we are going to employ . . .

HOW DO YOU THINK SEO WILL CHANGE OVER THE NEXT FEW YEARS?

As voice search becomes prevalent, successful brands will create content to answer very specific questions relating to their areas of expertise and business. There is a glut of content available, and most brands are creating content that is too general, covers topics that have been addressed a thousand times already, and has no real chance of ranking or getting any attention. Gaining attention and rankings will result from specificity and laser focus in content and creating content that very clearly answers one question for a customer.

LEARN MORE ABOUT RYAN

I have over a decade of digital marketing and SEO experience working with small local brands and Fortune 500 companies and maintain a busy schedule writing for industry blogs and speaking at national conferences.

It is my goal to make SEO and digital marketing concepts simple and easy to apply. Many businesses may not need a large agency or a new website, and I want to empower businesses with the knowledge to take their digital marketing to the next level.

⊕ WWW.RSJ8000.COM

BEN OREN

HOW DO YOU DETERMINE THE EFFECTIVENESS OF AN SEO CAMPAIGN?

Many marketers would claim an SEO campaign successful if it simply improves search engine rankings for certain keywords and/or drives an increase in organic traffic, since they do not control the factors typically associated with conversion (such as lead quality). However, in my view, to declare an SEO campaign successful, it's necessary to meet the objectives established with the client. These may be limited to improved visibility for chosen keywords but typically include higher lead volume or increased sales (for e-commerce sites).

Excluding campaigns intended purely to increase exposure, all other SEO campaigns need to factor in key performance indicators (KPIs) like conversion rate, number of pages viewed, and bounce rate. Monitoring these continuously ensures we're doing more than increasing organic traffic—we're getting the visitors that matter. If the keyword and competitor research is conducted thoroughly, any gaps in user experience (UX), pricing, and quality should surface early in the process and influence keyword selection initially. Proper initial keyword research is the foundation for setting clear expectations with the client.

WHAT IS THE SINGLE MOST EFFECTIVE SEO TACTIC YOU'VE LEARNED?

Hands down, the single most effective SEO tactic I've learned is the importance of deep and comprehensive on-page optimization. SEO is composed of two main areas: on-page and off-page. There is hardly any doubt about the importance of links for SEO, which is why most marketers spend considerable time and resources to increase the volume of inbound links. This is done through a variety of methods, including blogger outreach and content creation.

Conversely, on-page optimization is often looked at only superficially at the onset of a project, whereas its importance has grown exponentially with the introduction of artificial intelligence (AI) and the evolution of the Google "RankBrain" AI algorithm. Fixing errors in the site's code and improving the internal link structure, site speed, and crawl budget are all tasks that, when tackled effectively, can significantly improve both Google's bot assessment of a website and how users respond to it. This, in turn, helps rankings since user signals are becoming more and more important to rankings.

IF YOU COULD CARRY ONLY FIVE TOOLS IN YOUR SEO TOOLKIT, WHAT WOULD THEY BE?

The first tool would be Screaming Frog. It's one of the most user-friendly and high-quality crawlers out there today, and it has undergone significant improvement during the past year. The second tool is Ahrefs, which enables a thorough analysis of a client's link profile, ranked keywords, and more. The following two tools are intended for research: SEMrush and SimilarWeb will help you conduct competitor research at a higher level, assuming you opt for the paid version (the free version is quite basic). Finally, I'd be remiss if I didn't mention Google's tools: Google Analytics and Search Console. I treat these as a single tool, since they're connected and feed off of each other constantly. Using Google Analytics and Search Console in unison will enable you to analyze site traffic and site health.

WHAT'S THE SINGLE BIGGEST MISTAKE YOU SEE PEOPLE MAKE IN SEO?

It's not actually a professional mistake. It's a logical failure. Many marketers focus on sending detailed, comprehensive reports showing improved rankings; however, if this doesn't directly translate to leads and sales for the client, something is wrong. Essentially, those marketers are placing a disproportionate emphasis on rankings and incoming traffic, though these factors may not actually result in higher revenue. In the real world, traffic is not enough: Take the time to learn your client's endeavors and holistic objectives in order to build a truly effective strategy based on more than rankings.

WHAT ADVICE WOULD YOU GIVE TO PEOPLE WHO ARE LOOKING TO RUN SUCCESSFUL SEO CAMPAIGNS?

Research, and then research some more. Research should precede proposals, objectives, and any implementation. Conduct a thorough audit of your client's website to map all current problems and make a game plan to address each and every one according to clear priorities. This should yield thorough on-page optimization to kick off the project. Once the project is ongoing, divert your efforts from research to finding creative methods to earn links while continuously monitoring site metrics, rankings, and organic traffic volume.

HOW DO YOU THINK SEO WILL CHANGE OVER THE NEXT FEW YEARS?

Don't worry—I don't think inbound links are going to become obsolete anytime soon. I do, however, think that massive changes are already underway, and marketers need to adapt quickly. First, I predict that the importance of UX will continue to rise, as the algorithm places greater emphasis on mobile metrics. Moreover, AI is going to determine most rankings. Manipulation of the algorithm will be a thing of the past, since there will be multiple algorithms capable of self-correcting in real time for every single keyword, user, industry, country, and language. Google will continue to refine its predictive search offering according to our search patterns and interests, making search results more and more personalized.

LEARN MORE ABOUT BEN

I'm a multidisciplinary digital marketing expert with over twelve years of combined in-house and agency experience. I specialize in leading technical SEO, marketing strategy, and conversion at organizations ranging from start-ups to Fortune 500 companies. After heading two tech start-ups, one in retail and the second in marketing automation and reporting, I joined Bouclair as Director of Search & Innovation. I'm an avid contributor to the global online marketing community, publishing regularly on leading professional publications such as *Search Engine Journal*.

🌐 WWW.BENOREN.COM
💼 WWW.LINKEDIN.COM/IN/BENOREN

PAUL BAGULEY

MANAGING DIRECTOR, INTERNET SALES DRIVE LIMITED

HOW DO YOU DETERMINE THE EFFECTIVENESS OF AN SEO CAMPAIGN?

To determine how well an SEO campaign is working, we use a few methods. The first one is to check Google Analytics. We review the traffic coming from Google organic and other search engines and ensure that organic traffic is increasing month over month. Also, we review the traffic to make sure users are engaging with the website—so we know we're getting the right type of traffic and not just traffic for the sake of traffic. We assess this by reviewing bounce rate, time on site, and the number of pages and conversions. Another factor is keyword rankings: our goal is to show progress from keywords moving closer to page one and then correlate the value of these rankings to our client's traffic and conversions.

WHAT IS THE SINGLE MOST EFFECTIVE SEO TACTIC YOU'VE LEARNED?

It is important that when you get traffic via your keywords that the customer is the right one and that they land on a web page that will make them convert. That is why having a page that fits a purpose for one or multiple search terms is important—that can attract the search engine and attract the user to engage. This page should be optimized with a good meta title, H1 heading, banner, and useful content with a call-to-action.

IF YOU COULD CARRY ONLY FIVE TOOLS IN YOUR SEO TOOLKIT, WHAT WOULD THEY BE?

I use Moz Pro for its technical site audits and on-page recommendations. I've used Raven Tools for many years now; it's a great toolset for all-around SEO. Other tools I use are Screaming Frog, Advanced Web Ranking, and Google Search Console.

WHAT'S THE SINGLE BIGGEST MISTAKE YOU SEE PEOPLE MAKE IN SEO?

The most common mistake is just not having the fundamentals of SEO implemented correctly or even missing, such as having an issue with a robots.txt or an XML sitemap. We have new clients who have websites where no SEO has been put in place, and therefore they have issues like duplicate meta titles and meta descriptions. I feel it's important to have a website with the basics correct before you can move on to the next level and start bringing traffic to your website that will convert.

WHAT ADVICE WOULD YOU GIVE TO PEOPLE WHO ARE LOOKING TO RUN SUCCESSFUL SEO CAMPAIGNS?

Don't try and do everything. Focus on a specific area of your website and work on that initially to bring traffic to the site. Do optimize your site but don't try and rank for everything all in one go. Work on a service or a certain product category, get movement from there, and then build your SEO campaign step by step.

HOW DO YOU THINK SEO WILL CHANGE OVER THE NEXT FEW YEARS?

With the updates in Google over the last few years, we've seen the role of SEO change and evolve. I see this happening again and believe SEO is still going to grow and move with industry changes. With voice search becoming a bigger player in our field, as well as other new developments in local and augmented reality, new challenges will arise. SEOs will need to adapt to be successful.

LEARN MORE ABOUT PAUL

My name is Paul Baguley and I am the Managing Director of an SEO agency based in Nottingham, England, called Internet Sales Drive. I have been in digital marketing for over eight years, helping UK businesses build traffic and making conversions to their websites.

🌐 WWW.INTERNETSALESDRIVE.COM
✉ PAUL@INTERNETSALESDRIVE.COM
in WWW.LINKEDIN.COM/IN/BAGULEYPAUL
🐦 @BAGULEYPAUL

VLADIMIR FEFER

SEO MANAGER

HOW DO YOU DETERMINE THE EFFECTIVENESS OF AN SEO CAMPAIGN?

Everyone likes to look at overall traffic and revenue from organic, and those are both critically important. But those are lagging indicators of whether you're doing the right things to improve SEO. I like to look at entrances split by pages or groups of pages. I pay attention to whether the on-site improvements we've made have driven more traffic to that page or group of pages so that we can either do more (scale the tactic site-wide) or move on to other improvements.

WHAT IS THE SINGLE MOST EFFECTIVE SEO TACTIC YOU'VE LEARNED?

I work with large sites. Fixing site architecture—that is, improving internal links, navigation, and information architecture—is quite often the biggest win for sites with more than one million URLs, because it will improve crawling and indexing. You want to make it as easy as possible for the search engines to parse and understand your site.

IF YOU COULD CARRY ONLY FIVE TOOLS IN YOUR SEO TOOLKIT, WHAT WOULD THEY BE?

You need good site crawling tools, either Screaming Frog or Sitebulb (a newer one that I really like). If you're enterprise, you can probably afford DeepCrawl. You need a tool for research, and besides Google's Keyword Planner, I recommend Ahrefs and SEMrush. And you need Excel to put it all together.

WHAT'S THE SINGLE BIGGEST MISTAKE YOU SEE PEOPLE MAKE IN SEO?

People always think SEO doesn't take time or that it's a one-off activity. If you're doing SEO right, you're in it for the long term. It's a journey of a thousand optimizations that accumulate, but if you do it right, that traffic continues for a long time.

WHAT ADVICE WOULD YOU GIVE TO PEOPLE WHO ARE LOOKING TO RUN SUCCESSFUL SEO CAMPAIGNS?

First things first. You have to fix the fundamentals of your site and build from there. It's almost pointless to publish great content and build high authority links to your site if your site is not crawlable by Google because of the way you've structured it or the technology stack (like the latest JavaScript framework that Google can't handle yet).

HOW DO YOU THINK SEO WILL CHANGE OVER THE NEXT FEW YEARS?

I think the integration of AI and machine learning more deeply into Google's algorithms will help improve the overall SEO world because it will be harder to manipulate the SERPs.

LEARN MORE ABOUT VLADIMIR

I've been doing SEO for seven years, and I like digging into large sites to find opportunities. I love talking shop about SEO and can be reached via LinkedIn. I live in Chicago with my wife and three kids.

in WWW.LINKEDIN.COM/IN/VFEFER

CHRIS ROMERO

TECHNICAL SEO DIRECTOR, THE HOTH

HOW DO YOU DETERMINE THE EFFECTIVENESS OF AN SEO CAMPAIGN?

I usually start by looking at whether or not the web property speaks to the end user effectively. If I am looking for "X," does "Y" site provide the info, products, services I need in a way that is engaging? Impressions, click-through rate (CTR), search engine rankings, conversions, site speed, mobile readiness, and on-site content are all factors I look at, as well.

WHAT IS THE SINGLE MOST EFFECTIVE SEO TACTIC YOU'VE LEARNED?

Thirteen hundred words or more of effective copy speaking to a subject matter and answering user intent queries coupled with good link building are the quickest ways to rank any page.

IF YOU COULD CARRY ONLY FIVE TOOLS IN YOUR SEO TOOLKIT, WHAT WOULD THEY BE?

Ahrefs, SEMrush, SEOJet, DeepCrawl, and KWFinder.

WHAT'S THE SINGLE BIGGEST MISTAKE YOU SEE PEOPLE MAKE IN SEO?

The biggest mistakes I see commonly are keyword cannibalization and/or improper URL mapping.

WHAT ADVICE WOULD YOU GIVE TO PEOPLE WHO ARE LOOKING TO RUN SUCCESSFUL SEO CAMPAIGNS?

Map your URLs and keyword/topics according to what Google sees first by entering Google operator "site: domain.com keyword" and then looking at which page comes up first in Google's index. Then work on that page. Start with your easy wins, if you have any (keywords ranking in spaces 4–30), and focus on increasing ranking for those keywords. Make sure your website structure is on point and has good internal linking so that content and link juice will benefit you as much as possible. Also, add fresh content as often as you can.

HOW DO YOU THINK SEO WILL CHANGE OVER THE NEXT FEW YEARS?

I think video and funnel creation/optimization will replace a lot of websites.

LEARN MORE ABOUT CHRIS

I'm a filmmaker/stand-up comedian/actor turned SEO/SEM ten years ago. I've consulted with Universal, Disney, Google Chicago, Chase Reiner, and Clayton Johnson. I'm an avid reader and loving dad with nonstop energy. I enjoy auditing websites and backlink profiles. I oversee three thousand accounts at The HOTH as their technical SEO director. I'm also CEO of Full Scale SEO and an aspiring speaker and author.

- 🌐 THEHOTH.COM/ABOUT
- ✉ CHRIS@THEHOTH.COM
- 💼 WWW.LINKEDIN.COM/IN/ICHRISROMERO
- 🐦 @OHROMERO
- 📘 FACEBOOK.COM/MALE.COMEDIAN
- 📷 @ROMEROMEDIA

BILL SLAWSKI

HOW DO YOU DETERMINE THE EFFECTIVENESS OF AN SEO CAMPAIGN?

Individual campaigns have specific goals to reach. Often the metrics associated with these goals are what we look out for: more qualified traffic, more sales, more conversions, more subscribers, more followers, a stronger brand, and a more positive image associated with a brand or product or site.

WHAT IS THE SINGLE MOST EFFECTIVE SEO TACTIC YOU'VE LEARNED?

Being responsive to targeted audiences and answering questions they might have in easy-to-understand language can be very effective.

IF YOU COULD CARRY ONLY FIVE TOOLS IN YOUR SEO TOOLKIT, WHAT WOULD THEY BE?

Screaming Frog web crawler, Google Search Console, Bing Webmaster Tools, Google Analytics, and PageSpeed Insights.

WHAT'S THE SINGLE BIGGEST MISTAKE YOU SEE PEOPLE MAKE IN SEO?

This is technical, but the single biggest mistake I see people make is using the first page in a series of pagination pages as the canonical link element URL for every page in that pagination series.

WHAT ADVICE WOULD YOU GIVE TO PEOPLE WHO ARE LOOKING TO RUN SUCCESSFUL SEO CAMPAIGNS?

Listen to your targeted audience and know how they talk. Know which words they use to describe what you offer, the words they use to search for the goods or services you provide, and what they expect to see on your website's pages. Use those words to build confidence that they have come to a site that offers what they are looking for.

HOW DO YOU THINK SEO WILL CHANGE OVER THE NEXT FEW YEARS?

SEO is evolving to do more than match words in search queries with words in documents and web pages. It's about working toward helping to fill the situational and informational needs of searchers by better understanding the intent and meaning behind searches, regardless of whether they are typed or spoken or photographed.

LEARN MORE ABOUT BILL

I am Bill Slawski, and I am the Director of SEO Research for Go Fish Digital. I blog about search and SEO and patents from search engines at *SEO by the Sea*. I live in Carlsbad, California, a few miles from the Pacific Ocean.

- ⊕ GOFISHDIGITAL.COM
- ⊕ WWW.SEOBYTHESEA.COM
- ▥ WWW.LINKEDIN.COM/IN/SLAWSKI
- ▢ @BILL_SLAWSKI
- ▪ WWW.FACEBOOK.COM/BILL.SLAWSKI
- 8+ PLUS.GOOGLE.COM/+BILLSLAWSKI

KENNETH FONG

FOUNDER, LEAD TAGGER

HOW DO YOU DETERMINE THE EFFECTIVENESS OF AN SEO CAMPAIGN?

I determine the effectiveness of an SEO campaign by checking it against what the website is meant to provide for the business. In most cases, it's website visits and conversions. The number of people visiting a site and filling out the contact form is what determines how effective a campaign is (for lead generation campaigns). Monitoring where your traffic is coming in and which pages are converting highest will tell you what's working and what's not.

WHAT IS THE SINGLE MOST EFFECTIVE SEO TACTIC YOU'VE LEARNED?

Focus on improving the pages that are ranking on the second page of Google. Work on on-page SEO, such as improving the copy and increasing its length to go in-depth into a particular topic. Focus on driving links to the page to increase its authority and relevance. Pushing your pages to page 1 in the search results usually improves the traffic to the site pretty substantially, because over 75 percent of people searching on Google never go past the first page. If you do this successfully, you will be able to see positive movement in your SEO campaign quickly.

IF YOU COULD CARRY ONLY FIVE TOOLS IN YOUR SEO TOOLKIT, WHAT WOULD THEY BE?

Google Analytics, Google Search Console, SEMrush, Screaming Frog, and Ahrefs.

WHAT'S THE SINGLE BIGGEST MISTAKE YOU SEE PEOPLE MAKE IN SEO?

Not focusing on business objectives. People are too in the weeds when it comes to miniscule SEO tasks that do not matter in the bigger picture of things. For example, people spend too much time trying to figure out the best URL structure. Instead of focusing on that, focus on what will make the most significant impact in growing the business. If it's getting more leads for a particular service, then concentrate on the web pages that focus on the service. Having a targeted SEO strategy that helps grow the business is the only way you can become successful.

WHAT ADVICE WOULD YOU GIVE TO PEOPLE WHO ARE LOOKING TO RUN SUCCESSFUL SEO CAMPAIGNS?

Make sure you record a baseline of how the site is performing before you optimize it. Get a list of everything you would like to improve on. Record keyword rankings, conversion rate, rich snippet markup appearance, and everything else that you plan on improving so that you can show a before and after picture of all the successes of your work. Recording these items will help prove your value and provide great insight into what's working and what's not. Having this data will also help you build case studies that will show off your SEO abilities.

HOW DO YOU THINK SEO WILL CHANGE OVER THE NEXT FEW YEARS?

SEO will be much more fragmented. People are finding answers and doing research online in various ways. With the rise of smart home devices, people are starting searches with their voice instead of typing. It is more important than ever to have content that is easily digestible and can answer users' questions quickly and easily. Google is rolling out new features and functionalities where searchers do not need to click onto a site to find their answer because the answers will be on the search page itself. Finding home services, restaurants, hotels, and other businesses will be easier. Today you can find answers and businesses directly on Google. com instead of your website. This type of searching will continue to grow and evolve. It is important to structure your content so that Google can understand it and display your content right on the search results page. Leverage Schema.org or JSON-LD markup to help Google understand the structure of your content.

LEARN MORE ABOUT KEN

I've come from successful stints at marketing agencies and in-house marketing teams. I've merged my skill sets to form my digital marketing agency, Lead Tagger. I'm active on social media and provide daily marketing tips on my LinkedIn profile.

- WWW.LEADTAGGER.COM/FREE-SEO-AUDIT
- KEN@LEADTAGGER.COM
- WWW.LINKEDIN.COM/IN/KLFONG2

MICHAEL HODGDON

HOW DO YOU DETERMINE THE EFFECTIVENESS OF AN SEO CAMPAIGN?

SEO starts with a full website audit to determine status and baselines then KPIs like online sales, organic website traffic growth, keyword placement, SERP click-through rates, and social mentions and signals. Determining statistic baseline numbers and ultimately tracking KPIs are done via Google Analytics and Google Search Console. Effectiveness would be determined by improvement in KPIs and ultimately by the business's return on investment (ROI).

WHAT IS THE SINGLE MOST EFFECTIVE SEO TACTIC YOU'VE LEARNED?

If I had to pick one, I think it all starts with effective on-page optimization—things like meta tags, page speed/load time, and quality unique content.

IF YOU COULD CARRY ONLY FIVE TOOLS IN YOUR SEO TOOLKIT, WHAT WOULD THEY BE?

Google Analytics, Google Search Console, WebCEO, SEMrush, and Screaming Frog.

WHAT'S THE SINGLE BIGGEST MISTAKE YOU SEE PEOPLE MAKE IN SEO?

Poor planning. Proper planning can provide a blueprint that can be improved upon over time if you're executing SEO yourself and can provide an effective way to manage a vendor if you're outsourcing.

WHAT ADVICE WOULD YOU GIVE TO PEOPLE WHO ARE LOOKING TO RUN SUCCESSFUL SEO CAMPAIGNS?

Start with a solid written or typed plan focused by priority of present ranking factors. Be sure to set up tracking (Google Analytics, Google Search Console). Do your proper keyword research (Google Keyword

Planner). Use a software like WebCEO to track the SEO work you do and to assist in gauging success. Stay on top of SERP ranking factors and algorithm updates. Consistently perform SEO work, even if it's only a couple hours a month. Continue to educate yourself; read e-books, articles, and blogs like *Moz Blog*, *Search Engine Journal*, and *Search Engine Land*.

HOW DO YOU THINK SEO WILL CHANGE OVER THE NEXT FEW YEARS?

Mobile, security (SSLs), and voice search will continue to grow and will impact how websites are built. Technologies like AMP (Accelerated Mobile Pages) will continue to impact SERPs. Currently, websites are built for desktop, and mobile and tablet responsive designs are created as an afterthought. In the future, a website will be designed for mobile first and then responsiveness will accommodate desktop computers. Website SSLs (secure connections) have in the past been limited to e-commerce websites; they will become the standard for all websites.

LEARN MORE ABOUT MICHAEL

I have more than twenty years of demonstrated success running SEO and internet companies, with intimate knowledge of online advertising media, SEO, local SEO, Google My Business listings/verification, website design and development, advertising, and e-commerce. I've been featured in *Entrepreneur* magazine, *The New York Times*, *Los Angeles Times*, and *Colorado Springs Business Journal*.

⊕ WWW.INFRONT.COM
⊕ WWW.MICHAELHODGDON.COM
▥ WWW.LINKEDIN.COM/IN/MICHAELHODGDON
▢ @MICHAEL_HODGDON

TERRY REEVES

SEO

HOW DO YOU DETERMINE THE EFFECTIVENESS OF AN SEO CAMPAIGN?

SEO implies an increase in organic search traffic through website optimizations. These optimizations include meta elements, on-site content, and technical website issues that can impact a website's organic search engine visibility. The most common meta optimizations are a website's page titles and descriptions. Page titles should include keywords or phrases important to the topic of the page for which there is search interest. Well-optimized page meta elements can also improve a page's organic click rate and bounce rate, both of which have been proven to improve a page's organic search engine positions. Common technical issues that can impact a website's organic performance include improper or no page canonicalization, duplicate page issues, broken links, broken pages . . . the list can be long.

WHAT IS THE SINGLE MOST EFFECTIVE SEO TACTIC YOU'VE LEARNED?

Frequently, keyword research is the starting point for most new content added to a website. Though search data around specific words or phrases is an important part of the content creation process, having well-written, engaging content will always pay off in the long run. Including important keywords is just one part of that process. Keyword research is also often applied to previously created content in an attempt to improve organic performance. These pages should already have a baseline of words and phrases that send organic search traffic. Just adding additional keywords that have been identified as having a desired search volume is often the process for optimizing these existing pages; however, that is not the most effective page optimization technique. For these existing pages and for most sites, I have found Google's Search Console to be the best source for keywords and phrases that can enhance a page's organic search visibility and therefore improve a website's organic search performance. I've found that keyword research utilizing page-level keyword data provided by Google is one of the most effective SEO tactics any webmaster, SEO professional, or individual can use to make measurable search improvements to a website.

IF YOU COULD CARRY ONLY FIVE TOOLS IN YOUR SEO TOOLKIT, WHAT WOULD THEY BE?

There are really only four "tools" I carry in my toolkit. Google Search Console provides the most important data and information you need in order to understand and improve the health of any website. DeepCrawl provides important analyses of a website's architecture to identify and monitor technical issues that can improve SEO performance. Google's PageSpeed Insights is also a very important tool that any SEO should utilize to optimize a website. SearchEngineWatch.com and SearchEngineJournal.com provide a variety of information that is timely and always informative across all areas of digital marketing.

WHAT'S THE SINGLE BIGGEST MISTAKE YOU SEE PEOPLE MAKE IN SEO?

Believe it or not, spammy link building is still a thing. Private blog networks and the easy backlinks they provide are still being sold by link sellers and SEO agencies of all sizes. Dozens of times every month, I am contacted by individuals and agencies wanting to sell me "high domain authority" backlinks. Engaging with some of these link sellers has provided me with many example pages where keyword anchor text links are pointed to related websites from the pages of obvious blog networks and some very popular, high-trafficked websites. Aside from the obvious danger of this practice, it leads people who are not immersed in the SEO field to believe the sales pitch. The reality is, regardless of the actions and threats of search engines, powerful backlinks continue to influence the rankings of websites. Therefore, there will continue to be a marketplace for them. About a year ago, I had to explain the reasons why a backlink campaign from a very large SEO agency was not in the best interest of a very large online retailer. This director had been contacted by an agency that was selling a $20,000-per-month service that included twenty high-authority backlinks per month. The backlinks were not the only aspect of the service, but they were the "juice" that provided the most impact. We passed on the service.

WHAT ADVICE WOULD YOU GIVE TO PEOPLE WHO ARE LOOKING TO RUN SUCCESSFUL SEO CAMPAIGNS?

Fundamentals first. A good site structure and simple navigation are very important. I mentioned DeepCrawl as one of my preferred tools—it's perfect for sniffing out the many potential hidden technical issues any website can have. Create content that engages, informs, and answers the questions your website visitors may have. Then make sure that content is optimized by current SEO best practices. Spend time in Google Search Console; become familiar with the important data and information contained there. Google Search Console keyword and page data are also available within Google Analytics, which is a great resource for site performance. Become informed on up-to-date SEO-related information and don't believe everything you read online. There are still plenty of articles available online that explain tactics and strategies that are no longer relevant to a successful SEO campaign.

HOW DO YOU THINK SEO WILL CHANGE OVER THE NEXT FEW YEARS?

As happens, everything old is new again. In many ways, "good SEO" today has reverted back to what good SEO was back in the day. Fundamentals like effective meta, strong content, and clean site structure and design are back in a big way. The advance of mobile usage has helped push these fundamental changes. Mobile usability forces simpler websites that respond easily to any device without the need for maintaining separate platforms. Personally, I believe the biggest advances in SEO will probably happen within the AI area. RankBrain, currently reported to be one of Google's top ranking factors, is probably the first of many attempts at machine learning in an effort to improve the search experience. Combine machine learning with advances in personalization, and pretty soon search engines will know what we're looking for before we even tell the search engine what we seek. Notice I didn't say "type." :)

LEARN MORE ABOUT TERRY

As an SEO professional, I have serviced hundreds of web properties in three countries, from local small business websites to billion dollar online retailers. I built my first websites, bought my first pay-per-click (PPC) ads, and optimized my first website for search before there was a Google. SEO has provided me with many great relationships, opportunities, and experiences. I am sure it will continue to do so for many years to come.

⊕ WWW.TERRYREEVES.COM
✉ TERRY@TERRYREEVES.COM
in WWW.LINKEDIN.COM/IN/TERRYREEVES

MARK FITZSIMMONS

SEO/SEM PRACTICE LEAD, SWC TECHNOLOGY PARTNERS

HOW DO YOU DETERMINE THE EFFECTIVENESS OF AN SEO CAMPAIGN?

Measuring performance and effectiveness of your SEO campaign is vital to truly validate the ROI of your internet marketing efforts. Many simply report rankings, sessions, and page views as the measurable metrics of an SEO campaign. However, to truly validate your investment, you need to track conversions. Conversion data is much easier to compile and measure with e-commerce sites—you can track conversions to a monetary amount. However, a non-ecommerce site can also have trackable conversions without a traditional online shopping cart. The Search Engine Optimizer needs to determine what the calls-to-action are on the website and what can be associated as an end goal. By then creating goals and events around those agreed-upon user actions, conversions can be recorded and used to measure the ROI of the SEO campaign.

WHAT IS THE SINGLE MOST EFFECTIVE SEO TACTIC YOU'VE LEARNED?

Guest posts, link bait, keyword-rich H1s, backlink outreach—there will never be a shortage of tactics associated with SEO; depending on which SEO you ask, their personal favorites will vary. There's always the latest and greatest tactic that becomes the hot discussion in industry posts. Over years of performing SEO both in house and client-side, the one tactic—or more like strategy—that has had the most impact for me is being nimble. With dashboards, crawl reports, and conversion/goal tracking and real-time data being available 24/7 and with search engine environments changing instantaneously, SEOs need to be nimble and able to react accordingly. Having an understanding of website and campaign analytics allows SEOs to see what implementations they have made that are working and also what may be returning less than desirable results. This enables SEOs to make changes quickly and test and monitor their effectiveness. As an SEO, you even gain insight into issues that may be impacting results outside of SEO. For example, while performing a technical site audit, an SEO may discover a site has been hacked and then is able to bring in a developer to address the vulnerability quickly.

IF YOU COULD CARRY ONLY FIVE TOOLS IN YOUR SEO TOOLKIT, WHAT WOULD THEY BE?

The top five tools I use consistently are Screaming Frog, Moz, SEMrush, Google Search Console (I still like to call it GWMT), and Google Analytics. The combination of these tools provides me with insight into visitors, competition, campaign and site performance, and technical issues. If I could sneak one more took into that kit, it would be Ahrefs.

WHAT'S THE SINGLE BIGGEST MISTAKE YOU SEE PEOPLE MAKE IN SEO?

Working with clients exposes me to numerous sites in varied industries. Frequently, I come across sites with sitewide duplicate title tags, broken links taking visitors (and bots) to 404 pages, and sites resolving to both www. and non-www. versions. But the biggest mistake I see happens when a client or potential client does not have any analytics enabled on the site. Without utilizing analytics, how can you even begin to understand who is coming to your site, what they are doing on your site, and how they got there? Not having analytics affects conversion tracking, performance monitoring, finding technical issues, and even understanding UX. Without having analytics, there's no history of how the site is performing or benchmarks to measure against when implementing campaigns or fixes. There are plenty of options to choose for analytics, but since Google Analytics is free and just a small bit of code is needed on the site for it to work, there really is no reason not to have analytics installed.

WHAT ADVICE WOULD YOU GIVE TO PEOPLE WHO ARE LOOKING TO RUN SUCCESSFUL SEO CAMPAIGNS?

The best advice I have for someone looking to conduct a successful SEO campaign is to think it through. You don't just "do" SEO. You need to understand the product/service you are promoting, company goals, competition, and target market. Also, you need to determine how you are going to define success (or failure) of the campaign. By meeting with stakeholders; departments like marketing, sales, customer service, and any other people who can provide valuable insight, you can better think through and both strategize and visualize what the campaign will require. Following implementation of the campaign, you must continue to monitor, analyze, measure, evaluate, tweak, and test, test, test (#WashRinseRepeat).

HOW DO YOU THINK SEO WILL CHANGE OVER THE NEXT FEW YEARS?

Virtual reality (VR) and augmented reality (AR) will transform the way we interact and communicate. VR/AR is not just for video gaming or YouTube videos for kids. It will become the next platform in business. VR/AR is in the early stages of having immense potential for almost every business industry and product/service. All the new VR/AR content being developed will need to be discovered and indexed by the search engines, and SEO will have a major impact on that success. Those businesses that harness early adoption of generating VR/AR content will dominate the SERPs and benefit by attracting new audiences. The sooner companies (websites) are associated with high-quality, fresh, and compelling VR/AR content, the more backlinks and mentions those sites will receive. This, in turn, will benefit both domain authority and SERP rankings. SEO will be vital in optimization to help the search engines locate and promote VR/AR content and also in strategy to help guide site visitors into and through a conversion funnel.

LEARN MORE ABOUT MARK

I'm a seasoned internet marketer who specializes in Search Engine Optimization (SEO), Search Engine Marketing (SEM) and digital strategy. My exposure covers both in-house and client-facing agency environments, and I'm currently the SEO/SEM Practice Lead for the full-service IT consulting firm SWC Technology Partners, based in the Chicagoland area.

🔗 WWW.LINKEDIN.COM/IN/FITZSIMMONSMARK

RYAN D'SOUZA

SEO MANAGER, HYATT HOTELS CORPORATION

HOW DO YOU DETERMINE THE EFFECTIVENESS OF AN SEO CAMPAIGN?

The KPIs I look at to determine whether a campaign is successful are the classic SEO metrics: natural search visits, rankings, organic SERP, CTR, page authority/trust flow (number and quality of links earned/unique referring domains), and business metrics like revenue. I may also look at engagement metrics like bounce rate and time on page.

WHAT IS THE SINGLE MOST EFFECTIVE SEO TACTIC YOU'VE LEARNED?

The single most effective SEO tactic I've learned is link building, assuming on-page factors such as site crawlability and content optimization are already evaluated and implemented.

IF YOU COULD CARRY ONLY FIVE TOOLS IN YOUR SEO TOOLKIT, WHAT WOULD THEY BE?

Google Search Console, Majestic, DeepCrawl, Moz Pro (for 100,000+ terms, options are Conductor/SM/SeoClarity/BE/Linkdex), and Google Analytics.

WHAT'S THE SINGLE BIGGEST MISTAKE YOU SEE PEOPLE MAKE IN SEO?

I'm going to provide two mistakes rather than one because they're connected:

1. Forgetting that SEO is a holistic discipline. It's not "just" a function of one or two factors.

2. Providing SEO recommendations without taking brand guidelines, e-commerce implications, and user expectations into consideration.

Both points emphasize that SEO should address not only multiple SEO-related factors but also multichannel factors.

WHAT ADVICE WOULD YOU GIVE TO PEOPLE WHO ARE LOOKING TO RUN SUCCESSFUL SEO CAMPAIGNS?

Let's assume you're running an SEO campaign to promote a specific product. If you were involved in developing the page, great! Then we can talk about information architecture, SEO wireframing, and SEO-friendly design. If the page is already developed, ensure that all on-page factors (technical and content) such as crawlability/accessibility, URL, meta, schema, canonical, image, page load time, source code, hreflang tag, and content are optimized. From an off-page perspective, earn high-quality links to the page (high-quality = highly relevant links from authoritative sites). The skill involved in implementing the above will determine the success of your campaign. There are, of course, other factors that play a role and that we have limited control over, such as competition, algorithm updates, and market changes.

HOW DO YOU THINK SEO WILL CHANGE OVER THE NEXT FEW YEARS?

Search Engine Optimizers will have to assess the impact and opportunity that voice search queries will present and strategize accordingly. AI technology will play an even more significant role in determining rankings. Google will continue to monetize the SERPs with new types of search results.

LEARN MORE ABOUT RYAN

I'm the Global SEO Manager for Hyatt Hotels Corporation. Prior to Hyatt, I provided SEO support for Anheuser Busch, General Motors, Devry University, Avant, and a number of other brands. I've also managed SEM campaigns for Luxottica, Anheuser-Busch, and ESPN.

✉ DSOUZA_RYAN@YAHOO.COM
🔗 WWW.LINKEDIN.COM/IN/RYANRDSOUZA

GEORGE LANDES III

MANAGER, DIGITAL STRATEGY & EXECUTION, ARONSON ADVERTISING

HOW DO YOU DETERMINE THE EFFECTIVENESS OF AN SEO CAMPAIGN?

This will always vary based on business goals and objectives. If I'm measuring effectiveness based on revenue generated, then measuring KPIs such as cost per acquisition relative to business goals and objectives helps me determine whether my campaign is cost effective and is helping to drive ROI. If I'm measuring effectiveness based on organic growth and conversions (there's always a goal), then I'll be measuring effectiveness of relative KPIs to that goal. This includes overall organic growth, increases in non-branded organic traffic growth, quality of traffic (revenue driving and high engaging), and ROI if a monetary value exists within conversions or traffic benchmarks.

WHAT IS THE SINGLE MOST EFFECTIVE SEO TACTIC YOU'VE LEARNED?

How to think "big picture." In my experience, creativity and an ability to think big picture is one of the most effective tactics in a digital marketer's arsenal. It's a little difficult to explain, but often as we grow within the digital space, we become engulfed in one aspect of digital—whether it's SEO, PPC or social media, for example—that becomes our niche. I recognized early on that acquiring knowledge and application skills in all aspects of digital would make me a more well-rounded, versatile, and big-picture-thinking digital professional. In my experiences, I have had the opportunity to actively learn and engage in all aspects of digital, SEO, social media, content development, web development, and PPC. When it comes to digital strategies and SEO, understanding user behavior, understanding audiences, understanding your client, and being able to conceptualize a strategy utilizing the big picture has proven to be the most effective means to driving success. This is something I emphasize to my team members. Being able to think on a micro *and* macro level and then being able to understand how to utilize both is a proven tactic for success.

IF YOU COULD CARRY ONLY FIVE TOOLS IN YOUR SEO TOOLKIT, WHAT WOULD THEY BE?

Keyword Planner, Screaming Frog, Google Analytics, Google Search Console, and Majestic SEO.

WHAT'S THE SINGLE BIGGEST MISTAKE YOU SEE PEOPLE MAKE IN SEO?

They don't set expectations properly. SEO is a marathon; it's not a sprint. If you don't set that expectation up front, you are in for a real shootout shortly down the road.

WHAT ADVICE WOULD YOU GIVE TO PEOPLE WHO ARE LOOKING TO RUN SUCCESSFUL SEO CAMPAIGNS?

Be sure to always dot your i's and cross your t's. If you do that, you'll be setting yourself up for long-term SEO success.

HOW DO YOU THINK SEO WILL CHANGE OVER THE NEXT FEW YEARS?

We are already amidst a fundamental shift in SEO; users have begun making a fundamental shift in the way that they search. Google is no longer the keyword-based engine it was ten years ago—it's now an answer-based engine. Google has recognized this shift, which is why they've put so much emphasis on semantic search, the knowledge graph, and importance of quality informational content. Even more emphasis will be put on the quality of the informational content. Also, as voice search expands, we will look at ways we can optimize content around this new form of search.

LEARN MORE ABOUT GEORGE

For the past eleven years I've strived to better understand the landscape of what we call digital marketing. I have worked across a range of verticals to diversify my experiences, which has driven my ability to think "big picture." From working in small start-up agencies to experiencing the dynamics of large global agencies, I have gained extensive experience crafting both local and global marketing strategies for some of the world's most iconic brands, including Nike, Red Hat Linux, CooperVision, and beIN SPORTS. I truly love this space. I have worked with some brilliant and creative minds, and I continue my passion for SEO and digital marketing every day. However, my true joy is watching my team grow into well-rounded digital marketing professionals who show growth in knowledge and application. If someone I have cultivated can someday take my job, I will have been successful.

✉ GLANDES2I@YAHOO.COM
✉ G.LANDES@ARONSONADS.COM
in WWW.LINKEDIN.COM/IN/GEORGE-M-LANDES-III-I4B2OBI7

CRAIG CAMPBELL

HOW DO YOU DETERMINE THE EFFECTIVENESS OF AN SEO CAMPAIGN?

There are so many different metrics people use in the world of SEO to determine how effective a campaign is. I personally look at traffic, rankings, and sales. At the end of the day, clients will gauge your skills on all of these factors. There are other SEOs out there who will talk about many other indicators, but if you do not rank then you will not take advantage of any organic traffic online.

WHAT IS THE SINGLE MOST EFFECTIVE SEO TACTIC YOU'VE LEARNED?

SEO is about a number of different tactics pulling together to form an effective campaign, but link building is the most important part of any SEO campaign, as far as I'm concerned. That being said, on-page SEO needs to be done well to see the impact of the links you are building.

IF YOU COULD CARRY ONLY FIVE TOOLS IN YOUR SEO TOOLKIT, WHAT WOULD THEY BE?

The first of my five favorite SEO tools would have to be SEMrush to do my keyword research and competitor analysis. Ahrefs is my go-to tool for backlink analysis. There are a number of others, but for me this one provides the most accurate data. We then have ScrapeBox, which is a must-have tool for any digital marketer—it can be used for seeking link opportunities, checking whether links are "nofollow" or "dofollow," and checking whether links are still live. It also has a heap of other features. NinjaOutreach is a good tool to use for any outreach that I need to do. If you have not tried it, you should; it helps with outreach and automated follow-ups. DeepCrawl is one of the best site auditing tools on the market and is a must-have—regular site audits are a must to ensure a website is error free.

WHAT'S THE SINGLE BIGGEST MISTAKE YOU SEE PEOPLE MAKE IN SEO?

One of the biggest mistakes I see in SEO is people not using the correct tools to do research, analysis, and site auditing.

WHAT ADVICE WOULD YOU GIVE TO PEOPLE WHO ARE LOOKING TO RUN SUCCESSFUL SEO CAMPAIGNS?

Have the right setup, do the right research, and do not overthink SEO campaigns. So many people miss the basics or think SEO is something that it's not. It's fairly straightforward and simple; it's a game of common sense, as far as I'm concerned. If you implement the basics properly and continue to build your knowledge and test constantly, then you'll do fine.

HOW DO YOU THINK SEO WILL CHANGE OVER THE NEXT FEW YEARS?

SEO is constantly changing. Google's algorithms change and software and analysis tools are getting better. You need to keep on top of it. Automation and AI are big players in the coming years. The core basics do remain similar, but you need to keep on top of SEO and be prepared to continuously learn.

LEARN MORE ABOUT CRAIG

I'm based in the United Kingdom and have over sixteen years' experience in the SEO industry. I do SEO consultancy and training, and I'm a regular SEO speaker.

🌐 WWW.CRAIGCAMPBELLSEO.CO.UK
🔗 UK.LINKEDIN.COM/IN/CRAIGCAMPBELLO302
🐦 @CRAIGCAMPBELLO3

JULIAN SCOTT CONNORS

SR. MANAGER OF SEARCH INITIATIVES, CVS

HOW DO YOU DETERMINE THE EFFECTIVENESS OF AN SEO CAMPAIGN?

The effectiveness of any SEO campaign depends on multiple factors, such as vertical, target audience, and purpose. The key performance indicators (KPIs) for informational websites that look to build consumer engagement are going to differ from e-commerce brands that focus on maximizing repeat transactions. However, most brands can refer to the following to determine how well they are connecting with online consumers: total traffic, organic traffic, mobile vs. desktop traffic, pages per session, average time spent, bounce rate, goals/conversions, top landing pages per channel, and domain authority.

WHAT IS THE SINGLE MOST EFFECTIVE SEO TACTIC YOU'VE LEARNED?

The most effective tactic I've employed is called "Product Focused Linking," which leveraged a particular brand's products to provide disaster relief support after Typhoon Yolanda struck the Philippines. This brand was recognized internationally for their work-wear clothing and distributed thousands of jackets, jeans, gloves, and shoes in exchange for pictures featuring the products in use. Pictures were sent to various media outlets, social media influencers, and consumer review platforms. This singular campaign generated thousands of quality links from relevant sources, improved first page keyword rankings by 28 percent YOY, and increased quarterly profits by $1.2 million.

IF YOU COULD CARRY ONLY FIVE TOOLS IN YOUR SEO TOOLKIT, WHAT WOULD THEY BE?

DeepCrawl, BrightEdge, Keyword Planner, Google Analytics, and Google Search Console.

WHAT'S THE SINGLE BIGGEST MISTAKE YOU SEE PEOPLE MAKE IN SEO?

The biggest mistake I see throughout the SEO industry is too many people assuming that everything they read online is true and not relative to the author's personal experience. Too many SEOs do not take the time to test out their strategies in practical applications to determine the validity of their campaigns. In order to perfect your craft and to remain relevant as organic search continues to evolve, SEOs must commit themselves to retesting their strategies to find ways to maximize results.

WHAT ADVICE WOULD YOU GIVE TO PEOPLE WHO ARE LOOKING TO RUN SUCCESSFUL SEO CAMPAIGNS?

The best advice for aspiring SEO strategists is to focus on consumer behavior, which includes: who your audience is; what their search intent is (do something, know something, or purchase something); what specific terms they use when searching via desktop vs. mobile; what specific questions/dilemmas they are trying to resolve; which form of content (e.g., videos, buying guides, infographics, white papers) aligns with their search intent and will solicit the highest engagement/conversions; and how consumers engage with content based on location, interests, and devices.

HOW DO YOU THINK SEO WILL CHANGE OVER THE NEXT FEW YEARS?

SEO will continue to evolve in ways that focus on individual habits and needs. The more connected you are to the individual consumer, the better your campaign will perform when you try to create an optimized navigation, acquire relevant links, and develop intelligent content. Strategists need to invest time and energy in learning about mobile optimization since voice-recognition systems and devices will continue to become more mainstream among consumers. These devices will completely change how consumers receive content and information because only one or two answers are provided, as opposed to a list of ten or more domains.

LEARN MORE ABOUT JULIAN

I am the Founder and President of SEO Without Borders and the Sr. Manager of Search Initiatives at CVS. Over the last ten years, I have developed complex, wide-scale search and social campaigns for brands that include P&G, Staples, Duracell, Dickies, Papa John's, and more. I'm a published author on the concept of "Social SEO" and "Your Most Common SEO Questions Answered." I also contribute to a number of recognized publications like *Search Engine Land* and *Entrepreneur* magazine.

WWW.LINKEDIN.COM/IN/JULIANCONNORS

@JCONNORSSEO

CHAPTER 2
GOOGLE ADWORDS

A SIMPLE EXPLANATION OF GOOGLE ADWORDS AND PAID SEARCH

Paid search, sometimes called search engine marketing (SEM), refers to paid ad listings on search engines. Google AdWords is the world's largest paid search platform, so often the terms "paid search," PPC, or SEM refer to Google AdWords.

Paid search is a big business. Google alone receives billions of dollars every year from advertisers who show their ads on Google.

With Google AdWords, advertisers pay for ads on the search engine results page (SERP), the listings pages on search engines. When you see an advertisement at the top of Google, that's a paid search listing. The advertiser is paying for their ad to show there and will pay a monetary cost-per-click (CPC) when a person clicks on that ad.

By selecting keywords that a business's target customer might search for, advertisers are able to show highly targeted advertisements to people who are searching for their exact product or service. Once someone clicks on the ad, they will typically be taken to the company's website or a custom-ized landing page. From the advertiser's perspective, the goal is usually to get people to "convert"—perform a desired action, like purchasing prod-uct or submitting contact information on the website or landing page.

Search engines like Google operate like an auction house for these ads. The more popular the keyword, the more companies pay for a click to their ad from that keyword—their "bid" for that keyword. Advertisers are constantly jockeying for position by adjusting bids and improving the quality of their Google AdWords campaigns.

One important feature of Google AdWords is called "remarketing" (or "retargeting"). Remarketing campaigns are used to show ads to people who have already visited a website or app. Have you ever browsed prod-ucts on a website, left the website, and then saw ads for those products in other areas of the web? That is an example of a Remarketing campaign. Often, the goal of a Remarketing campaign is to drive a person to purchase a product or service that they've already shown an interest in.

"Quality Score" is an important metric for Google AdWords specialists. Quality Score is a Google-generated estimate of the quality of an advertiser's Google AdWords ads, keywords, and landing pages. Higher quality scores can lead to lower bid prices and better ad positions.

Search campaigns are only one of multiple campaign types that advertisers can use through AdWords. Advertisers can also use campaigns such as Display campaigns to show ads on websites across the web, Universal App campaigns to drive app installs, or Shopping campaigns to promote e-commerce products. Google is continuously adding new campaign types to AdWords and updating the platform to better serve advertisers.

GOOGLE ADWORDS SPECIALISTS SOUND OFF

DAVID CHAPMAN

DIRECTOR OF MARKETING, WEBRAGEOUS

HOW DO YOU DETERMINE THE EFFECTIVENESS OF AN ADWORDS CAMPAIGN?

Measuring the effectiveness of a paid search campaign starts with understanding a company's individual goals. These goals can vary greatly. For some companies, the main goal is awareness (driving new customers to the site). In most cases, however, the goal is centered on two basic metrics: conversions (driving more) and cost per conversion (lowering the cost per action). Still, measuring the success of a campaign runs deeper than simply measuring the number of conversions. For example, a conversion for a company may be a customer calling to book a particular service. In this case, driving a high quantity of calls where people don't book wouldn't be profitable. In other cases, a conversion may mean e-commerce sales for products of varying price, so the value of each conversion may vary considerably. Therefore, measuring the success of a campaign depends not only on the conversion but also on the quality of that conversion.

WHAT IS THE SINGLE MOST EFFECTIVE ADWORDS TACTIC YOU'VE LEARNED?

Developing landing pages that convert. No tactic is going to work unless you can turn clicks into conversions. Paid search is only going to continue to become more competitive. Also, the way people search is going to continue to evolve. Having a clear understanding of best practices and the ability to adapt to the changing search environment is the foundation of a high-performing paid search campaign.

IF YOU COULD CARRY ONLY FIVE TOOLS IN YOUR ADWORDS TOOLKIT, WHAT WOULD THEY BE?

Microsoft Excel, AdWords Editor, the AdWords Preview Tool, SpyFu Kombat, and CallRail. AdWords has made significant improvements to their reporting and data visualization tools over the years, but I still find myself turning to Excel to gain a better understanding of performance data. I use AdWords Editor to quickly build and optimize campaigns. The Preview Tool allows me to see how ads are displayed. SpyFu Kombat is great for discovering new successful keywords that competitors are bidding on, plus finding negative keywords I may not have considered. Finally, CallRail gives us the ability to better track call conversions.

WHAT'S THE SINGLE BIGGEST MISTAKE YOU SEE PEOPLE MAKE IN ADWORDS?

Not testing continuously is a huge mistake. Paid search success boils down to testing and measuring a lot of things. The number of variables is immense. You have to love doing paid search, or you'll never be very good. It's critical to test not just new ads and new keywords, but bid changes (which can be done in an experiment to best gauge the effectiveness of these changes), and especially landing page optimizations. Great landing pages are 50 percent of success with paid search!

WHAT ADVICE WOULD YOU GIVE TO PEOPLE WHO ARE LOOKING TO RUN SUCCESSFUL ADWORDS CAMPAIGNS?

There is no simple shortcut to run a successful campaign. The most important thing is to structure your campaigns as per industry best practices, which is to create campaigns based on your website categories/services and then organize relevant keywords into ad groups and write ad-group-specific ads. Then let your campaigns run, review the data, and start optimizing. Additionally, to avoid knee-jerk reactions, make sure you have enough data before making adjustments.

HOW DO YOU THINK ADWORDS WILL CHANGE OVER THE NEXT FEW YEARS?

Over the next few years, I expect to see an increase in the number of options available to automate management tasks in paid search. With suggested ads and the ever-growing list of automated bidding options available, we can already see this pattern surfacing. For the PPC account manager, this will likely mean a shift in how their time is spent. Less time will be spent in the weeds on day-to-day management tasks, and more time will be devoted toward guiding the overall campaign strategy. An account manager will focus their efforts even more on keeping up with industry changes, processing whether they make sense for a client, and driving a campaign toward reaching these individual goals.

LEARN MORE ABOUT DAVID

I've been with Webrageous since 2001 and managed PPC since 2004. I love skiing and racing Ultimate 20 sailboats. Webrageous is the only company I am aware of that offers a sixty-day risk free trial for PPC management.

⊕ WWW.WEBRAGEOUS.COM

KRISTI GEORGE

HOW DO YOU DETERMINE THE EFFECTIVENESS OF AN ADWORDS CAMPAIGN?

I determine the effectiveness of a campaign by the results it produces. With paid advertising like Google AdWords, multiple factors build on each other. You have to have the right keywords to create impressions, but you also need a strong list of negative keywords in order to keep the impressions relevant and your bounce rate low. PPC ads need to be descriptive with a call-to-action that produces a high click-through rate as well as a high conversion rate. At the end of the day, if your PPC lead-generation campaign has increased relevant traffic and leads from your website, then it is effective.

WHAT IS THE SINGLE MOST EFFECTIVE ADWORDS TACTIC YOU'VE LEARNED?

The best thing I have learned and have been successful with in PPC is competitor targeting. If your client has a competitor who is the "Kleenex" of their industry (a well-known brand), then use their brand name as a keyword so that when that competitor's name or product is typed in, your client's ad appears. To avoid a low quality score for those terms, you can create a page on your site that talks about how your product is similar to the "Kleenex" brand. That way search engines can find the relevance, rank you organically, and the click won't cost as much in your PPC campaign. This is a great way to steal some of the action from big names in your industry.

IF YOU COULD CARRY ONLY FIVE TOOLS IN YOUR ADWORDS TOOLKIT, WHAT WOULD THEY BE?

If I could carry only five tools in my toolkit, they would be SEO Moz, Google AdWords, KeywordSpy, WordStream, and social media advertising. Google AdWords is a great platform for general paid advertising, and social media sites like LinkedIn and Facebook are great for niche targeting, like displaying ads to a particular company, job title, hobby, etc. Besides creating ads and campaigns in AdWords, there are other tools like Google Keyword Planner, which is helpful for discovering potential search terms and their monthly search volume for any given region. For keyword rankings, I use Moz. Besides tracking weekly progress of key-word rankings in the SERPS, Moz also allows you to compare against your top competitors and monitor major site crawl issues; it also provides a backlink analysis and opportunities and provides a whole community of knowledge regarding SEO. Knowing how you rank organically can help you to better strategize your PPC efforts.

Another tool I use for competitor analysis to assist with PPC and keyword development is KeywordSpy. This is a great tool to see what keywords your competitors are targeting; it will tell you if they are doing PPC and if so, what their ads are, as well as their recent performance. Finally, I use WordStream to help with suggestions and areas of improvement for the campaigns to align with Google best practices. In a smaller agency where help is limited, WordStream is a great resource.

WHAT'S THE SINGLE BIGGEST MISTAKE YOU SEE PEOPLE MAKE IN ADWORDS?

The single biggest mistake that I have seen in PPC is when people "set it and forget it." Paid advertising shouldn't be like a casserole in a Crockpot. It needs attention and needs to be worked on constantly, especially when Google decides to change its algorithm. When clients ask me what it is I'm charging for every month when managing their PPC campaigns, I tell them it's a combination of analyzing and adjusting. One major task is in the negative keywords. I analyze the list of terms people are using to see my ads at least twice a month and then add irrelevant words to the negative search term list.

Being a Google Partner means keeping campaigns up to best practices. For example, when Google announced that every Search ad group needs three expanded text ads, I had to update campaigns for my clients that didn't already follow that rule. I find there are always areas to improve upon in PPC campaigns, whether it's adding new products or keywords or something as granular as reducing or increasing the amount spent for ads on mobile vs. desktop.

WHAT ADVICE WOULD YOU GIVE TO PEOPLE WHO ARE LOOKING TO RUN SUCCESSFUL ADWORDS CAMPAIGNS?

I would recommend to anyone who is looking to run a successful paid advertising campaign to partner with a person or a team that can execute a plan to help you achieve your goals and ultimately improve your online presence. I see so many people who "know a guy" that they trust to optimize their website and in the long run they end up throwing away a lot of valuable marketing dollars. For example, so many people who want to be on the first page of search engines will start by running a Google pay-per-click campaign.

Where instead, if they had a strategy in place with a professional SEO analyst like myself, I would advise them to never pay for clicks until they have an organic SEO strategy in place. Otherwise, if you're targeting keywords in pay-per-click that are not optimized on your website, you will have a lower quality score for that term and can pay up to 800 percent more for a click. Instead, create a strategy for the core terms, products, or services that you desire to be found for and dominate the SERPs. Then deploy a paid campaign, and your advertising budget will go much farther.

HOW DO YOU THINK ADWORDS WILL CHANGE OVER THE NEXT FEW YEARS?

The smarter the algorithm gets, the more we'll need to step our game up in the years to come. With paid advertising, it is not about simply paying to show up—there is a real strategy involved. I think as Google's algorithm evolves, people in PPC advertising need to be certified and up to date with how to effectively get their ads to show and how to dominate the search results when people are searching for their product or services.

LEARN MORE ABOUT KRISTI

I am Founder of Nonna—a digital marketing agency based in Wisconsin. Early on, I began my career at Naveo where I learned to manage a large client base in various industrial B2B markets. As an expert in Search Engine Marketing, I have a passion for helping small and medium sized businesses reach their goals by growing their brand online. I have developed a strategy to rank most of my clients on the first page organically within a few months. I have also had a lot of success with paid advertising and social media marketing. With a dual major in Marketing and Business Management and over a dozen Google certifications, I understand everything from branding and understanding a customer and how they buy to marketing to that audience through various channels—which gives me an advantage over most similar sized agencies.

⊕ WWW.NONNASEO.COM

BRIAN YARO

HOW DO YOU DETERMINE THE EFFECTIVENESS OF AN ADWORDS CAMPAIGN?

A paid search campaign is effective when it's meeting the business goals and objectives of the company. Too often paid search is viewed only as a bottom-of-funnel conversion channel, and important customer-centric keywords are removed based solely on last click attribution performance. A successful and effective paid search campaign utilizes strategic keyword sets that make companies discoverable and relevant when customers are searching in moments of need. Measurement needs to be performed with a holistic view of the campaigns, and separate KPIs should be set for each keyword set based on their role in achieving the business goals.

WHAT IS THE SINGLE MOST EFFECTIVE ADWORDS TACTIC YOU'VE LEARNED?

The 80/20 rule. Machine learning and advancements in algorithmic optimization technologies have now far surpassed the capabilities of even the smartest paid search experts. We utilize a paid search management technology that was developed by a rocket scientist and is able to learn in real-time and make optimizations every thirty minutes. Depending on the account, we are able to implement up to 80 percent of the keywords into the technology, while our team can focus on the most important 20 percent.

IF YOU COULD CARRY ONLY FIVE TOOLS IN YOUR ADWORDS TOOLKIT, WHAT WOULD THEY BE?

Machine learning technology, search query reports, dynamic ad creative, keyword research tools (Google Keyword Planner), and a real-time KPI tracker.

WHAT'S THE SINGLE BIGGEST MISTAKE YOU SEE PEOPLE MAKE IN ADWORDS?

Without question, pausing and removing converting keywords that *appear* less efficient solely based on a last click attribution model. The easiest way to tank a performing paid search account is to "bonsai tree" it to the point that it has no opportunity to grow and mature. Upper and lower funnel keywords have a far larger impact on each other than last click measurement can identify. Removing upper funnel keywords typically results in diminishing returns on lower funnel keywords.

WHAT ADVICE WOULD YOU GIVE TO PEOPLE WHO ARE LOOKING TO RUN SUCCESSFUL ADWORDS CAMPAIGNS?

Start with the first party data you have on your customer. Who are they, where are they, what are those moments of need your business has the answer for, what other options do they have in the marketplace? Next, identify the business goals for the company and how those goals align with your customer data. Also, identify what the various touch points are within your customer's journey where it's critical for you to be there. Finally, review various attribution models to determine which provides the best measurement view based on your customer and business model. The outcomes from this process provide the framework on how to build, structure, measure, and grow your paid search campaigns. And of course, be certain to incorporate paid search management technology to guide much of the granular day-to-day decision-making.

HOW DO YOU THINK ADWORDS WILL CHANGE OVER THE NEXT FEW YEARS?

The ongoing advancements in technology, audience, and attribution will change the role of paid search in a business's media mix. Paid search has been falling behind other digital media channels in the last few years because of the impact that tech, audience data, and attribution has had within remarketing, display, mobile, and social. However, now paid search is catching up—Google is investing incredible resources to ensure that it does.

LEARN MORE ABOUT BRIAN

I lead the overall Paid Media practice at Lever Interactive—from strategy to client relationships, as well as new business. Prior to joining Lever Interactive, I was a Senior Manager on the SEM team at Milestone Internet Marketing overseeing more than sixty clients in the hospitality and public storage verticals. Before Milestone, I served as a Paid Media & Social Manager at Starcom, serving a critical role in growing the Kraft Brands paid media efforts. My exposure to these varying verticals and channels has provided insights and learnings that I now apply at Lever Interactive.

⊕ WWW.LEVERINTERACTIVE.COM

🔲 WWW.LINKEDIN.COM/IN/BRIAN-YARO-25856313

JAY NASH

SR. PROGRAMMATIC MARKETING MANAGER

HOW DO YOU DETERMINE THE EFFECTIVENESS OF AN ADWORDS CAMPAIGN?

It is critical to have organizational alignment on one KPI, whether that be cost per lead (CPA/CPL), cost per app download, or revenue/spend (ROI). Whenever possible, I recommend using these metrics, as they ultimately help to determine the efficiency of your media buys as it is related to spend. Revenue and leads are the ultimate goal, but if you can't attain them at an efficient cost, then it adversely affects your margins. It is also very important to look at secondary metrics that speak to the quality of sites and performance across frequency of impressions. Certain sites might have low viewability that can drive up your ad cost. It is imperative to look at viewability, CPM, CPCs and conversion rate by publisher so you can eliminate (blacklist) underperforming inventory sources. It is also important to test and evaluate performance at different frequency levels, as well.

WHAT IS THE SINGLE MOST EFFECTIVE ADWORDS TACTIC YOU'VE LEARNED?

In order to achieve optimal performance results in performance display campaigns, it is vital to have a well structured and diverse audience approach. Structuring campaigns by different targeting types and making sure each is mutually exclusive is critical to success. For example, you want to bucket your retargeting audiences in their own campaigns and prospecting audiences in different campaigns. To take this a step further, you want to break out your retargeting audiences based on what pages they interacted with on your site and how long ago they visited (recency). Since people can qualify to be eligible for retargeting off of multiple pages on a site, you want to bucket site visitors into the closest page they hit before leaving.

For example, if someone visited your home page, a category page, product page, and shopping cart, and then didn't purchase, you want to exclude shopping cart visitors from all other pages. This is because they are higher intent than someone who just visited your home page and should be served ads at a great frequency with higher bids and potentially be offered an incentive to transact. If you didn't apply this exclusion, then the visitor (cookie) would be eligible for retargeting in all four segments. Not only does this inflate the frequency at which they receive ads, but it also "waters down" the performance differences that you would otherwise notice between homepage visitors and those who hit the shopping cart.

IF YOU COULD CARRY ONLY FIVE TOOLS IN YOUR ADWORDS TOOLKIT, WHAT WOULD THEY BE?

The first one I would recommend is integrating a data management platform (DMP), which allows for activation of your CRM database. This enables immense retargeting and lifecycle messaging opportunities that you cannot get from just relying on website pixels. The second tool I would recommend is measuring the incremental value of your media campaigns to determine lift from those who just see ads as opposed to clicking on them. Post-click attribution is used widely because it is easy to track and widely accepted by analytics teams. While there definitely is value in post-click transactions, they are often influenced strongly by other channels. There should be some post-impression lift applied to post view impressions, and you can identify the right lift percentage by running a test/control lift test.

I would also recommend using moat.com, where you can find display ads from competitors and top brands. Finally, I would recommend continuously testing creative performance (based on CTR and conversion rate), utilizing your top paid search keywords to run contextual display targeting, and utilizing lookalike segments built off of your best customer.

WHAT'S THE SINGLE BIGGEST MISTAKE YOU SEE PEOPLE MAKE IN ADWORDS?

I can answer this one easily: over-frequency of impressions. Retargeting is typically the best performing tactic in the display toolkit, and because of this, marketers want to push as much volume there as possible. This is not the correct approach, because retargeting is limited by audience size. Instead, you should have a diverse retargeting portfolio with twenty to fifty audiences, and each should have different frequency levels. In order to determine the correct frequencies, marketers should look at ROI by retargeting audience and conversion rates across varying frequency levels that they have tested. A general rule of thumb is that advertisers should target recent site visitors (within twenty-four hours) with much higher frequency. However, if someone has not been to your site in one week, this frequency should decrease and continue to do so as the time frame increases. It is also crucial that advertisers exclude recent converters from remarketing. I far too often make an online purchase and am retargeted with the same product I just bought. This not only makes the brand look naïve, but it is also a waste of media spend.

WHAT ADVICE WOULD YOU GIVE TO PEOPLE WHO ARE LOOKING TO RUN SUCCESSFUL ADWORDS CAMPAIGNS?

Be thoughtful in your approach to setting up audiences and aligning your creative messaging to those audiences. The more specific you can get with your targeting and messaging, the better the campaign will perform. Advanced AdWords display campaigns will have more than one hundred audiences that span the gamut of retargeting, contextual targeting, affinity targeting, in-market targeting, lookalike targeting, and whitelist targeting (top performing site lists). Test multiple audiences, bids, frequencies, and sites, and then iterate on what works. Always be measuring, always be testing, and always make your audiences mutually exclusive.

HOW DO YOU THINK ADWORDS WILL CHANGE OVER THE NEXT FEW YEARS?

Publishers are finding new ways to monetize their websites with additional spaces for video, native, and customized ad units. The same core programmatic principles that are used to correctly set up, optimize, and succeed in performance media will stay the same, but the ad formats and inventory sources will continue evolving. Because of this, advertisers need to prepare themselves now by testing new forms of media. These new forms of media rely on more content-heavy assets that either provide consumers additional insight or tell a story through video.

LEARN MORE ABOUT JAY

I have over eight years' experience in performance marketing across display, paid search, social media, native, video, and mobile. Recently, I brought all performance media buying in-house at a Fortune 500 B2B supplier. In my current role, I oversee a team of in-house programmatic native media buyers in the financial marketing sector.

✉ JRNASH52@GMAIL.COM
🔗 WWW.LINKEDIN.COM/IN/JAYNASH52

JONATHAN NG

DIGITAL ADVERTISING, PPCCONSULTING.COM

HOW DO YOU DETERMINE THE EFFECTIVENESS OF AN ADWORDS CAMPAIGN?

There are many metrics that can be used to determine the effectiveness of an AdWords campaign. However, companies are in business to make a profit, so it's important to evaluate effectiveness through their lens and not on metrics that don't matter to them. For example, if you're running a lead-generation campaign with the goal of connecting with prospects, effectiveness is determined by the cost-per-lead. For an e-commerce campaign, it's important to look at the total revenue and total cost. For companies running brand awareness campaigns, they will want to focus on how often their ad is being seen.

WHAT IS THE SINGLE MOST EFFECTIVE ADWORDS TACTIC YOU'VE LEARNED?

Remarketing helps you keep your brand visible to people who have been to your website by serving them ads around the web. It's also a strategic way to target people who have abandoned the sales funnel. Many advertisers see a higher return on advertising spend with remarketing over other ad channels because you're targeting people after they've interacted with your business.

If you could carry only five tools in your AdWords toolkit, what would they be?

1. Google AdWords Editor—an application for managing AdWords accounts

2. Google Analytics—tracks and reports website traffic

3. Tools for optimizing a landing page—the testing and personalization tools used depends on the situation

4. Excel—data analysis tool

5. Google AdWords Keyword Planner—research keywords and find new ways of targeting

WHAT'S THE SINGLE BIGGEST MISTAKE YOU SEE PEOPLE MAKE IN ADWORDS?

A not-so-obvious mistake people make with AdWords is searching for their own ad on Google search to see its position and then not clicking on the ad. This affects quality score and can increase the price you pay per click, as well as lower your ad position. If you want to see your position without harming your campaign, you can look at the average position (Avg. Pos.) column within the AdWords interface or use the Google Ad Preview Tool.

WHAT ADVICE WOULD YOU GIVE TO PEOPLE WHO ARE LOOKING TO RUN SUCCESSFUL ADWORDS CAMPAIGNS?

Many people struggle to run a successful Google AdWords campaign because they do not know how AdWords works, which results in them making the same costly mistakes over and over. It's important to learn about the service before jumping in and stay up to date as AdWords evolves. Also, it's important to learn about optimizing a landing page. Even if you manage campaigns properly, if you send the right traffic to a bad landing page, people won't convert.

HOW DO YOU THINK ADWORDS WILL CHANGE OVER THE NEXT FEW YEARS?

Google AdWords will continue offering new audience targeting options. As a result, more companies will use AdWords to keep their sales funnel full by showing ads to a lot of highly targeted people before they reach the bottom of the funnel. Another benefit of targeting the entire sales funnel is that people will be more likely to buy from you when it's time to make a purchasing decision because they're already familiar with your company.

LEARN MORE ABOUT JONATHAN

I've been involved in digital marketing since launching my first PPC advertising campaign in the year 2000.

🌐 WWW.PPCCONSULTING.COM

🔲 WWW.LINKEDIN.COM/IN/THEJONATHANNG

🔲 @THANKYOUJON

🔲 FB.ME/JONATHANNGOFFICIAL

BRAD PUTNEY

HOW DO YOU DETERMINE THE EFFECTIVENESS OF AN ADWORDS CAMPAIGN?

Each campaign will have several key performance indicators that are cru-cial to judge the success of a campaign. However, more often than not, we're watching and optimizing toward three numbers: (1) click-through rate, (2) Conversions, and (3) cost per conversion or acquisition. The click-through rate is the best measure of the relevancy of keywords to ad text and keyword to landing page content. Conversions are the last and final action we desire a website visitor to take, whether that's a purchase, phone call, or some type of form fill. We also drive down the cost per acquisition to increase the return on ad spend.

WHAT IS THE SINGLE MOST EFFECTIVE ADWORDS TACTIC YOU'VE LEARNED?

The most effective tactic, or maybe advice, for a search campaign is to try not to be all things to all people. To run an effective campaign, your ad doesn't have to show for every keyword search or even be in the num-ber-one position every time. Use the data in your campaigns and Google Analytics to find what's working and what's not. Stop going after keywords that *you think* searchers are using and optimize for keywords that search-ers *are* using by looking at your search terms reports.

IF YOU COULD CARRY ONLY FIVE TOOLS IN YOUR ADWORDS TOOLKIT, WHAT WOULD THEY BE?

The five tools or reports that I find most important, in no particular order, are: AdWords Search Terms Report, the Auction Insights Report, the Search Impression Share Report, Google Search Console search analytics, and Google Search Console crawl stats.

WHAT'S THE SINGLE BIGGEST MISTAKE YOU SEE PEOPLE MAKE IN ADWORDS?

I've diagnosed and repaired hundreds of AdWords campaigns, and the simplest mistakes seem to be the most prevalent. First, I see Search campaigns using the wrong match type for the keywords in the ad groups. Using the wrong match types will generate hundreds if not thousands of irrelevant impressions and drive non-performing, non-converting traffic to your website. Second, many inexperienced campaign managers will take the position of "set it and forget it." Google AdWords campaigns must be maintained, managed, and optimized on a regular basis. A campaign that is regularly adjusted will see continuous improvement in performance.

HOW DO YOU THINK ADWORDS WILL CHANGE OVER THE NEXT FEW YEARS?

As anyone who's familiar with search knows, the only constant is change, and we are forever learning, adopting, and adapting. Critical to search in the next few years will be mobile; both AdWords campaigns and websites must be mobile-friendly and optimized. Also important, both today and in the near future, is the explosive growth of voice search. Searchers use different words when talking into their devices, therefore campaign managers must adjust their keywords and ad text to remain relevant. Further out on the horizon is AI and machine learning, which will change the way we build and manage campaigns.

LEARN MORE ABOUT BRAD

I eat, breathe, and sleep Google AdWords and paid search campaigns at True North Consulting. To date I've built, repaired, and managed more than five hundred AdWords campaigns. I'm certified in all AdWords disciplines, as well as Google Analytics. In 2015 I was selected as a Google AdWords All-Star and spent three days at the GooglePlex in Mountain View. On days away from the office I work to manage my addiction to all things boats and boating by getting out on the water with my wife and my beagle, Eddy.

🌐 TRUENORTHCONSULTINGCLOQUET.COM
🔗 WWW.LINKEDIN.COM/IN/BRADPUTNEY

ALLISON SCHAFFER

PAID SEARCH MANAGER, IPROSPECT

HOW DO YOU DETERMINE THE EFFECTIVENESS OF AN ADWORDS CAMPAIGN?

First, review primary KPIs and goals to ensure the paid search campaigns are reaching those. In addition, if paid search is driving a significant percentage of overall site traffic, I'd suggest monitoring business metrics to see if shifts in paid search investment and tactics are helping to drive the business forward.

WHAT IS THE SINGLE MOST EFFECTIVE ADWORDS TACTIC YOU'VE LEARNED?

Right now, Similar Audiences has been key in the growth of many clients. While remarketing to users through remarketing lists for search ads (RLSA) or Customer Match can be effective from a lower funnel perspective, Similar Audiences allows us to reach potential new customers that we already know have a higher likelihood of converting. New customer acquisition has been a huge focus for a lot of companies, and Similar Audiences is the perfect targeting tactic in order to efficiently reach this audience.

IF YOU COULD CARRY ONLY FIVE TOOLS IN YOUR ADWORDS TOOLKIT, WHAT WOULD THEY BE?

Excel, Google Keyword Planner, DoubleClick Search bidding rules, Audience Insights, and AdGooroo.

WHAT'S THE SINGLE BIGGEST MISTAKE YOU SEE PEOPLE MAKE IN ADWORDS?

Focusing too much on a lower funnel, last click goal, such as revenue or purchases. Many companies will have a strict ROI or Return on Advertising Spend (ROAS) goal that must be hit, but sometimes that comes with the cost of focusing on only branded or long tail non-branded keywords. In order to fuel the funnel and drive new customer acquisition, clients still need to keep in mind that budget should be allocated toward awareness-focused tactics, even though the results may not be immediately apparent.

WHAT ADVICE WOULD YOU GIVE TO PEOPLE WHO ARE LOOKING TO RUN SUCCESSFUL ADWORDS CAMPAIGNS?

First, align on what your primary KPI and goal will be and ensure that this goal will drive your company's business. From there, ensure campaign tactics are aligned with this primary KPI, targeting campaigns at as granular a level as possible.

HOW DO YOU THINK ADWORDS WILL CHANGE OVER THE NEXT FEW YEARS?

The future of paid search is audience targeting and has been shifting that way since the launch of RLSA, Customer Match, and Similar Audiences. We're now able to layer on more data than we ever could, allowing us to segment and target campaigns at an even more granular level to help companies reach their goals. In addition, the transition to voice search is going to shake up the industry significantly as virtual assistants continue to pop up in everyone's homes. Digital marketers are on the lookout for how we can adapt to the shift in search queries as voice search adoption rates increase.

LEARN MORE ABOUT ALLISON

After graduating from Northwestern University in 2012, I have worked in the digital marketing space for more than five years on a variety of large-scale clients, including Hewlett-Packard, Pier 1 Imports, Choice Hotels, Massage Envy, Culligan, and Ameriprise Financial. I am currently a paid search manager at iProspect in Chicago, Illinois. In my free time, you will find me at CrossFit, cooking, or traveling abroad.

in WWW.LINKEDIN.COM/IN/ALLISON-SCHAFFER-GONZALEZ-55179323

SCOTT SALWOLKE

GOOGLE ADWORDS CONSULTANT

HOW DO YOU DETERMINE THE EFFECTIVENESS OF AN ADWORDS CAMPAIGN?

With Google AdWords, there are a number of factors you can look at to determine how successful a campaign is, from click-through rate to the Quality Score of keywords to the cost-per-conversion of campaigns. Yet none of these really matters unless the advertiser is getting new business from the campaign. From the outside, it could look like the greatest campaign ever, but if the phone calls and form submissions don't lead to actual business, then none of that really matters. This is one reason you need to have conversion tracking for your campaigns and follow up to make sure conversions have become quality leads.

WHAT IS THE SINGLE MOST EFFECTIVE ADWORDS TACTIC YOU'VE LEARNED?

To constantly review the data and to be constantly testing, which go hand in hand. Even when I've had campaigns that had very high click-through rates, I've continuously tested new ads against the successful ones and often found ads that did even better. This is why you should always be proactive with your campaigns and not just let them run on their own, even if they seem to be successful. The competition isn't likely to be letting their campaigns become stagnant, and neither should you.

IF YOU COULD CARRY ONLY FIVE TOOLS IN YOUR ADWORDS TOOLKIT, WHAT WOULD THEY BE?

Many of the best tools are from Google and are free, such as Google Analytics, which many websites already have installed. Yet advertisers need to make sure the analytics and AdWords are properly linked, or all the data won't be recorded properly. Keyword Planner is a good tool for finding keywords to target. Google Search Console is important for acquiring data related to your website, some of which can help you with your AdWords campaign. For example, if you find your site does poorly on mobile, then you need to fix that. If that isn't an option right away, then you might want to bid lower on mobile in AdWords. AdWords Editor is a free tool from Google that you download onto your computer. You can make changes to your campaign offline and then load them online. You can save a lot of time by using this tool, which also provides warnings about potential problems with ads or keywords. SEMrush is a great tool learn about your competition and what they're doing online.

WHAT'S THE SINGLE BIGGEST MISTAKE YOU SEE PEOPLE MAKE IN ADWORDS?

The biggest mistake I see people make is not having campaign-specific landing pages. For some it's not an option, as they can't easily make updates to their sites. Yet I've seen many companies who could afford to have it done but didn't want to take the time or expense to develop them. Even if there's a cost involved, it can often be made up in a short time by the increase in conversions. If the ad campaign focuses on a particular service or product, you don't want to send people to your home page, where they might have to search for what they're looking for. With a landing page, you can focus on what interested the person in the ad that convinced them to click on it in the first place.

WHAT ADVICE WOULD YOU GIVE TO PEOPLE WHO ARE LOOKING TO RUN SUCCESSFUL ADWORDS CAMPAIGNS?

The biggest thing is to be constantly monitoring the campaigns. You need to regularly read the Search Terms Report to find what actual phrases triggered ads. You might find new phrases to test, as well as those that don't apply for the business. With any that don't apply, you need to add some part of the phrase to your negative keywords list. You must also continuously test your ads to see if you can improve on your click-through rate, even if you already have a strong CTR. Since Google is constantly adding new features, advertisers should evaluate each one to see if it might benefit their ad campaigns. You can't take a "set it and forget it" approach to your campaign, or you'll pay for it in the long run.

HOW DO YOU THINK ADWORDS WILL CHANGE OVER THE NEXT FEW YEARS?

The biggest change to pay-per-click will be the increase in usage of voice search. When people use Alexa or Google Home, their device often gives them just one result. That could change if these devices start to have screens, but it will still make it a challenge for these platforms to incorporate ads into their voice query results. If you're in an industry where people typically research before making a purchase, it might not have much impact. For some businesses, however, it could limit exposure unless the company is the best in their field or already used by the consumer.

LEARN MORE ABOUT SCOTT

I have a background slightly different than most in my field. For twenty years I was a writer and journalist, but it was when I was hired to write for a website that I discovered SEO. In 2004 I started my own agency with an emphasis on SEO. I added pay-per-click a couple of years later, and that is now the main focus of my agency, Ad Hoc Marketing. The advantage of Google AdWords is that you can control your message and who sees it. You can spend a lot of time on SEO but not know the results for a long time. With PPC you can get results in a relatively short time. I'm certified yearly by both Google AdWords and Bing Ads and active in the pay-per-click community. With so many changes to both platforms, it's become a full-time job just to keep up with everything.

⊕ WWW.ADHOCMARKETING.COM

✉ SEM@ADHOCMARKETING.COM

ROB WATTS

PPC CONSULTANT, BRIGHTON, UNITED KINGDOM

HOW DO YOU DETERMINE THE EFFECTIVENESS OF AN ADWORDS CAMPAIGN?

It depends entirely on what the client needs and any goals they may have set. It's really important to manage expectations before you start working on any campaign, as well as agreeing on how success should be measured. Beyond this, I think it's important to communicate results in whatever format works for the client—and where possible—demonstrate progress in order to keep the client invested. If the client is happy and expectations are met, then that is an effective campaign.

WHAT IS THE SINGLE MOST EFFECTIVE ADWORDS TACTIC YOU'VE LEARNED?

Be efficient and treat your client's budget as if it were your own. It may sound really simple, but a lot of PPC managers fall into the trap of forgetting the basics when attempting to grow an account. It can be dangerous to try to achieve results too quickly, but if you don't have an eye for detail, you can very quickly waste your client's budget.

IF YOU COULD CARRY ONLY FIVE TOOLS IN YOUR ADWORDS TOOLKIT, WHAT WOULD THEY BE?

I have to admit I'm pretty old school in that respect, as there's honestly very few tools that I use on a regular basis. I guess the basics—Google Analytics, AdWords Editor, and Microsoft Excel—are the ones I use the most, and I pretty much get most of what I need from them. There are so many tools on the market that promise certain things. It's easy to think they can be a quick route to transforming an account, but unless you're spending tens of thousands of dollars per month on AdWords, there's really no substitute for experience and attention to detail. Oh, and pivot tables!

WHAT'S THE SINGLE BIGGEST MISTAKE YOU SEE PEOPLE MAKE IN ADWORDS?

Not understanding how keyword match types work. I see this so often and I'm always surprised when I see an account spending a large amount of money but making fundamental errors in this way. If you don't understand how match types work, it's going to be difficult to ever get your account performing optimally, regardless of whatever else you might be doing to optimize your campaigns.

WHAT ADVICE WOULD YOU GIVE TO PEOPLE WHO ARE LOOKING TO RUN SUCCESSFUL ADWORDS CAMPAIGNS?

If you're new to AdWords, make sure you understand how match types work, how quality score works, and how ad rank is calculated. If you don't understand those, then there's little point in learning anything else. Start with the basics and know them inside out and upside down. You'll be surprised how far that knowledge extends to other areas of an AdWords account. If you're a little more experienced, then start building audiences and use them as much as you can. Remarketing lists for search ads (RLSA) was a game changer for me, but still I see it used less often than it should be. If you get this right, it can unlock a lot of performance in your account.

HOW DO YOU THINK ADWORDS WILL CHANGE OVER THE NEXT FEW YEARS?

I expect the shift will continue more toward mobile, and audience bidding will begin to take over from keywords to some extent. I think we will see voice search having an impact on optimization techniques, as well.

LEARN MORE ABOUT ROB

I'm a freelance PPC consultant based in Brighton, United Kingdom. I've worked in digital for almost a decade now and have been fortunate to work with several major global brands and some fantastic award-winning agencies. These days I prefer to work with start-ups and smaller businesses looking to grow or expand their business online.

⊕ WWW.ROBWATTSPPC.CO.UK

KASPARS BRENCANS

PPC EXPERT, BEST PPC MARKETING

HOW DO YOU DETERMINE THE EFFECTIVENESS OF AN ADWORDS CAMPAIGN?

The number-one factor will always be: Is the client making money from this campaign? If the answer is no, then it's not effective. There isn't a better breakdown than that. Our company focuses directly on clients' ROI, and we do whatever it takes to be profitable. If it's an online store, obviously the return will be measured in dollars. Meanwhile, if it's a lead gen campaign, then the ultimate goal is to communicate results with the client to understand the quality of the leads. If it's a brand awareness campaign, the ultimate question is whether we're balancing having the lowest costs vs. being in front of the right audience who would be interested in being involved with the particular company.

WHAT IS THE SINGLE MOST EFFECTIVE ADWORDS TACTIC YOU'VE LEARNED?

Google AdWords is a tricky platform. The best tactic is actually pretty simple: structure your campaigns and ad groups in a way that if someone else looked at the account, they would actually understand what is going on there. Next, as far as ad groups go, make sure your ad groups have only a handful of very closely related keywords in each and write very specific ads to each of these groups. Don't be afraid to have tons of ad groups. Meanwhile, even though you have many ad groups—you do have to make sure the ads are specific to your product/service, but these ads have to stand out from what others are searching for. Each ad group has to have at least three ads to start with, and they all have to have a different value proposition for testing/optimization purposes.

To touch upon my last statement, for example, search in Google for "ppc company" and you'll see how every single company offers either "free account audit or evaluation" or a "free quote." Now, here's a great opportunity to enter this market with a completely out-of-box approach, such as writing ads offering something along the lines of "Start your PPC campaign by October 15th and get a free set of remarketing ads."

IF YOU COULD CARRY ONLY FIVE TOOLS IN YOUR ADWORDS TOOLKIT, WHAT WOULD THEY BE?

I actually prefer to do many things on my own. Automation is good, but it can be limiting. I prefer to analyze things on my own. If I could, I would list Excel/Google Sheets here five times—that's how important it is in my everyday life.

1. Excel

2. AdWords Editor

3. Unbounce

4. Google Optimize

5. Data Studio

WHAT'S THE SINGLE BIGGEST MISTAKE YOU SEE PEOPLE MAKE IN ADWORDS?

I would say the 1(a) problem I've noticed in unsuccessful accounts lie in improper account setup. Google is very picky about what is being served, considering their Quality Score is playing such a huge role (changing average CPC costs to be able to vary in the range of −400 percent to +50 percent). 1(b) is not using/understanding how match types work. 1(c) using the same/similar keywords in different ad groups. 1(d) not using negative keywords. Many companies give AdWords a chance, fail, and then give up the hope of advertising in this platform. Note that all the issues I mentioned above go hand-in-hand in 95 percent of cases.

WHAT ADVICE WOULD YOU GIVE TO PEOPLE WHO ARE LOOKING TO RUN SUCCESSFUL ADWORDS CAMPAIGNS?

Make sure you don't make the mistakes I mentioned in the previous question, and remember that Google will always favor advertisers that have been in the game for longer. It's called the "ad account history." Once a campaign has run, I highly suggest not moving keywords from that campaign around in the account, as Google will consider them new keywords. Furthermore, NEVER delete any keywords that you want to move around or test match types; simply pause them, add a label, and make duplicates of the keyword in whichever way you envision. Same goes with ads: if you delete, move, or update an ad, it will lose its historical data and will be considered a completely new ad.

HOW DO YOU THINK ADWORDS WILL CHANGE OVER THE NEXT FEW YEARS?

Honestly, I believe that one day, organic results in Google will be completely gone. AdWords for ETA (extended text ads) already take up the fold on mobile searches, and Google tried to test with double eighty-character description lines—increasing the ad real estate by another half-inch per ad on either platform. Also, Google wants to turn into a pay-per-result platform and therefore stray further away from keywords to focus on in-market audiences.

LEARN MORE ABOUT KASPARS

I'm a PPC Marketing Expert in Chicago who believes that PPC without CRO is the same as having a wedding without music. I'm probably best known for asking, "Did you test that already?"

⊕ BESTPPC.MARKETING
✉ KASPARS@BESTPPCMARKETING.COM
ⓛ WWW.LINKEDIN.COM/IN/BRENCANS

MEG RAIANO

MANAGING DIRECTOR, RECREATIVEAGENCY

HOW DO YOU DETERMINE THE EFFECTIVENESS OF AN ADWORDS CAMPAIGN?

It really depends on the clients/tactics and what their key metrics are. For a campaign that drives users to gated content, the measure of success would be form fills/downloads. For clients who don't have any recognition and are trying to drive more traffic to their site—which will, in turn, create more brand awareness—their main goal would be visits or clicks.

WHAT IS THE SINGLE MOST EFFECTIVE ADWORDS TACTIC YOU'VE LEARNED?

I've learned that each tactic needs other tactics to support it in order to be effective. If you take AdWords ads, for example, it's necessary to build some kind of strategy outside of AdWords that will enhance the user experience of those clicking through the ads. That includes keyword research, site analytics, landing page strategies, and others. Highly effective campaigns are entirely dependent on the way they are being supported through other tactics.

IF YOU COULD CARRY ONLY FIVE TOOLS IN YOUR ADWORDS TOOLKIT, WHAT WOULD THEY BE?

Google's Keyword Planner tool, Google Analytics, call tracking integration, Google's URL builder, and SpyFu.

WHAT'S THE SINGLE BIGGEST MISTAKE YOU SEE PEOPLE MAKE IN ADWORDS?

The single biggest mistake I see is—overwhelmingly—people are using super broad keywords that could be tied to people searching for a myriad of different things. By using these keywords, you will lower your quality score, lower your potential click-through rate, and lower conversions overall, not to mention spending tons of marketing dollars on irrelevant or unspecific keywords.

WHAT ADVICE WOULD YOU GIVE TO PEOPLE WHO ARE LOOKING TO RUN SUCCESSFUL ADWORDS CAMPAIGNS?

The best piece of advice I can give someone looking to run successful AdWords campaigns is to do your research; explore your analytics and SpyFu reports to see where your strengths and weaknesses are for keywords, both for SEO and PPC, and then use that to your advantage when creating new campaigns and ad groups; and do your keyword research. Also, don't try and do it yourself if you're not familiar. Hire someone to help you, show you how to do it, or fully do it for you. A lot of my clients come to me saying, "We set this up ourselves and it seemed to be working, but we're really not sure what we're looking at." By hiring someone with PPC experience—either within your company or outsourcing to an agency—you'll get better bang for your buck right off the bat, and you'll have less headache in the end.

HOW DO YOU THINK ADWORDS WILL CHANGE OVER THE NEXT FEW YEARS?

Google is constantly changing and updating their algorithms. I think with the addition and growth of paid social media ads, Google AdWords will eventually expand into the social realm and try to increase its reach overall.

LEARN MORE ABOUT MEG

reCreativeAgency was born out of my love for digital marketing and photography. Before making the move to Connecticut, I started my digital marketing career in Long Island at a small boutique business in Port Washington. After moving to Connecticut and getting my feet wet in the agency arena, I now get to focus on some of my favorite things: small businesses in the beer, wine, and puppy industries. When not working, you can often find me hiking with my dogs in Litchfield County or checking out new local breweries. It's work, right?

⊕ WWW.RECREATIVEAGENCY.COM
✉ MEG@RECREATIVEAGENCY.COM
▣ @RECREATIVE_CT
▣ @WILL_WHEATEN

SHAUN BOND

CEO, PPC SAMURAI

HOW DO YOU DETERMINE THE EFFECTIVENESS OF AN ADWORDS CAMPAIGN?

An effective AdWords campaign should put your ads in front of people who are interested in the services or products you offer, for the cheapest click costs possible. Sounds logical, right? However, you'd be amazed how many people run campaigns without defining a conversion event or how much they spend on searches that have never produced a conversion event. Google "Reduce Wasted Ad Spend In Your AdWords Account" for a great article from searchengineland.com on how to dramatically reduce wasted spend in an account, thus increasing the effectiveness of the campaign and the ROI for the client.

WHAT IS THE SINGLE MOST EFFECTIVE ADWORDS TACTIC YOU'VE LEARNED?

It's essential to organize your campaign structure in a way that is granular enough to enable good management decisions. One campaign per major location and one campaign per device is the best approach I've seen. This allows you to control bids and budget for each major location you are targeting, plus it gives flexibility to adjust for the different performance of each device type. Mobile performs very differently than desktop, and using a device/location bid modifier does not give you the level of control needed to squeeze the most out of your campaigns. I'm also a fan of a broad match modifier (BMM)/exact structure, which can be very effective for clients but also offers incredible automation potential.

IF YOU COULD CARRY ONLY FIVE TOOLS IN YOUR ADWORDS TOOLKIT, WHAT WOULD THEY BE?

1. PPC Samurai (of course!) – designed to help automate the ongoing components of campaign management using your own "secret-sauce" strategies, so you don't spend all your time down in the trenches

2. PPC Campaign Generator – great for helping for initial campaign builds, finding keyword themes, and identifying negative keywords

3. AdWords Editor – incredible free tool from Google to help make mass changes to your campaigns

4. SEMrush – fantastic competitor research and insights

5. Respected knowledge bases – like searchengineland.com and search-enginewatch.com, so you can keep up to date with the latest AdWords trends and tips

WHAT'S THE SINGLE BIGGEST MISTAKE YOU SEE PEOPLE MAKE IN ADWORDS?

They forgo ad testing because it can be very time consuming; it becomes a "tomorrow" activity. We all know we should do it, but it can be so onerous, we tend to put it off. However, A/B split testing is the single most important activity that can be done to progressively increase click-through rate (CTR) and Quality Score (QS), thus reducing click costs for clients. Additionally, it should be done by using statistically significant data, not gut feel. We need to find ads that are underperforming and replace them with new tests to continually search for better performing ads. There are some split-testing calculators online that can help you run ad tests on a small scale; otherwise use a tool like PPC Samurai for automated testing.

WHAT ADVICE WOULD YOU GIVE TO PEOPLE WHO ARE LOOKING TO RUN SUCCESSFUL ADWORDS CAMPAIGNS?

Select your keywords carefully. Get your campaign structure right. Run at least two ads per ad group (so you can split test). Watch your search queries closely. Add negative keywords. Expand on keywords that are working well. Watch location and device performance and move budget to your best performers. Bid manually unless you have loads of conversion data, in which case the Google auto bidding options can work well. Don't forget ad extensions. If hiring an agency, make sure they have specialists, and check the change history report in your AdWords account to ensure they're making regular tweaks.

HOW DO YOU THINK ADWORDS WILL CHANGE OVER THE NEXT FEW YEARS?

I think automation will become increasingly important as AdWords becomes more complex and margins become thinner in the global economy. I also think Google will introduce more AI into bidding, device, and geo targeting. Competition between businesses will increase as they struggle to get their ads into desirable page positions. I believe Google will introduce some serious remarketing capabilities, expanding the current capabilities to include retargeting users who have been to sites similar to that of the client.

LEARN MORE ABOUT SHAUN

I am the co-owner and creator of PPC Samurai, a tool designed to help AdWords agencies compete globally through automation of their own "secret-sauce" management strategies. I also own an AdWords agency (and have done so for over ten years) with experience managing AdWords accounts ranging from small local businesses up to large multinational listed companies. PPC Samurai was born of my own need, as I wanted to automate workflows that I determined, and nothing else in the market offered that. Automation allows for efficiency—and it's true, efficiency is my favorite word in the English language! PPC Samurai is now being used in eighteen countries by a broad range of agencies; as a result, it provides me with the wonderful opportunity to spend considerable time with some of the brightest minds in the AdWords world. I love helping them implement automation of unique and varied management techniques while brainstorming cutting edge strategies to keep them well ahead of their competition.

⊕ WWW.PPCSAMURAI.COM

▥ WWW.LINKEDIN.COM/IN/SHBOND

▐ WWW.FACEBOOK.COM/GROUPS/PPCSAMURAI

CHAPTER 3
FACEBOOK ADS

A SIMPLE EXPLANATION OF FACEBOOK ADS

Facebook Ads allow advertisers to target people on the world's most popular social media platform: Facebook.

Facebook offers a multitude of advertising solutions for businesses to interact with their customers via their advertising platform, Facebook Ads.

If you've used Facebook recently, you've likely seen ads for businesses relevant to your interests. For instance, if you commonly shop for clothes online, you may see Facebook Ads for clothing companies that offer fashions you might like. This isn't a coincidence. Facebook offers the ability for businesses to advertise to their target market based on their likes and behaviors on Facebook. Therefore, people's actions have a direct influence on the ads that they see on Facebook.

For this reason, Facebook can be a highly effective advertising channel; it allows advertisers to target very specific groups of people who are likely to buy their product or service. Facebook stores *a lot* of information about people, and this data allows advertisers to create highly specific audiences to target with ads.

Facebook Ad campaigns are objective-based. Objectives may include: getting people to fill out a quote form in an ad, drive traffic to a website, guide people to an in-person store, or even get more likes and followers to a Facebook page.

Similar to the Google AdWords Quality Score, Facebook Ads provides a "relevancy score" that influences how Facebook delivers ads to an audience and the cost to the advertiser. The goal is to ensure that people see ads that matter to them, leading to a better experience for people and advertisers alike.

You'll also hear Facebook Ads specialists allude to the Facebook Pixel, an analytics tool provided by Facebook that allows advertisers to measure the effectiveness of their campaigns and understand the actions taken from Facebook Ads on a website or landing page.

It's important to note that Facebook Ads alludes to the advertisements and paid-engagement in Facebook, not organic "community management" or other unpaid strategies to reach an organization's goals on Facebook.

FACEBOOK ADS
SPECIALISTS
SOUND OFF

MEG BRUNSON

FOUNDER & CEO, EIEIO MARKETING

HOW DO YOU DETERMINE THE EFFECTIVENESS OF A FACEBOOK ADS CAMPAIGN?

Facebook offers a variety of analytics to measure the effectiveness of Facebook Ads within their Ads Manager tool. Every business will have a slightly unique measure of success, so the precise analytics that we use to determine the effectiveness of a Facebook Ad Campaign will vary from client to client. One stat that I always like to track and measure is the cost-per-impression. Cost-per-impression is a valuable statistic for establishing a baseline comparison across different platforms. It's also a good way to determine whether increases in Ad spend are the result of higher bidding in the marketplace or whether there is an element of the ad itself not converting as well as past Ads have. I will also track the stats at each step in the customer journey (or funnel), depending on what the ultimate goal of the campaign is. So for example, if the goal is to sell an item, I will track clicks to view that item, how many times the item was added to a cart, how many times a purchase was initiated, and how many times the item was purchased. This not only helps us identify our customer journey and where our funnel may be leaky but it allows us to measure the effectiveness of our Facebook Ad based on our ultimate goals.

WHAT IS THE SINGLE MOST EFFECTIVE FACEBOOK ADS TACTIC YOU'VE LEARNED?

Video content has proven to be favored by users on the Facebook platform, and it's inexpensive to place your video in front of your ideal audience using Facebook's comprehensive targeting options. These targeting options also include the ability to create an audience of people who have viewed your video content. Because we know that it's easier to sell to a warm audience (people who know, like, and trust you), a wildly successful tactic is to run a Facebook Video View Ad in order to warm up an audience of new/cold prospects. These videos should deliver value to your viewers in order to build up that rapport with your business. Then, run a second campaign retargeting that warm video-viewer audience with another Ad that has a stronger call-to-action, encouraging them to work their way further down your sales funnel toward a conversion. This two-step process, warming up a cold audience with a promoted video before serving them an Ad calling for a conversion, is a highly-effective Facebook Ads tactic.

IF YOU COULD CARRY ONLY FIVE TOOLS IN YOUR FACEBOOK ADS TOOLKIT, WHAT WOULD THEY BE?

The tools I cannot afford to be without are: the Facebook Pixel, Google Tag Manager, Canva, a cell phone, and Zapier. The Facebook Pixel is a piece of code that is essential for tracking, retargeting, and optimizing Ad Campaigns. It's the building block to success and needs to be installed on every website ASAP. Google Tag Manager is an amazing tool that not only makes installation of the Pixel easy, it simplifies the ability to set up complex event tracking without in-depth coding knowledge. When it comes to running Ads on Facebook, it's the creative that will stop the user from scrolling, making quality creative essential to the success of marketers. Canva is a free (with low-cost add-on options) graphic design tool that is easy to learn and use for making quality images. Because video is so highly engaging, especially live video, a cell phone would be my next essential tool for capturing video clips. Finally, Zapier is a digital program that connects various programs and platforms. It allows us to automate many processes, such as lead generation, mailing lists, scheduling, and other notifications. These are the five tools I use most often when running successful Facebook Ads Campaigns.

WHAT'S THE SINGLE BIGGEST MISTAKE YOU SEE PEOPLE MAKE IN FACEBOOK ADS?

The single biggest mistake made by marketers regarding Facebook Ads is choosing the wrong objective. It's easy to fall into the habit of boosting posts because Facebook makes it so easy, but in most cases, a boosted post is not the best Ad for a business to run. The objective you choose for your Ads (when creating in the Ads Manager tool) tells Facebook what result you want to see. You can choose from things like leads (you want names, email addresses, and/or phone numbers), traffic (you want people to go to your website) or conversions (you want people to make a purchase). But it's also not quite that simple. Once you realize how that part works, people jump from running boosted posts to running conversion ads. But you also have to get fifty conversions in one week's time (and ideally twenty-five conversions per day, per ad set) in order for the Ads to optimize effectively. What that means is that if you are not able to hit that conversion goal based on your current budget, then you need to run an ad to optimize for a step (or more) "higher" in your sales funnel. For example, optimize for traffic instead of conversions until you are able to raise your budget or until you are generating enough conversions to change the objective. Without a doubt, when people say that Facebook Ads don't work for their business, they tend to be running the wrong type of Ads for their business goals.

WHAT ADVICE WOULD YOU GIVE TO PEOPLE WHO ARE LOOKING TO RUN SUCCESSFUL FACEBOOK ADS CAMPAIGNS?

Take the time to learn the platform. Facebook offers FREE training modules at Facebook.com/blueprint. These Blueprint courses walk through the basics of Facebook Ads, and they are actually a prerequisite for Facebook employees to take, as well. There are many other Facebook courses available from a variety of sources, but when at all possible, I highly recommend learning from the source. That being said, a paid course from an expert can also provide a great supplement to the Blueprint courses. Paid courses typically come with some level of support from the expert who produced the course, which is invaluable when learning the processes on your own.

HOW DO YOU THINK FACEBOOK ADS WILL CHANGE OVER THE NEXT FEW YEARS?

Facebook changes all of the time. As more and more people join Facebook and more and more businesses are competing for Ad space, we will likely see prices rise incrementally, as they have been for the past few years. This makes it more important than ever to familiarize yourself with Facebook Ads and learn how to leverage them for your business now so that when things become more expensive, you're already getting the ROI you need to remain competitive.

LEARN MORE ABOUT MEG

I am a former Facebook employee who currently lives in Phoenix, Arizona, with my husband and four daughters. I loved working at Facebook and learning all of the tips, tricks, and best practices directly from the source. Marketing is one of my favorite ways to help people—both helping to grow businesses and helping people find new products and services that they didn't know they can't live without! I left Facebook in 2017 and founded EIEIO Marketing, a digital marketing agency that focuses on Facebook Ads. When you think of Facebook, remember EIEIO: Engage, Interact, Educate, Influence, and Optimize. It's our philosophy, and it's what we do for our clients every single day. I also host a podcast and other materials related to supporting parent entrepreneurs through topics related to entrepreneurship, marketing, and raising entrepreneurial children.

- 🌐 WWW.EIEIOMARKETING.COM
- 🌐 MEGBRUNSON.COM
- ✉ MEG@EIEIOMARKETING.COM
- 🔗 WWW.LINKEDIN.COM/IN/MEGBRUNSON
- 🐦 @THEMEGBRUNSON
- 📘 WWW.FACEBOOK.COM/THEMEGBRUNSON
- 📷 @THEMEGBRUNSON
- 📌 @THEMEGBRUNSON

MARLY SCHUMAN

PARTNER, ASSOCIATE DIRECTOR OF PAID SOCIAL

HOW DO YOU DETERMINE THE EFFECTIVENESS OF A FACEBOOK ADS CAMPAIGN?

Setting clear KPIs and benchmarks is key in determining effectiveness of your Facebook Ads. I ensure that my objective lines up with these KPIs before setting up a campaign. If I am testing something new, I try to rely on industry benchmarks or results from other clients within my agency. Another important consideration is evaluating whether it is scalable. For example, if my campaign's ROAS is one hundred dollars but I spent only five dollars, I wouldn't consider that a successful campaign. Whenever I set up a test, I try to ensure the spend is at least a few thousand dollars—ideally more—and that it can be expanded.

WHAT IS THE SINGLE MOST EFFECTIVE FACEBOOK ADS TACTIC YOU'VE LEARNED?

The strongest Facebook tactic I've utilized that I would pass on to pretty much any client is Lookalikes. Using a CRM list (an email list of customers), Facebook can find users potentially like those current customers. Lookalikes are consistently my strongest click and purchase driver. I've tested them out for multiple clients and products and they always work, especially if your goal is to generate online sales or drive traffic to a website. A huge benefit is that you're able to scale out a tiny customer list into a list of several million users more likely to have an affinity for your brand.

IF YOU COULD CARRY ONLY FIVE TOOLS IN YOUR FACEBOOK ADS TOOLKIT, WHAT WOULD THEY BE?

The most important tools in Facebook Ads really depend on what your objectives are and what your brand is trying to achieve. A consumer packaged goods (CPG) brand is going to rely on completely different objectives than a retail brand. With that said, five of the most critical tools are measurement studies, Dynamic Product Ads, vertical video, the Facebook Pixel, and Lookalike targeting.

WHAT'S THE SINGLE BIGGEST MISTAKE YOU SEE PEOPLE MAKE IN FACEBOOK ADS?

Facebook has been progressing from a "like" and engagement driver to a more reach-focused platform, and many brands still don't want to face the facts. Due to the Facebook algorithm, organic content just isn't seen. Still, many brands focus far too many of their efforts on creating content that few people will see and doing so to gain meaningless likes or engagements.

WHAT ADVICE WOULD YOU GIVE TO PEOPLE WHO ARE LOOKING TO RUN SUCCESSFUL FACEBOOK ADS CAMPAIGNS?

Being successful on Facebook is largely about quality creative and targeting the right audience. More specifically, tailoring your creative for the audience you're trying to reach. I often see brands trying to be very prescriptive about who they are targeting, but what's the point if you're just going to use a general message? More niche audiences tend to cost more to reach so make the more effective use of your dollars.

HOW DO YOU THINK FACEBOOK ADS WILL CHANGE OVER THE NEXT FEW YEARS?

Facebook is going to have to keep competing with other social platforms, especially for the attention of the younger age groups who are spending a lot of their time on other social networks like Snapchat. Instagram is capturing a lot of those users, but Facebook still seems to be missing out. It is also becoming more common for brands to go digital first, so there is going to be more and more competition on Facebook. This is pushing many to be more innovative with ads. With that, Facebook will need to continue developing new ad types to allow brands to tell their full story on the platform.

LEARN MORE ABOUT MARLY

I have been working in social media for over eight years, so I have seen the space progress in terms of the way brands use the platform and the platforms they focus on. I currently work at Mindshare, a GroupM agency, helping develop and refine social media strategy for major brands.

in WWW.LINKEDIN.COM/IN/MARLYSCHUMAN

ANDREW LIWANAG

SR. ADVERTISING MANAGER, NATIVE & SOCIAL,
COMPARECARDS AT LENDINGTREE

HOW DO YOU DETERMINE THE EFFECTIVENESS OF A FACEBOOK ADS CAMPAIGN?

I work in performance marketing—we determine success by profits and Return on Advertising Spend (ROAS). Many companies that advertise on Facebook are putting marketing dollars toward branding campaigns or signup campaigns; their goals are different than mine, which leads to different strategies and buying models. Performance marketing doesn't rely heavily on CTRs, CPAs, or engagement metrics, as long as dollars are coming in. For example, Campaign A can have a CPC of $10 with a total spend of $1,000, and Campaign B can have a CPC of $1 with a total spend of $1,000. To most brand marketers, that is an easy win for Campaign B. To me, if Campaign A returned $1,100 and Campaign B returned $900, I would scale Campaign A.

WHAT IS THE SINGLE MOST EFFECTIVE FACEBOOK ADS TACTIC YOU'VE LEARNED?

Target testing. When working in a highly competitive industry, scraping for every marginal win is the difference between a profitable campaign and a non-profitable campaign. Targeting can affect multiple things. If you find the right target, it can improve all engagement metrics like CTR, CPC, and CPA; this means it reaches a highly qualified audience and can lower your costs overall.

IF YOU COULD CARRY ONLY FIVE TOOLS IN YOUR FACEBOOK ADS TOOLKIT, WHAT WOULD THEY BE?

Kenshoo—it's a third-party integration service that is very useful when the Facebook account has reached scale. The biggest help is their ability to build campaigns with fully customizable parameters automatically built into each individual ad. This saves a ton of time. Excel—I have ten files open at all times. It makes it easy to combine data sets from different platforms (in my case, in-house data and FB front-end data) into one beautiful sheet you can pivot; make fancy charts on for c-suites; and make quick and agile decisions. In-house multi-attribution reporting—the most important data is the data you collect yourself. We've built an entire system that is custom to us with modeled, first click, last click attribution, as well as pulling API reporting from multiple sources. Audience Insights— Facebook has some of the best data in the world, and it's all first-party. Plug in your most valuable pixel/audience and see what Facebook gives you. Google Analytics—a great tool to check in the early stages of a campaign. You can combine it with front-end Facebook metrics to figure out if (1) your target audience is not as qualified, (2) your landing page is not performing well, or (3) there are bot traffic issues.

WHAT'S THE SINGLE BIGGEST MISTAKE YOU SEE PEOPLE MAKE IN FACEBOOK ADS?

Not letting their campaigns run long enough. I've had many experiences where I would run campaigns for a short amount of time, see Facebook's metrics look very poor initially, and shut off the campaign. Many of those times, one of two things would happen: Facebook would be still determining who to serve ads to for best performance, or the campaign would be profitable but it took time to fully understand what the user intends. Facebook is a push medium. Unlike SEM, these users are not searching for specific items to purchase, they are browsing—the conversion funnel is higher.

WHAT ADVICE WOULD YOU GIVE TO PEOPLE WHO ARE LOOKING TO RUN SUCCESSFUL FACEBOOK ADS CAMPAIGNS?

If you work in performance marketing, be prepared for losses and to learn from them. Chances are you'll learn from what your audiences are doing and can convert them at a later date. Make sure you have a persona in mind before launching a campaign; this will save you marketing dollars in testing.

HOW DO YOU THINK FACEBOOK ADS WILL CHANGE OVER THE NEXT FEW YEARS?

Facebook seems to be going through a shift in their strategy with the recent changes to ad policy. In the long run, the quality will be better, but it will be more competitive and more expensive in the coming years. I think Instagram is a gold mine that performance marketers are yet to crack; it is dominated by big-brand marketers. The first ones to do so will reap the benefits for a couple years until competitors catch up.

LEARN MORE ABOUT ANDREW

I'm an overly-confident digital advertising manager who enjoys spending tons of money to make tons of money. I advertise in major social media channels like Facebook, LinkedIn, Twitter, and Pinterest in a very competitive industry and more than ten different native advertising channels. I consult and manage advertising and freelance writing for local businesses around Chicago in my free time.

- ⊕ ANDREWLIWANAG.COM
- ✉ ANDREWLIWANAG@GMAIL.COM
- 🔲 WWW.LINKEDIN.COM/IN/ANDREWLIWANAG

VALERIE DEL TORO

PAID SOCIAL MEDIA SPECIALIST, COX MEDIA GROUP

HOW DO YOU DETERMINE THE EFFECTIVENESS OF A FACEBOOK ADS CAMPAIGN?

There are many ways to measure performance; you just need to make sure your measurement fits your objective. For example, if you are seeking a lower funnel conversion objective, such as a lead generation campaign, you will want to stay on top of your click-through rate (CTR), cost per click (CPC) and cost per lead (CPL). If you are running a branding campaign, such as a reach and frequency campaign, you will also need to look closely at your cost per mille (CPM or cost per one thousand impressions) and your relevancy scores.

WHAT IS THE SINGLE MOST EFFECTIVE FACEBOOK ADS TACTIC YOU'VE LEARNED?

Without a doubt, the most effective tactic I've learned is this: know your audience. It's vital to learn what types of creative, copy, CTA buttons, placements, devices, etc., appeal the most to your target audience and then execute on them. If you test often, you will find trends, and in those trends, you will find answers on how to most effectively reach, educate, interest, and convert people into customers. It's also important to make sure you are excluding placements, devices, CTAs, objectives, etc., that do not do well for your brand.

IF YOU COULD CARRY ONLY FIVE TOOLS IN YOUR FACEBOOK ADS TOOLKIT, WHAT WOULD THEY BE?

Facebook Ads Manager App, Hootsuite Ads, AdRoll, Google URL Builder, and Kissmetrics.

WHAT'S THE SINGLE BIGGEST MISTAKE YOU SEE PEOPLE MAKE IN FACEBOOK ADS?

More often than not, people are too quick to optimize. It can take Facebook up to forty-eight hours before it learns who to serve your ad to and which ad is performing the best. Too often people will see one lead come in and immediately turn off other ads, which is a big mistake. You should give your campaigns at least two full days of performance before making any decisions on how to optimize.

WHAT ADVICE WOULD YOU GIVE TO PEOPLE WHO ARE LOOKING TO RUN SUCCESSFUL FACEBOOK ADS CAMPAIGNS?

Test, test, and test some more. It's essential to your overall success to understand which audience, objective, and type of creative works best when combined, whether it be for evergreen ads or specials and promos. Each type of campaign or promotion has a sweet spot, and testing is the best way to find it.

HOW DO YOU THINK FACEBOOK ADS WILL CHANGE OVER THE NEXT FEW YEARS?

I think we are going to continue shifting toward auto ads based on AI, like the ones rolling out on Google right now, to help us determine which ads, placements, and devices perform best for specific users. Currently, we are coming to these conclusions for ourselves, whether it be by creating Lookalike Audiences or by third-party behavioral data science from companies such as Oracle Data Cloud. I think this continual shift toward auto ads will help make the process of learning what tactics work much more accurate and efficient.

LEARN MORE ABOUT VALERIE

I am a digital marketing enthusiast, social media guru, and paid social rockstar. I have worked as a digital marketing strategist for the past eight years and as a social media specialist for the past five years. I am passionate, hardworking, and dedicated to my craft. I have hopes of making it to a TED stage one day so I can help others with my professional and personal insights.

in WWW.LINKEDIN.COM/IN/VALERIEDTORO

@SOCIALMEDIAPOWERHOUSE

KYLE J. VOLENIK

SENIOR PAID SEARCH AND SOCIAL MEDIA SPECIALIST, EMPOWER

HOW DO YOU DETERMINE THE EFFECTIVENESS OF A FACEBOOK ADS CAMPAIGN?

Effectiveness is driven by the KPI. Ultimately, impacting the cost per acquisition is the main goal, but consistently creating opportunities to learn and enhance KPIs is how one can measure effectiveness.

WHAT IS THE SINGLE MOST EFFECTIVE FACEBOOK ADS TACTIC YOU'VE LEARNED?

Precise Facebook Pixel placement to drive users through the sales funnel further can work wonders on campaigns. This engages audience members throughout the funnel and drives them to making a decision on your brand.

IF YOU COULD CARRY ONLY FIVE TOOLS IN YOUR FACEBOOK ADS TOOLKIT, WHAT WOULD THEY BE?

Facebook's native platform, Google Analytics, Google Tag Manager, DoubleClick and Excel. Always Excel.

WHAT'S THE SINGLE BIGGEST MISTAKE YOU SEE PEOPLE MAKE IN FACEBOOK ADS?

People's biggest mistake is not taking paid social media seriously, especially Facebook. With the organic algorithm changes occurring in the near future, paid is only going to get more competitive and more important. Brands need to have a serious paid strategy.

WHAT ADVICE WOULD YOU GIVE TO PEOPLE WHO ARE LOOKING TO RUN SUCCESSFUL FACEBOOK ADS CAMPAIGNS?

Understand what types of ads are available and where in the customer journey to engage users with those ads. Map this out and use pixels, audience segmentations, and other insights to refine your content to drive users to perform desired actions.

HOW DO YOU THINK FACEBOOK ADS WILL CHANGE OVER THE NEXT FEW YEARS?

Facebook is going to change drastically in the next few years; I anticipate some form of regulation to greatly impact the channel.

LEARN MORE ABOUT KYLE

I work with small and large businesses within the tech, start-up, and CPG verticals. With more than ten years experience in executing initiatives ranging from social media projects to fully developed digital strategies, I help brands launch and enhance their online presence to positively impact their bottom line.

✉ KVOLENIK@GMAIL.COM
☎ 740-244-2417
in WWW.LINKEDIN.COM/IN/KYLEVOLENIK

SAM SPRAGUE

FOUNDER, SPRAGUE MEDIA

HOW DO YOU DETERMINE THE EFFECTIVENESS OF A FACEBOOK ADS CAMPAIGN?

There is only one way to determine the effectiveness of a Facebook Ads campaign, and that is ROI. If you gave me one dollar and I gave you back four dollars, we'd do business all day right? But if you gave me one dollar and I gave you eighty-five cents back, then it would make no sense at all. That's how you end up broke!

WHAT IS THE SINGLE MOST EFFECTIVE FACEBOOK ADS TACTIC YOU'VE LEARNED?

The single most effective Facebook Ads tactic I've learned is Sequential Advertising. Or in layman's terms, laser-focused retargeting. It's important to understand the buyer's journey and their mind-set. Most people don't convert on that first touch; thus, it is in your best interest to make sure you follow up with them. You need to build trust and authority with your audience before they will give you a penny!

IF YOU COULD CARRY ONLY FIVE TOOLS IN YOUR FACEBOOK ADS TOOLKIT, WHAT WOULD THEY BE?

There are really only two tools you need to create and manage successful Facebook Ad campaigns: Ads Manager and Facebook's tracking Pixel. You need to be able to tell which campaigns are running smoothly and which are not, be able to optimize, and double down on the campaigns that are going strong, and cut off the campaigns that aren't pulling their weight.

WHAT'S THE SINGLE BIGGEST MISTAKE YOU SEE PEOPLE MAKE IN FACEBOOK ADS?

The single biggest mistake I see people make while running Facebook Ads is that they run one ad, try to sell their product/service, spend one hundred dollars on it, and don't see any results. Afterwards they say, "Oh, Facebook Ads is BS! You can't make any money from it." If you want to leverage Facebook, you need to be prepared to invest in your business like it's YOUR business! Testing the temperature with your toe can be deceiving and is the biggest mistake you can make.

WHAT ADVICE WOULD YOU GIVE TO PEOPLE WHO ARE LOOKING TO RUN SUCCESSFUL FACEBOOK ADS CAMPAIGNS?

The best advice I could give anyone who is looking to run Facebook Ads is to create the best damn offer you can! Put yourself in your buyer's shoes and answer the question "What's in it for me?" Give them something of value to help build that initial trust. You'll know it's valuable by asking yourself this question: "Should we charge for this?" If the answer is yes, then test it. If no, then go back to the drawing board.

HOW DO YOU THINK FACEBOOK ADS WILL CHANGE OVER THE NEXT FEW YEARS?

The biggest change I think we'll see in the future of Facebook Ads is that everyone and their dog will have a chatbot. There are already chatbots for just about everything, but you can actually create automated bots to give you the weather, help you cook dinner, qualify leads, and sell products. It's going to be an interesting next few years for sure!

LEARN MORE ABOUT SAM

I love helping companies and entrepreneurs acquire, nurture, and grow using paid social media channels, specifically Facebook Advertising. The purpose is to increase visibility, grow your fan base, supercharge engagement, drive traffic, give sales a boost, and give branding a kick in the pants! Our strategies make a marketing and sales team's life a breeze and provide no brainer results and data-oriented performance for co-founders and C-level executives. If you want to empower your sales team, expand your brand, or just need a consult, connect with me.

⊕ SPRAGUEMEDIA.COM

TUCKER FERWERDA

DIGITAL MARKETING CONSULTANT

HOW DO YOU DETERMINE THE EFFECTIVENESS OF A FACEBOOK ADS CAMPAIGN?

To determine the effectiveness of a campaign, I always make sure I do my homework before running ads. Most companies move to Facebook Ads too quickly and become frustrated because their ads aren't working. This is because they haven't done their homework. Before I even start thinking of ads, I research my customers and find out what their wants and needs are. After doing this, I create the offer based on what I find out, put that in sales funnel, and then start creating Facebook campaigns. This completes 95 percent of the work up front.

WHAT IS THE SINGLE MOST EFFECTIVE FACEBOOK ADS TACTIC YOU'VE LEARNED?

Split-testing buyer's audiences. It's never about finding the right ad, but HOW to find the right ad. Split-test buyer's audiences to find out which audience will purchase from you. A buyer's audience is an audience that people are already buying from. Don't target cats and dogs if you're selling leashes. Target PetSmart and other products and companies that people are already buying from. Run as many audiences as you can in the beginning to find out which audiences work best. Cut the audiences that don't perform and perfect the audiences that do.

IF YOU COULD CARRY ONLY FIVE TOOLS IN YOUR FACEBOOK ADS TOOLKIT, WHAT WOULD THEY BE?

Depending on the project, my favorite tools are ClickFunnels, ActiveCampaign, Google Sheets, Calendly, and Gmail. I'm always using these tools and checking my stats on a regular basis. You don't need much to be successful. Sure, all the bells and whistles are nice to have, but in reality all you need is a solution to someone's problem. The more you can engage the right people, the quicker your results will happen. Now go sell some stuff!

WHAT'S THE SINGLE BIGGEST MISTAKE YOU SEE PEOPLE MAKE IN FACEBOOK ADS?

Giving up too quickly. People are SO impatient when it comes to digital marketing. It makes me go bonkers. They have the "I'm going to make a million dollars in a month" mind-set. It never works that way if you're just starting out and not yet set up for success. This is why I research exactly what my customers need and what my competitors are doing. No sense in reinventing the wheel, right?

WHAT ADVICE WOULD YOU GIVE TO PEOPLE WHO ARE LOOKING TO RUN SUCCESSFUL FACEBOOK ADS CAMPAIGNS?

Do your homework, don't think you know the answers to your customer's problems without asking them, and test. No matter what, you're going to pay to play, whether you're paying with time, trial and error, your own cash, or by hiring an expert. But the rewards are just around the corner when you nail it! Facebook Ads are one of the best ways to market any industry and niche, and people are making millions off it every day. Keep perfecting your craft!

HOW DO YOU THINK FACEBOOK ADS WILL CHANGE OVER THE NEXT FEW YEARS?

Facebook Ads will become more expensive, smarter, and more valuable. This is why I always tell my students and clients that they need to start mastering Facebook Ads now. Advertising platforms will come and go, but Facebook is one of the leaders in the advertising space. I call it the "Artificial Intelligence of the Internet." It's so smart that it can place your products and services right in front of the people who are already looking to buy from you.

LEARN MORE ABOUT TUCKER

I used to be a warehouse junkie; now I grow companies. I'm an author, a Facebook Ads expert, a digital marketer, and a business consultant for millionaires and multimillion-dollar companies. We run a digital marketing agency to run their digital marketing. I have been featured in major publications like *Inc.* and *Huffington Post*, been asked to speak at marketing events, hosted my own marketing events, and taught digital marketing skills to over 3,100 people. My goal is to help you get insane results with digital marketing.

⊕ WWW.PRELAUNCHPROFIT.COM
✉ TUCKER@PRELAUNCHPROFIT.COM

ANTHONY DULIEUX

SOCIAL MEDIA PLATFORM STRATEGIST, LOOP

HOW DO YOU DETERMINE THE EFFECTIVENESS OF A FACEBOOK ADS CAMPAIGN?

The effectiveness of a Facebook Ads campaign will depend on a few questions you need to ask yourself before starting the campaign: What is your brand/company objective for this campaign? What scale of impact on this objective do you want to have? If the campaign provides the pre-determined impact, you can say it's been a success. I always determine the effectiveness using the big picture. Your campaign's impact on the brand and on users must always be your principal KPI. There is no single "magic" metric that can provide you a yes/no answer on the success of a campaign. You need to extrapolate the data and give it context in the business reality. However, if we're talking purely technical (i.e., we remove the brand point of view), an effective campaign is when you've done your tests and know that you can't change anything technically to get better results. Then the only variable left is the content itself.

WHAT IS THE SINGLE MOST EFFECTIVE FACEBOOK ADS TACTIC YOU'VE LEARNED?

The most effective tactic I've learned is to use Facebook Ads every day and constantly experiment. Every day, behavior is changing, costs of ads are changing, and the platforms themselves are changing. You cannot say for sure that your choices today will be the right ones tomorrow. An example: a Facebook Ads reach campaign could be more effective in getting conversions than a conversion campaign. The best thing to do is the same for any test: run different campaigns with only one variable. Testing objectives, placements, audiences, creative, one at a time. Once done, I know 99.9 percent of the right choices to run the most effective campaign. And for the next campaign, I'll have to do it all over again.

IF YOU COULD CARRY ONLY FIVE TOOLS IN YOUR FACEBOOK ADS TOOLKIT, WHAT WOULD THEY BE?

The only things I would need to carry would be an internet kit and a computer. The other things I would need are a business, an open-minded brain, and only one little plug-in on my browser: Facebook Pixel Helper. The advantage of Facebook Ads is that you don't necessarily need many tools to do a good job.

WHAT'S THE SINGLE BIGGEST MISTAKE YOU SEE PEOPLE MAKE IN FACEBOOK ADS?

At the moment, I see an impressive number of so-called "Facebook Ads experts" that sell themselves as providing a cast-iron guaranteed tactic for success. The biggest mistake is to assume to know what Facebook Ad campaign type and settings will work best. This isn't an exact science. There is no 100 percent right answer. The closest we have are best practices on how to find out what works best for your company, your brand, your product, and your specific objective. Another mistake I see a lot is to take numbers and metrics for granted and stick with them instead of placing each metric in its context. It's a balance to look at the data we see and the reality of each user behind these numbers. Marketers on Facebook Ads stopped thinking with the big picture in mind and started using data as a religion, when most of the time they don't fully understanding the meaning of these stats. A perfect example is the mid-roll ads during videos. A user doesn't necessarily want to actively watch (some won't watch at all), but the metric will show them as a view, and some marketers will call that a success.

WHAT ADVICE WOULD YOU GIVE TO PEOPLE WHO ARE LOOKING TO RUN SUCCESSFUL FACEBOOK ADS CAMPAIGNS?

Keep an open mind on the big picture at all times, and don't focus on specific metrics. Don't think "x" likes or views or clicks necessarily equates to success. Always have in mind that behind every result is a user: a person. Another big piece of advice is that Facebook Ads are not an exact science. If you practice business-oriented thinking and learn the settings and possibilities of Facebook Ads, you'll run effective campaigns.

HOW DO YOU THINK FACEBOOK ADS WILL CHANGE OVER THE NEXT FEW YEARS?

Facebook Ads aren't on the way up anymore. They're not new. The big wave of companies shifting their media budgets into social ads is happening right now, and the platform will eventually be too saturated to be as cheap and effective as it once was. There are already a number of publishers and marketers that are experimenting with new ways to market their audiences. Facebook will battle on for as long as possible and as with any shift, even in digital, it won't change overnight. But either Facebook itself will create change, or we will see the emergence of other platforms. Facebook is trying and will continue to try to come back to a more social platform, but I could see them creating another platform that combines social with the "traditional" website. All companies would then use at least one of their platforms, closing the gap in the web/app space between social and commercial use.

LEARN MORE ABOUT ANTHONY

I am currently working in a digital agency on various brands, mainly PUMA, Corona, Audi, and Durex. My role is to be a sort of consultant on social media and of course Facebook Ads and also provide courses to social teams and potentially other teams. My objective is that the knowledge and logic of social media and Facebook Ads is understood at every level of the agency, from content creation to project management and website/app development.

 WWW.LINKEDIN.COM/IN/ANTHONY-DULIEUX-53091B42

AARON ZAKOWSKI

FACEBOOK ADS EXPERT, ZAMMO DIGITAL

HOW DO YOU DETERMINE THE EFFECTIVENESS OF A FACEBOOK ADS CAMPAIGN?

I focus on running Facebook Ads for Software as a Service (SaaS) companies. As such, our primary objective is usually to generate as many free trial signups as possible within a target price. Therefore, I determine the effectiveness of our ads based on the average cost per free trial signup. Other metrics give me a general sense of the health of the campaign, but the CPA for free trials determines true success or failure.

WHAT IS THE SINGLE MOST EFFECTIVE FACEBOOK ADS TACTIC YOU'VE LEARNED?

The most effective tactic with Facebook Ads is to rely on Facebook's algorithms to optimize for you. Lots of people think they know what's best for their campaigns, so they do lots of research into audiences and things like that. In reality, we always have the best success when we give Facebook as much control as possible. For example, Lookalike Audiences that Facebook creates for us are usually our best performing audiences (especially when the Lookalike is based on a conversion pixel audience). We also like to make sure to use relatively large audiences (five hundred thousand to two million people) when prospecting to cold audiences. This gives the algorithm the space to optimize and deliver ad impressions to the people they think are most likely to convert.

IF YOU COULD CARRY ONLY FIVE TOOLS IN YOUR FACEBOOK ADS TOOLKIT, WHAT WOULD THEY BE?

1. Canva.com – This is my favorite tool for making new ad creative.

2. Facebook Ads Manager – This is where we create all campaigns, ad sets, and ad creative.

3. AdEspresso Ad Gallery – This free tool lets us review thousands of ads that other companies have launched and gives us ideas and inspiration for our ads.

4. Google Docs – This is where we create and organize all of our process documents. Staying organized and having systems is very important to running Facebook Ads so that you don't rush to make emotional decisions about your ads. Google Docs makes it easy to manage and share process documents with my whole team.

5. Excel – Excel is a data geek's best friend. And Facebook Ads are all about data. I frequently export Facebook data into Excel so that I can use pivot tables and other data manipulation tools to discover the trends and opportunities in the data. Excel helps me to make better, data-backed decisions.

WHAT'S THE SINGLE BIGGEST MISTAKE YOU SEE PEOPLE MAKE IN FACEBOOK ADS?

The biggest mistake I see people make is that they aren't using Lookalike Audiences. The other big mistake is that people aren't testing enough fresh ad creative. Testing new ads needs to be a consistent part of the advertising process.

WHAT ADVICE WOULD YOU GIVE TO PEOPLE WHO ARE LOOKING TO RUN SUCCESSFUL FACEBOOK ADS CAMPAIGNS?

The best advice I would give is to first determine what your best performing audiences are. Then make sure to keep testing lots of new ad creative. Remember that ads burn out relatively quickly on Facebook, so you always need to be coming up with new creative ideas. Be sure to mix up your ads with link ads, videos, and image ads. Use lots of different angles for images and text. In our agency, we have a system that we test at least five to ten new ads for every client every week (even when a campaign is running well). This helps to make sure that we are never stuck in a position where all of our ads have burned out, and we'll always have profitable ads to run.

HOW DO YOU THINK FACEBOOK ADS WILL CHANGE OVER THE NEXT FEW YEARS?

Facebook Ads are evolving very quickly, and more advertisers are hopping on the platform all the time. That means that in order to succeed, long-term advertisers will need to stay aware of changes in the technology and in the trends of ad creative. This is the only way to keep your costs down. I also predict that Facebook will expand their Audience Network and make it more profitable. This will create a lot more ad placements on third-party sites. I imagine it will be grow to be something very similar to the Google AdSense program.

LEARN MORE ABOUT AARON

I am the CEO of Zammo Digital Marketing, where I help leading SaaS start-ups accelerate user acquisition and achieve scale through Facebook Ads. I've managed over $2 million in Facebook Ads, generating over five hundred thousand leads and signups for clients such as eBay, InVision, Cuisinart, Webydo, Treehouse, and many more. I also share my best Facebook Ads strategies on my blog.

🌐 WWW.AARONZAKOWSKI.COM

BEN DAHL

DIRECTOR OF MONETIZATION, BLITZMETRICS

HOW DO YOU DETERMINE THE EFFECTIVENESS OF A FACEBOOK ADS CAMPAIGN?

Facebook uses the term "Campaign" in its organizational hierarchy, so technically speaking, you will have campaigns that are not optimized for conversions that are still playing a part in driving sales. For example, a video view campaign builds a warm audience for a traffic or conversion campaign to sell to at a lower cost. ROI is the end goal, but you need to optimize your campaigns for their micro goals, like video views or clicks, to see the return you want. This is where most of our clients get overwhelmed by the infinite number of combinations by which you can measure your Facebook Ads campaigns. The best thing you can do is use custom columns and organize them so they resemble your funnel. For example, for a video view campaign, you want to see how many unique people your ads have reached (reach), the number of times they have seen your video (frequency), the number of three-second video views, the number of ten-second video views, the CTR on your ad, unique link clicks, website conversions as they are relevant to your campaign, and your cost-per for all the former metrics. When you organize your columns like this, you can see exactly where in the funnel your campaigns break down and test new solutions.

WHAT IS THE SINGLE MOST EFFECTIVE FACEBOOK ADS TACTIC YOU'VE LEARNED?

Retargeting video views. It's the most powerful form of targeting available on any ad platform. That said, it's not an auto-win. People are sitting in their living room, scrolling rapidly through their newsfeed and stopping for an average of five to six seconds on videos. Most importantly, they are not ready to buy. You must properly qualify your customers on Facebook. There are a couple tactics I've seen work. One is using a

Lookalike Audience to generate video views then retargeting those who watched at least ten seconds. This is a light qualification tactic. Because ten seconds is about twice the length of the average watch time on Facebook, you know these people were at least moderately interested in your content and brand. The other tactic is running a more broadly targeted Lookalike, behavioral, or demographic audience to generate video views and targeting people who watched at least 75 percent of the videos in that campaign. This tactic will cause you to spend more in reaching your audience but less in conversions since it sets the qualifying bar much higher.

IF YOU COULD CARRY ONLY FIVE TOOLS IN YOUR FACEBOOK ADS TOOLKIT, WHAT WOULD THEY BE?

For targeting, the single most effective asset Facebook offers is Lookalike Audiences. They let you "clone" your customers on Facebook on a massive scale. It's Facebook's way of saying, "Here. We want you to win, so just use this and don't overthink things." You can build your Lookalike Audiences from your most valuable custom audiences and refine them further with Audience Insights. Another tool that everyone should use is Acxiom, Facebook's data partner. Acxiom provides you all the data points that Facebook's targeting doesn't. You can export their audiences for free straight into your ad account and start running the most targeted ads possible. When it comes to reporting and monitoring ads, custom conversions are still exciting, but offline event sets are becoming even more powerful for industries where you can't track the sale online. Facebook's offline conversion tracking is improving rapidly, which will allow marketers to get more meaningful insights for industries that previously were relying on tracking in-store visits or using engagement metrics as KPIs for their Facebook campaigns.

WHAT'S THE SINGLE BIGGEST MISTAKE YOU SEE PEOPLE MAKE IN FACEBOOK ADS?

People tend to either overthink or drastically underthink their Facebook Ads targeting. It can be hard to look at. You open up their ad sets to find there are fifty unrelated interest categories lumped into one audience, and all you can think is, "Oh no, this is how you've been spending thousands of dollars?" Of course, I've also seen clients running campaigns to entire states without any detailed targeting. In effect, they're trying to sell to millions of completely random people. Their ads become intrusive billboards in the newsfeed. They just press that "Boost Post" button and off they go wasting twenty dollars at a time. It's easy to get carried away and it's easy to get lazy. Don't. Just be logical. Keep your audiences relevant and simple.

WHAT ADVICE WOULD YOU GIVE TO PEOPLE WHO ARE LOOKING TO RUN SUCCESSFUL FACEBOOK ADS CAMPAIGNS?

Imitate industry leaders, split test, stay organized, and keep learning. Imitation is a great way to start if you want to succeed. Seeing how someone records a video, lays out a landing page, or writes copy and using their template or style for your company or brand is a great way to ensure some degree of success. Then you need to split test everything. Split test landing pages and canvases. Split test ad copies. Split test images and videos. And run your split tests to multiple audiences. Give Facebook the reins to optimize the work you've put in. When you find what works, do more of it and keep testing. When I say to stay organized, I mean use naming conventions and organize your ads from the top down. Campaigns should be named by business goal and Facebook objective. Name ad sets by their content and their audience. Name ads by their content, link, and version. This also means you have to stop boosting posts. Finally, keep learning, because this stuff is ever changing. Every new development opens the door for new opportunity, and you can take advantage only if you're paying attention.

HOW DO YOU THINK FACEBOOK ADS WILL CHANGE OVER THE NEXT FEW YEARS?

Facebook isn't going anywhere in the short term. It is expanding into new territory all the time to keep people on the platform longer. New targeting options will arise, I'm sure, but the foundational principles will remain the same. The primary change will not come from within Facebook but from the noise coming to the platform. More and more people are jumping on the Facebook train. Even the reluctant local businesses are starting to boost posts and care about their business pages. The most difficult thing will be standing out. My advice? Start now and invest in quality, engaging video.

LEARN MORE ABOUT BEN

As the Director of Monetization at BlitzMetrics, I focus on content creation for the brand and scaling the company's passive income by selling courses and guides. We teach others around the world how to grow their agency and execute on a proven process that we have used for clients like the Golden State Warriors and Nike. There is nothing more rewarding than seeing businesses grow and brands explode as a result of our education. Through our university partnerships, I'm also able to educate and mentor high school and college students on digital marketing and building a personal brand. Add me on social; I love connecting with new people. You can also catch me at a social media conference or rock concert near you.

- ⊕ WWW.BLITZMETRICS.COM
- ✉ BEN.DAHL@BLITZMETRICS.COM
- 🔗 WWW.LINKEDIN.COM/IN/BEN-DAHL
- 🐦 @BENDAHL
- 📘 WWW.FACEBOOK.COM/BEN.A.DAHL

CHRIS MADDEN

CO-FOUNDER, MATCHNODE

HOW DO YOU DETERMINE THE EFFECTIVENESS OF A FACEBOOK ADS CAMPAIGN?

We get as close to a hard ROI as possible, so we're comparing how many dollars were invested versus how many dollars are generated as directly as we can. Of course, customer lifetime value differs for each client, so we often help refine understanding of LTV so that we can compare it to CPA (cost per sale or cost per lead, etc.). It's important to have a shared definition of success at the outset so we all have the same view of "campaign effectiveness" after the fact.

WHAT IS THE SINGLE MOST EFFECTIVE FACEBOOK ADS TACTIC YOU'VE LEARNED?

Within Facebook Ads, it's optimizing for the conversion: the simple act of telling Facebook's algorithm what you define as a conversion but also writing ad copy and creative that hints at what is to come after the ad is clicked. This continuity should be refined throughout the funnel to remove friction and minimize cognitive dissonance for the user and what she experiences. When she is appropriately included in an audience and a message is relevant between the ad, the landing page, the call-to-action, and even the "thank you" page, you are on the right track to improving conversion rates and ROI.

IF YOU COULD CARRY ONLY FIVE TOOLS IN YOUR FACEBOOK ADS TOOLKIT, WHAT WOULD THEY BE?

1. The Facebook Pixel for tracking conversions and creating audiences
2. Mobile-optimized landing pages
3. A thirty- to sixty-second video or two
4. A good variety of static images we can test in ads
5. Clear data from the client on customer lifetime value and ROI so we can iterate quickly and build audiences off their data

WHAT'S THE SINGLE BIGGEST MISTAKE YOU SEE PEOPLE MAKE IN FACEBOOK ADS?

Facebook Ads are difficult to really make work well without a nuanced understanding of the platform and the business context in which you are operating. Too often, people with an incomplete understanding of audience targeting options or conversion optimization (for example) will take the very simple step of boosting a post. When that does not result in a business outcome they desire, they throw up their hands and say, "Facebook doesn't work for my business."

WHAT ADVICE WOULD YOU GIVE TO PEOPLE WHO ARE LOOKING TO RUN SUCCESSFUL FACEBOOK ADS CAMPAIGNS?

Facebook Ads changes so quickly, often multiple times per week, so you have be really interested and passionate about Facebook as an ad platform to read about and use all of the new features and stay up to date with the changes. Successful Facebook Ad campaigns require daily monitoring and management, and the outsized "wins" are often on the margins of the newest thing when the latest feature works well. If you were running Facebook Ads and immediately tested things (to list a few areas of emphasis in the past couple of years) like mobile Newsfeed ads, video as ad creative, and custom audience combinations right as they were released, you were likely rewarded with cheap CPMs and high ROI. You need to stay on the edge of testing the "next thing" on Facebook Ads.

HOW DO YOU THINK FACEBOOK ADS WILL CHANGE OVER THE NEXT FEW YEARS?

Facebook will continue to innovate in an effort to stay ahead, and it's no secret that they will look for profitable ground in areas like Messenger bots, augmented reality, virtual reality, and other next generation environments that will drastically impact ad creative and content. This will likely include some sort of wearable (think contact lenses, glasses, etc.) and ads that blend digitally augmented reality and the physical "real" world. There will be a continued focus on data and cross-device "people-based" identity.

Perhaps the greatest change could come from blockchain technologies that threaten to upset the centralized giants (Facebook and Google) in a transition by which people maintain control of their identities and data around their online behavior.

LEARN MORE ABOUT CHRIS

I'm Co-founder of Matchnode, a Chicago growth marketing agency that works with great B2C businesses with revenues between $1 million and $500 million. Matchnode focuses on digital strategy, traffic generation, and conversion optimization to help great businesses grow, including New Balance Chicago, Indiana University, LendingTree, and Byline Bank.

⊕ WWW.MATCHNODE.COM
✉ CHRIS@MATCHNODE.COM
🖸 @MATCHNODE

CHAPTER 4
SOCIAL MEDIA MARKETING

A SIMPLE EXPLANATION OF SOCIAL MEDIA MARKETING

Social Media Marketing, commonly referred to as SMM, is a way for businesses to reach their prospects and customers via social media like Facebook, Twitter, Instagram, YouTube, and LinkedIn.

Often, SMM revolves around creating and sharing "sticky" content on social media to reach marketing and branding goals—content that will gain and hold a user's attention.

SMM can include the promotion of various forms of media on social media, such as video, blog posts, white papers, infographics, images, and livestreams.

A goal of SMM is to produce content that people will share with their own social networks to increase brand exposure and customer reach.

Most of the large social networks encourage users to provide detailed geographical, behavioral, demographic, and personal information, which allows marketers to tailor their messages to what is most likely to resonate with those users.

One advantage of SMM is that feedback from customers is acquired in real-time. Due to the interactivity of social media, businesses can view comments and interactions on their social media posts that indicate the effectiveness of the service or product.

Marketers are increasingly using social media to make their brand appear more personable or to give a specific voice to their brand.

As the large social media networks evolve and as new networks emerge, SMM specialists must keep up with the changing technology in order to understand consumer preferences and effectively reach their customers.

SOCIAL MEDIA MARKETING SPECIALISTS SOUND OFF

SABRINA TORRES

HOW DO YOU DETERMINE THE EFFECTIVENESS OF A SOCIAL MEDIA MARKETING CAMPAIGN?

The effectiveness of any campaign always circles back to "What were our goals with this campaign, and did we meet them?" With social media, that might mean that a campaign was effective if we increased engagement or brand mentions. It could mean gaining video views and website clicks. Or it can mean virality! The key is to begin with having measurable and achievable goals. Then—and only then—can you determine what is effective in your social media campaigns. Because even virality doesn't equal success if it doesn't bring you any closer to your goals.

WHAT IS THE SINGLE MOST EFFECTIVE SOCIAL MEDIA MARKETING TACTIC YOU'VE LEARNED?

This is going to sound entirely too simple, but the single most effective tactic I've learned for my client's social media profiles is to ask questions. The core of social media is still personal connection and relationships, no matter how automated and analytical we can get. Followers need a reason to engage with brands online. The simple act of asking questions opens the line of communication with followers; it is an invitation to a conversation. Conversations turn brand followers into brand enthusiasts. Plus, the more engagement your posts get, the more the algorithms view your content as relevant and the more your content will show up in feeds. It's an all-around winner.

IF YOU COULD CARRY ONLY FIVE TOOLS IN YOUR SOCIAL MEDIA MARKETING TOOLKIT, WHAT WOULD THEY BE?

The first tool I would carry in my social media toolkit would be Post Planner. It allows me to find content and schedule it, all in one place. The second would be Canva, which is the perfect tool for crafting creative and brand consistent visuals for all social media platforms. The third is Asana, because project organization is vital to campaign success. Fourth is BuzzSumo to find the top performing social content. And last but not least is the emoji. Never underestimate the power of emojis in social media.

WHAT'S THE SINGLE BIGGEST MISTAKE YOU SEE PEOPLE MAKE IN SOCIAL MEDIA MARKETING?

The single biggest mistake that people make in Social Media Marketing is trying to be everywhere at once and everything to everyone. What ends up happening is that they do five social media platforms poorly and since they don't get any benefit from their efforts, they write off social media altogether. The key is to pick two or three social media platforms based on where your target market goes online and hit those platforms hard. Perfect them. Don't waste time on Snapchat if your target market is over thirty. Don't waste time on Pinterest if you're a local business. Know your market, know your ideal social media platforms, and stop wasting time and resources in all the wrong places.

WHAT ADVICE WOULD YOU GIVE TO PEOPLE WHO ARE LOOKING TO RUN SUCCESSFUL SOCIAL MEDIA MARKETING CAMPAIGNS?

To run a successful social media campaign, you first have to have data to base your actions on. So it all has to begin with testing different types of content and monitoring how people respond. You have to be willing to try new things, get creative, and take risks! At the end of the day, you can have a perfectly branded and polished social media campaign but if it doesn't excite and engage your following, it won't be a success. Get to know your followers; get to know their pain points and their passion points. Once you know what makes your market tick, you can craft a social media campaign that will get a response and a return.

HOW DO YOU THINK SOCIAL MEDIA MARKETING WILL CHANGE OVER THE NEXT FEW YEARS?

We already know that the world of social media turns more and more toward video content, and I believe video will be king for the next few years. But there are two other trends that I believe we'll see taking over social media in the near future. One is chatbots, which are emerging as a tool for customer service and email replacement on Facebook Messenger. The other is augmented reality and virtual reality. As these technologies rise, we will undoubtedly see them integrated into our social media, so keep your eye out. Those brave enough to take on the newest trends will often gain the greatest rewards from them!

LEARN MORE ABOUT SABRINA

I am a social media specialist who helps business owners around the globe by making their social media pop in a busy online world. From my home in Nashville, Tennessee, I put my caffeinated energy to good use for my clients, who range from solo start-ups to multimillion-dollar organizations. I believe in the power of organic growth, engaging content, red lipstick, and coffee. Lots and lots of coffee.

⊕ WWW.BETRULYSOCIAL.COM
✉ SABRINA@BETRULYSOCIAL.COM
🐦 @BETRULYSOCIAL

RACHEL PEDERSEN

ENTREPRENEUR, FOUNDER, CEO, SOCIAL MEDIA UNITED, SOCIALWORKS DIGITAL

HOW DO YOU DETERMINE THE EFFECTIVENESS OF A SOCIAL MEDIA MARKETING CAMPAIGN?

Without a clear goal, no social media campaign can be deemed successful. It would be like blindfolding yourself and throwing darts at an empty room! An effective social media campaign is determined first and foremost by the goal it is trying to achieve. Was the goal virality? Was the goal increased following on a specific platform? The best way to determine the effectiveness of a social media campaign is to identify the KPIs of the goal and then launch the campaign and measure the outcome against that specific campaign's goals.

WHAT IS THE SINGLE MOST EFFECTIVE SOCIAL MEDIA MARKETING TACTIC YOU'VE LEARNED?

The most effective social media tactics I've learned all stem from one thing: knowing your market intimately. What are their desires? What are their goals? What makes them laugh, cry, share with friends? When building out a social media campaign, reverse engineer the emotions of your target market and craft each post as if it were written for ONE person. By writing for one, you will reach many.

IF YOU COULD CARRY ONLY FIVE TOOLS IN YOUR SOCIAL MEDIA MARKETING TOOLKIT, WHAT WOULD THEY BE?

Believe it or not, I am a huge fan of tools that make sense for any business—tools that don't cost a fortune. Maybe it is the bootstrapped businessperson in me. The five tools I carry in my social media toolkit are Canva, Post Planner, Google Keyword Planner, Facebook Audience Insights, and ScreenFlow. Canva: an easy graphic design for non-graphic designers. Post Planner: a content creation and curation platform that also schedules social media posts. Google Keyword Planner: a free and simple way to discover what topics are in high demand from your market. Facebook Audience Insights: the easiest way to immediately determine the details on your target market. ScreenFlow: a low-cost video editor that allows any entrepreneur to create attractive videos. These five tools are used every single day by me and other top social media managers to achieve successful social media results.

WHAT'S THE SINGLE BIGGEST MISTAKE YOU SEE PEOPLE MAKE IN SOCIAL MEDIA MARKETING?

Hands down, the biggest mistake I see people making with social media (besides the obvious gray hat/black hat techniques like buying followers or spamming) is assuming that the market cares about your product. Sorry, I know this is harsh! It comes down to psychographics—an intimate understanding of the emotions of your market. Here's the lowdown: the market cares about themselves. The more you can make your social media about them as individuals, the more successful your social media will be.

WHAT ADVICE WOULD YOU GIVE TO PEOPLE WHO ARE LOOKING TO RUN SUCCESSFUL SOCIAL MEDIA MARKETING CAMPAIGNS?

When you're looking to run successful social media campaigns, look to those who are already running successful campaigns. A big hint: don't just look at celebrities. Their social media campaigns are not the norm for most businesses. Instead, research those who are doing well in similar industries but aren't Fortune 500 companies. Find the companies whose businesses have been bootstrapped to success and take notes on what you see so you can do the same.

HOW DO YOU THINK SOCIAL MEDIA MARKETING WILL CHANGE OVER THE NEXT FEW YEARS?

Without a doubt, one of the major changes for social media that will occur over the next few years will be the integration of augmented reality or full-on virtual reality. People are looking to escape their day-to-day, and their desire to turn to social for this escape will be increased. While this is still quite a few years out, there will definitely be an increased tie-in between real life and the assisted realities that many intend to create. Amidst this major change, I do believe that the major platforms and mediums will shift.

LEARN MORE ABOUT RACHEL

I'm "The Queen of Social Media," CEO of SocialWorks Digital marketing agency, a full-time social media consultant and strategist, and Founder of Social Media United. My journey began in 2016 while working in my 9-to-5 (actually, it was an 8-to-5) day job. Within six months, I replaced my income and built a clientele that I love working with; today I teach others how to do the same thing. I have been called a top social media marketer and consultant, worldwide viral sensation, and leading authority on storytelling through social media and Facebook Ads—the crazy part is that it's all true! You can learn more about my work on my website. I am also a mother to two (almost three) beautiful children and a wife to my supportive husband.

⊕ WWW.SMUTRIAL.COM
⊕ WWW.RACHELPEDERSEN.COM

RON CULP

CONSULTANT AND PROFESSIONAL DIRECTOR, GRADUATE PROGRAM
IN PUBLIC RELATIONS AND ADVERTISING, DEPAUL UNIVERSITY

HOW DO YOU DETERMINE THE EFFECTIVENESS OF A SOCIAL MEDIA MARKETING CAMPAIGN?

Sales increases remain the best way to measure success of any product-related campaign. However, if the campaign's aim is to change attitudes or convey thought leadership, initial determination of effectiveness can be judged by the degree of engagement siding with your position. Ultimately, the client will determine success or failure of a campaign. That factor underscores the need to keep the client engaged throughout the planning and implementation process.

WHAT IS THE SINGLE MOST EFFECTIVE SOCIAL MEDIA MARKETING TACTIC YOU'VE LEARNED?

Infographics can convey the most amount of information in a non-commercial manner, thus gaining credibility beyond other online and digital content. Reader fatigue can effectively be overcome via a compelling infographic that visually simplifies often complex information and data. Attractive, well-designed infographics have a longer shelf life than other social tools, often ending up being pinned to Pinterest boards and woven into blog posts of authors eager for interesting storytelling artwork.

IF YOU COULD CARRY ONLY FIVE TOOLS IN YOUR SOCIAL MEDIA MARKETING TOOLKIT, WHAT WOULD THEY BE?

Organizations with whom I work operate on limited marketing budgets, so the toolkit generally focuses on two keywords: free and cheap. For starters, especially for individuals striving to increase their social media presence, Klout allows for quick, easy validation of social media influence. In addition to Google Analytics Ecommerce and Google Consumer

Surveys, I would round out my top five with Hootsuite and Sprout Social, both of which offer free trials and fair monthly pricing for small firms and organizations and can help you grow your social media presence.

WHAT'S THE SINGLE BIGGEST MISTAKE YOU SEE PEOPLE MAKE IN SOCIAL MEDIA MARKETING?

Current infatuation with social media sometimes drives organizations into an "all-in" strategy that slights other important marketing channels. Even with small budgets, don't ignore basic blocking and tackling in public relations. A great media placement can produce valuable third-party validation that provides important content coveted by social media.

WHAT ADVICE WOULD YOU GIVE TO PEOPLE WHO ARE LOOKING TO RUN SUCCESSFUL SOCIAL MEDIA MARKETING?

If this is your first foray into a social campaign, stick with the basics. Determine the top three channels that most of your customers have in common and focus on those initially. I encourage clients and nonprofits to focus on the Big Three: Twitter, Facebook, and LinkedIn. Master those first before venturing elsewhere. I am continually surprised with how quickly some people get bored with the Big Three and switch to other seemingly more sexy channels long before maximizing the enormous potential of Twitter, Facebook, and LinkedIn.

HOW DO YOU THINK SOCIAL MEDIA MARKETING WILL CHANGE OVER THE NEXT FEW YEARS?

Say goodbye to desktop computers and even laptops. The shift to mobile will be complete within the next few years. Also, both augmented and virtual reality will be routine, not just the fun curiosity it is with most consumers today. And artificial intelligence will answer most of our questions and fill in the blanks before we even complete many keystrokes on our mobile devices.

LEARN MORE ABOUT RON

I'm a consultant and Professional Director of the Graduate Program in Public Relations and Advertising at DePaul University. Previously, I held senior communications roles at Ketchum, Sard Verbinnen, Sears, Sara Lee, Pitney Bowes, and Eli Lilly. I've been listed for the past nine years in Crain's Who's Who in Chicago Business, and I've received PRSA's Gold Anvil Award and Arthur W. Page Society's Hall of Fame Award.

- WWW.CULPWRIT.COM
- @CULPWRIT
- WWW.FACEBOOK.COM/CULPWRIT

DAVID GINSBURG

SOCIAL MEDIA MARKETING SPECIALIST

HOW DO YOU DETERMINE THE EFFECTIVENESS OF A SOCIAL MEDIA MARKETING CAMPAIGN?

Metrics are determined with each client prior to any campaign launch. We map KPIs to goals to ensure we're aligned before any execution happens. It's also critical for clients to understand the need for paid social campaigns to achieve any results at scale.

WHAT IS THE SINGLE MOST EFFECTIVE SOCIAL MEDIA MARKETING TACTIC YOU'VE LEARNED?

Remarketing, especially via Facebook and Instagram's suite of tools, is a terrific way to generate results with tight budgets. Small businesses in particular need to wring every efficiency from their ad budgets, and on-platform remarketing is proving to be a powerful method of doing so.

IF YOU COULD CARRY ONLY FIVE TOOLS IN YOUR SOCIAL MEDIA MARKETING TOOLKIT, WHAT WOULD THEY BE?

Sprout Social for content scheduling and analytics; Facebook Ads Manager; Pocket for saving third-party content for future use; Canva for creating and editing still images and infographics for use across social channels; and of course, my iPhone!

WHAT'S THE SINGLE BIGGEST MISTAKE YOU SEE PEOPLE MAKE IN SOCIAL MEDIA MARKETING?

The "one size fits all" approach to Social Media Marketing! Take the time to optimize your content to meet the parameters of each active channel you're using. Instagram posts laden with @ symbols and hashtags look terrible on Facebook. Video and photo content should be sized for each platform, and the accompanying posts formatted for each. And, it should be noted, if you're going to use any live video platforms (Facebook Live,

Instagram Live, Twitter, LinkedIn), have a detailed plan for doing so. Don't just open the app on your phone and start babbling.

WHAT ADVICE WOULD YOU GIVE TO PEOPLE WHO ARE LOOKING TO RUN SUCCESSFUL SOCIAL MEDIA MARKETING CAMPAIGNS?

Have clear, attainable goals and a detailed strategy to guide your program. What are you hoping to achieve? How will your business benefit from the deployment of your precious resources? How are your competitors using these tools both positively and negatively? Make sure you know what you're doing or hire someone that does—your business will be better served for doing so.

HOW DO YOU THINK SOCIAL MEDIA MARKETING WILL CHANGE OVER THE NEXT FEW YEARS?

Social marketing is evolving at a lightning clip. It was only a few years ago that the "build it and they will come" ethos was still effective. Now it requires a dedicated budget to achieve any measurable business results. New platforms are launching and gaining audiences, and content has shifted from blogs and text posts to images to GIFs and now video serving as the coin of the social realm. Expect live video to continue gaining adoption. Facebook will rival Google as a contextual search platform.

LEARN MORE ABOUT DAVID

I'm a Social Media Marketing specialist with over nine years of experience helping small and medium-sized businesses develop content-driven programs that grow brand awareness and generate revenues.

🌐 ROSEATWATERSOCIAL.COM
✉ DAVID@ROSEATWATERSOCIAL.COM
🔗 WWW.LINKEDIN.COM/IN/DAVIDGINSBURG

STEPHANIE CREDEDIO

SOCIAL MEDIA SPECIALIST

HOW DO YOU DETERMINE THE EFFECTIVENESS OF A SOCIAL MEDIA MARKETING CAMPAIGN?

Determining the effectiveness of a campaign is dependent on the goal that is set. In most of my experience, we measure social media campaigns using various metrics such as engagement rate, audience growth, CTC (Click-To-Conversion), CPC, impressions, and reach. For determining effectiveness on creative social media content, engagement (likes, comments, shares) is extremely valuable to understand what's resonating with the audience.

WHAT IS THE SINGLE MOST EFFECTIVE SOCIAL MEDIA MARKETING TACTIC YOU'VE LEARNED?

While there are plenty of learning opportunities in a growing industry that never turns off, a good tactic in Social Media Marketing is to produce high-quality content over high-quantity content. The more valuable, helpful, and insightful the brand messages are, the better the results. After all, content is king!

IF YOU COULD CARRY ONLY FIVE TOOLS IN YOUR SOCIAL MEDIA MARKETING TOOLKIT, WHAT WOULD THEY BE?

A scheduling tool for content, such as Hootsuite; listening tool to monitor conversations on the brand; graphics/editing tool, such as Canva for quick ad hoc designs; Hashtagify to search for trending hashtags; and Sniply to shorten links.

WHAT'S THE SINGLE BIGGEST MISTAKE YOU SEE PEOPLE MAKE IN SOCIAL MEDIA MARKETING?

The biggest mistake I see people make is having a lack of passion for social media. To work in this industry, you need to be creative, willing, and dedicated to the work you're projecting onto each channel, as each social media platform is very unique. If you're lacking passion, you're not going to be able to provide the consumer the experience they're looking for, the content will be dry, and your brand will have no personality.

WHAT ADVICE WOULD YOU GIVE TO PEOPLE WHO ARE LOOKING TO RUN SUCCESSFUL SOCIAL MEDIA MARKETING CAMPAIGNS?

The best advice I'd give someone would be to challenge your team to create the best work you can, especially if your budget isn't sky high. Gather inspiration from other brands who are effective in social media. Also, keep in mind that the next big social media trend may not be the best approach for your brand—think before acting.

HOW DO YOU THINK SOCIAL MEDIA MARKETING WILL CHANGE OVER THE NEXT FEW YEARS?

Social media is constantly changing, growing, and evolving to meet the demands of what people want. I see video increasing and more niche-based social media platforms on the rise. Effective social media campaigns will have a heavy focus on creating experiences and building relationships vs. direct selling.

LEARN MORE ABOUT STEPHANIE

I have a knack for marketing strategy, social media content, and everything in-between. I'm a proactive, positive communicator who is highly motivated and enthusiastic—and also a fitness instructor. I have been working in the manufacturing industry for more than three years, and currently I manage the social media strategy for Elkay Manufacturing, America's number-one stainless steel sink company. If I'm not working on my computer, I'm most likely at the gym—probably still working from my iPhone. I'm constantly connected and dedicated to the work I am involved with.

WWW.LINKEDIN.COM/IN/STEPHANIECREDEDIO
@SCREDEDIO

ERIN GLEASON

DIGITAL MARKETING MANAGER, CAMPING WORLD

HOW DO YOU DETERMINE THE EFFECTIVENESS OF A SOCIAL MEDIA MARKETING CAMPAIGN?

Social media is changing daily. To keep up with the latest trends, research is key. I research what's new or what's coming, and then after implementing new tactics I track what works and what doesn't. I commonly use Google Analytics to track effectiveness. For example, when I create a post that links to the company's website, I use Google Analytics to track the amount of traffic that page received two weeks prior to the post, during the time the post was boosted or on an ad, and one month after the link was posted. My goal is to determine if boosting the post or creating an ad has an impact on the overall traffic to that specific page.

WHAT IS THE SINGLE MOST EFFECTIVE SOCIAL MEDIA MARKETING TACTIC YOU'VE LEARNED?

Social media has turned into a pay-to-play marketplace. For Facebook specifically, their algorithm has changed where content that is non-boosted has a small chance of reaching a fan's newsfeed. If a company wants their name and content to be seen by fans and potential fans, they need to use Facebook boosted posts and ads.

IF YOU COULD CARRY ONLY FIVE TOOLS IN YOUR SOCIAL MEDIA MARKETING TOOLKIT, WHAT WOULD THEY BE?

My top tools are Google Analytics to track the popularity of pages before, during, and after a social media campaign. That, and a social media management tool to track data for all social media channels, create reports, and to allow me to post to all company social media pages simultaneously.

WHAT'S THE SINGLE BIGGEST MISTAKE YOU SEE PEOPLE MAKE IN SOCIAL MEDIA MARKETING?

The biggest mistake I see people make when managing social media channels is not tracking the results of every post and ad that is created. By not tracking results, one cannot determine what works and what doesn't for a company.

WHAT ADVICE WOULD YOU GIVE TO PEOPLE WHO ARE LOOKING TO RUN SUCCESSFUL SOCIAL MEDIA MARKETING CAMPAIGNS?

If you want to run a successful social media campaign, know your audience and track your results. Boosted posts and ad campaigns give you the option of targeting specific people based on their location, age, gender, and interests. These people can be fans and nonfans of your page. Knowing who you want to target and how to connect to them with your text and putting a budget behind the post or ad will make your campaign successful.

HOW DO YOU THINK SOCIAL MEDIA MARKETING WILL CHANGE OVER THE NEXT FEW YEARS?

Social media changes daily. It's hard to predict where we will be in a few years, as new apps and channels are constantly created and explode in popularity. Example: Snapchat.

LEARN MORE ABOUT ERIN

I have been in the Social Media Marketing field for more than eight years, working for independent businesses, agencies, and franchises. In those years, I have gained experience in managing all social media channels: working with social media management tools; creating content for the channels, blogs, and newsletters; creating radio ads and creative visuals; editing videos; and managing online reputation. I also have experience working with PR firms and on crisis management teams.

in WWW.LINKEDIN.COM/IN/ERIN-GLEASON

AUSTIN CHU

MEDIA MARKETING CONSULTANT

HOW DO YOU DETERMINE THE EFFECTIVENESS OF A SOCIAL MEDIA MARKETING CAMPAIGN?

I'd be lying if I said the effectiveness of a social media campaign is not measured by the ROI on the campaign. However, I also determine the effectiveness of a social media campaign by the type of feedback we receive from our audience—how they are responding to it and whether or not they find our story to be relatable. I appreciate audience members who are straightforward and authentic in their responses regarding the effectiveness of our social media campaigns.

WHAT IS THE SINGLE MOST EFFECTIVE SOCIAL MEDIA MARKETING TACTIC YOU'VE LEARNED?

Be genuine. Social media is all about widespread storytelling and garnering an audience who want to hear your story. People are bombarded with advertising on social media every second they are on it, so make sure you own your story. Be genuine.

IF YOU COULD CARRY ONLY FIVE TOOLS IN YOUR SOCIAL MEDIA MARKETING TOOLKIT, WHAT WOULD THEY BE?

My tools in my Social Media Marketing toolkit seem to change all the time, with bigger and better tracker apps and up and coming platforms. I have become open to saying yes to different toolkits, trying them out for a season, and making up my mind about their effectiveness within a few months. It is important to trust your seasonal, consistent campaigns; be patient and trusting in those campaigns and the tools used for them.

WHAT'S THE SINGLE BIGGEST MISTAKE YOU SEE PEOPLE MAKE IN SOCIAL MEDIA MARKETING?

The single biggest mistake I see business owners make in Social Media

Marketing is believing their campaigns are going to be magically seen by tens and thousands of viewers without any direction and attention from the business. I have seen small to medium-sized business owners harness the power of social media and skyrocket their followers and viewers and use the power to their advantage. They're on their hands and knees, spreading their content, privately messaging friends and family, posting on their personal sites, and doing everything they can to spread their marketing. Friends, it works. But you have to put in the time to post, share, and send.

WHAT ADVICE WOULD YOU GIVE TO PEOPLE WHO ARE LOOKING TO RUN SUCCESSFUL SOCIAL MEDIA MARKETING CAMPAIGNS?

Be patient. There will be times when you will have unsuccessful social marketing campaigns. However, with a growth mind-set, learn from those unsuccessful marketing campaigns. If you're not there yet, figure out the missing piece in your campaign. Was it your demographic? Age group? Message? For small business owners, make sure you are not throwing out the same advertising that your competition is putting out there. Believe in your message, truly, and others will pick up on your genuine storytelling. You can't fake good storytelling.

HOW DO YOU THINK SOCIAL MEDIA MARKETING WILL CHANGE OVER THE NEXT FEW YEARS?

I believe Social Media Marketing will become more personalized to the individual and be all about—you guessed it—storytelling to that individual. More and more, the marketing experience is being personalized toward the individual based on past shopping lists, sites visited, etc. I see social media going in that direction further by having the ability to track what music our audience members listened to that week or what they are thinking of buying their friends for their birthdays—personal likes and behaviors. Because of personalization, social media marketers need to be ready to refresh their ideas and figure out what consumers like about various marketing campaigns and what they find to be ridiculous or off-putting. The more we learn about what people like and dislike in marketing, the more we'll be able to cater to what they want to see more of.

LEARN MORE ABOUT AUSTIN

By the time this book is published, I will be a graduate of Wheaton College, Illinois, with a degree in elementary education and special education. Graduating from a liberal arts college and being a naturally entrepreneurial-minded individual, I grew to love the notion of education and marketing. When I got my first job as a media marketing consultant in college, I realized this industry had all to do with teaching. A teacher by day and a media consultant by night and weekends and other random times of the day, I enjoy working with passionate small to medium-sized businesses to help them navigate how to market their businesses on the interweb.

✉ AUSTINCHU95@GMAIL.COM

DAN PALOMA

HOW DO YOU DETERMINE THE EFFECTIVENESS OF A SOCIAL MEDIA MARKETING CAMPAIGN?

If you're using social media, you should be measuring it. But don't measure just for the sake of having metrics. Instead, measure your social activities so you can learn what's successful, what isn't, and how you can improve. An effective social media campaign should have the right balance of high impressions, link clicks, and ROI.

WHAT IS THE SINGLE MOST EFFECTIVE SOCIAL MEDIA MARKETING TACTIC YOU'VE LEARNED?

The single most effective Social Media Marketing tactic I have learned is to always provide good quality content. Whether that content is a photo, a video, a link, or any other content, it should always be something that my followers will appreciate, love, and learn from. My ultimate goal is to connect and engage with my target audience.

IF YOU COULD CARRY ONLY FIVE TOOLS IN YOUR SOCIAL MEDIA MARKETING TOOLKIT, WHAT WOULD THEY BE?

Facebook Business Manager to manage my Facebook and Instagram Ads, Canva for graphics design, Hootsuite for scheduling content and measuring social media analytics, Grammarly to check that my content is always grammatically correct, and Feedly for content curation.

WHAT'S THE SINGLE BIGGEST MISTAKE YOU SEE PEOPLE MAKE IN SOCIAL MEDIA MARKETING?

The biggest Social Media Marketing mistake businesses make is that they don't just suddenly start and they don't persevere. Another big mistake is posting the same content, in the same format, at the same time on ALL social networks. Inexperienced brands often fail to realize the need to optimize and differentiate their output to suit the different audiences and features of each social platform.

WHAT ADVICE WOULD YOU GIVE TO PEOPLE WHO ARE LOOKING TO RUN SUCCESSFUL SOCIAL MEDIA MARKETING CAMPAIGNS?

My advice is to take the time to learn how Social Media Marketing works for your specific business. While the fundamentals are similar across the board, businesses will have to alter their strategies slightly in order to capture the attention of their target audiences. In the beginning, consume as much content and free resources as you can. From there, you can focus on your specific goals and objectives.

HOW DO YOU THINK SOCIAL MEDIA MARKETING WILL CHANGE OVER THE NEXT FEW YEARS?

I believe Social Media Marketing will change and improve for the better over the next few years. And we have so much to look forward to as this new era of social media develops. We should stay ahead of the competition by watching for developments, experimenting with new releases, and adapting quickly to the changing tides.

LEARN MORE ABOUT DAN

I've been working as a virtual assistant for six years, and I am now specializing in Social Media Marketing and management. I have helped over one hundred clients around the globe as their social media manager and VA. I have established my own social media and virtual assistant agency called Social Guy Media, and my goal is to help businesses (start-ups or big companies) grow their sales and traffic through social media and digital marketing. I also coach and train aspiring social media managers about this field and teach them how to have a stable income working as a social media manager and virtual assistant.

⊕ WWW.SOCIALGUYMEDIA.COM
✉ DANPALOMA@SOCIALGUYMEDIA.COM
✉ DANPALOMA.VA@GMAIL.COM
☎ +639233621365
▥ WWW.LINKEDIN.COM/IN/DANPALOMA
▣ WWW.FACEBOOK.COM/SOCIALGUYMEDIA

KAYLYN PARKER

HOW DO YOU DETERMINE THE EFFECTIVENESS OF A SOCIAL MEDIA MARKETING CAMPAIGN?

I determine the effectiveness of an organic social media campaign by measuring and analyzing the amount of genuine engagement we are getting after a specified time frame. More so than likes and followers, engagement by way of comments, replies, messages, and sharing is a true indication that followers are loyal to and impressed by a brand and its content. Measuring engagement also provides an opportunity to understand what an audience cares about: which pieces of content, in what style, and at what time. You can learn so much about your customers by analyzing engagement.

WHAT IS THE SINGLE MOST EFFECTIVE SOCIAL MEDIA MARKETING TACTIC YOU'VE LEARNED?

The single most effective social media tactic I've learned is how to garner massive attention to a piece of content for free. I've learned how to create content (e.g., article, video, photo, or post) a particular audience will love, the most optimal time to post it, the most effective attention-grabbing copy to complement the content, and how to drive attention to it without spending any money. It's provided my clients with free followers, great engagement to analyze and measure, and additional opportunities for press, leads, and retargeting. The key to this is to get tons of initial engagement on the social media post from friends, loyal customers, and family to get the "viral snowball" going.

IF YOU COULD CARRY ONLY FIVE TOOLS IN YOUR SOCIAL MEDIA MARKETING TOOLKIT, WHAT WOULD THEY BE?

If I could carry just five tools in my social media toolkit, I would carry: Canva, Asana, SocialPilot, Onlypult, and Google Drive. Canva is an amazing tool for creating graphics, social media posts, and even proposal templates quickly and easily. Asana is my master workflow planner—definitely something I couldn't live without! I love using the schedulers SocialPilot and OnlyPult: SocialPilot for most platforms and OnlyPult for Instagram. While I often schedule or create posts within the platform themselves, having a scheduler for when I'm away is lifesaver. Finally, Google Drive houses my calendar, inbox, and a matrix of files I could not live without!

WHAT'S THE SINGLE BIGGEST MISTAKE YOU SEE PEOPLE MAKE IN SOCIAL MEDIA MARKETING?

The single biggest mistake I see people and businesses making with their social media efforts is that they fail to be authentic. In a world where consumers are starting to tune out to adverts and posts that read like spam, it is imperative that businesses, entrepreneurs, CEOs, and influencers alike start incorporating authenticity into their social media plan. We must start thinking about the consumer when we create posts and asking ourselves what our audience would find most valuable. People connect with and are much more likely to buy from brands that get truly personal online instead of gunning for the sale online.

WHAT ADVICE WOULD YOU GIVE TO PEOPLE WHO ARE LOOKING TO RUN SUCCESSFUL SOCIAL MEDIA MARKETING CAMPAIGNS?

The advice I would give people looking to run a successful social media campaign is to get extremely clear on who your ideal customer is, first and foremost. By truly understanding who your audience is, you can create content they are sure to love and follow along with. No business truly appeals to everyone. So by asking yourself how you can help your ideal customer with your content (versus advertising to him or her), you will start to attract your most loyal fans who will be excited to buy from you and spread word to their friends.

HOW DO YOU THINK SOCIAL MEDIA MARKETING WILL CHANGE OVER THE NEXT FEW YEARS?

In the next few years, social media is going to drastically change. We are already trending toward more personalized social media campaigns, and this concept is sure to take off. Business leaders will be more widely followed on social media than the brands they represent because we as consumers are craving human interaction and the need to be involved in something greater than ourselves. I also believe video and voice content will be the most consumed content over the next few years, video because of our desire to connect and see behind-the-scenes and voice because we are busy and value our time.

LEARN MORE ABOUT KAYLYN

I'm a social media strategist, consultant, and mentor, and I'm passionate about changing the way businesses use social media to amplify their message. I truly believe all businesses and industries can flourish by using social media to build relationships and awareness, cultivate communities, and generate an impact. Cookie cutter marketing is a thing of the past. A customized social media presence that converts is the way of the future. I use this approach to build massive exposure around my own clients' brands and have since begun mentoring upcoming social media managers around the globe in hopes of spreading this ideology far and wide.

- WWW.KAYLYNPARKER.COM
- WWW.MANAGESOCIAL.MEDIA
- WWW.FACEBOOK.COM/KAYLYNJOYPARKER
- @KAYLYNJOYPARKER
- @KAYLYNJOYPARKER
- WWW.LINKEDIN.COM/IN/KAYLYNPARKER

DANIELLA PETING

MANAGER, SOCIAL COMMUNICATIONS AND DIGITAL CHANNEL STRATEGY – SCIENTIFIC PUBLICATIONS, JAMA NETWORK

HOW DO YOU DETERMINE THE EFFECTIVENESS OF A SOCIAL MEDIA MARKETING CAMPAIGN?

To determine the effectiveness of a social media campaign, I need to determine the campaign goals first. These goals should be SMART: Specific, Measurable, Achievable, Results-focused and Time-bound. Once these goals are established, I can then develop the campaign plan. The plan should consider (1) audience demographics, preferences, and behaviors, (2) content available and needed, (3) the time of year and duration of the campaign, (4) the social networks available and best suited for the campaign, and (5) resources needed to execute the campaign (time, money, people, etc.). Once the plan is finalized and implemented, the campaign needs to be monitored weekly and optimized as needed. At the end of the campaign, report the campaign's performance, good or bad. Transparency, authenticity, and consistency are more valuable to your team and objectives than skewed results.

WHAT IS THE SINGLE MOST EFFECTIVE SOCIAL MEDIA MARKETING TACTIC YOU'VE LEARNED?

I've acquired many effective social media tactics over the years, but the most effective one is to listen to your audience. If you monitor your social media audiences, you can learn (1) who they consider influencers, (2) what they want to consume, (3) when they want content, (4) the social networks they prefer, and (5) the types of content they prefer. You can then use this information to make better and more informed decisions when developing your strategy for your company or for your individual campaigns.

IF YOU COULD CARRY ONLY FIVE TOOLS IN YOUR SOCIAL MEDIA MARKETING TOOLKIT, WHAT WOULD THEY BE?

Social networks and users change, but five tools I need in my social media toolkit today are two additional team members, one amazing publishing tool, one comprehensive and insightful listening tool, and one manageable and affordable employee advocacy tool. With new features being added frequently to social networks like Facebook and LinkedIn, it's important to have the resources needed to support the demands of your stakeholders, both internally and externally. Additional team members can help you publish content, analyze its performance, listen to conversations about your brand online, identify influencers, engage with your communities, educate your internal stakeholders, and advocate for personal social media adoption throughout the organization to increase your company's reach and influence in the market.

WHAT'S THE SINGLE BIGGEST MISTAKE YOU SEE PEOPLE MAKE IN SOCIAL MEDIA MARKETING?

In some ways, social media is still unchartered territory, so mistakes will be made; however, some mistakes can be avoided. One such mistake is to adopt too many platforms. Just because there are a dozen or so social networks you can join doesn't mean you need to join them all. Make sure that the social networks you select can be supported with the resources you have today and that your customers are using those social networks. There's no need to invest in a social network that won't provide you with a positive ROI or help you achieve your company's or campaign's goals.

WHAT ADVICE WOULD YOU GIVE TO PEOPLE WHO ARE LOOKING TO RUN SUCCESSFUL SOCIAL MEDIA MARKETING CAMPAIGNS?

Do your homework. Social media audiences change, so make sure that your strategy and tactics not only meet your campaign's objectives but meet your audience's preferences and behaviors, as well.

HOW DO YOU THINK SOCIAL MEDIA MARKETING WILL CHANGE OVER THE NEXT FEW YEARS?

Eventually companies will discover that social media is a vocation worthy of its own identity and not an add-on to an existing role. With advancements in the social networks—advertising, AI, long-form content, ecommerce, etc.—practitioners need to educate their stakeholders and advocate for more and better resources in order to meet/exceed company goals/objectives.

LEARN MORE ABOUT DANIELLA

I'm an award-winning social media strategist with more than 15 years of B2B, B2C, agency and in-house experience in commercial real estate, education, finance, manufacturing, nonprofit, publishing, retail and tele-communications. Throughout my career, I've led several social media initiatives focused on crisis communication, lead generation, customer service, employee advocacy, influencer engagement and awareness. I'm currently the manager, social communications and digital channel strategy – scientific publications for the JAMA Network. In this role, I establish and implement social media best practices for the JAMA Network and lead its social media strategy.

🌐 JAMANETWORK.COM
🔗 WWW.LINKEDIN.COM/IN/DNPETING
🐦 @DNPETING

MINDI ROSSER

SOCIAL MEDIA MARKETING STRATEGIST

HOW DO YOU DETERMINE THE EFFECTIVENESS OF A SOCIAL MEDIA MARKETING CAMPAIGN?

Social media ROI is critical to measuring the effectiveness of a Social Media Marketing campaign. Social media ROI is based on the KPIs you choose for your campaign. For many Social Media Marketing campaigns, website traffic and generated leads are the main KPIs. Ideally, you want your costs in manpower and technology to be less than the revenue (in marketing qualified leads) generated from your campaign.

WHAT IS THE SINGLE MOST EFFECTIVE SOCIAL MEDIA MARKETING TACTIC YOU'VE LEARNED?

When in doubt, always personalize your marketing efforts. It may take more time than the typical automation that most social media marketers do, but your brand will be perceived as authentic and customer focused.

IF YOU COULD CARRY ONLY FIVE TOOLS IN YOUR SOCIAL MEDIA MARKETING TOOLKIT, WHAT WOULD THEY BE?

LinkedIn, CoSchedule, Buffer, TweetDeck, and Google Analytics.

WHAT'S THE SINGLE BIGGEST MISTAKE YOU SEE PEOPLE MAKE IN SOCIAL MEDIA MARKETING?

They don't have a plan and simply start posting on social media sites without determining their brand voice, creating a content calendar, and basing it all on an effective strategy.

WHAT ADVICE WOULD YOU GIVE TO PEOPLE WHO ARE LOOKING TO RUN SUCCESSFUL SOCIAL MEDIA MARKETING CAMPAIGNS?

Ask your network to find out who specializes in the type of Social Media Marketing campaign you want to run. You can save yourself a lot of hassle and wasted resources by finding a specialist. Ask them out for a coffee or a quick fifteen-minute chat or invite them to be a guest on your blog/ podcast. Be sure there's something in it for them and come up with a great list of questions to ask.

HOW DO YOU THINK SOCIAL MEDIA MARKETING WILL CHANGE OVER THE NEXT FEW YEARS?

Social Media Marketing will become more specialized and personalized in the next few years. Marketers will not be able to get away with mass messaging and blasting their content across social media channels. Fans, followers, and prospects will expect personalization rather than be pleasantly surprised when it happens.

LEARN MORE ABOUT MINDI

I help B2B businesses—and their leaders—look awesome on social media. Why? My underlying mission is to empower women and men to overcome adversity in their lives so they can become strong leaders more than capable of pursuing their dreams, their calling, and their purpose. How I do this through Social Media Marketing is giving those with a message to share (their purpose) a megaphone (social media systems) to share that message and find their tribe. A community-oriented B2B social media marketer with agency, consulting, and start-up experience, I craft niche Social Media Marketing programs and manage their day-to-day operations. I specialize in building integrated Social Media Marketing programs, social media employee advocacy programs, and influencer outreach and social selling programs. I am most passionate about building and engaging with B2B communities using an authentic marketing approach.

- WWW.MINDIROSSER.COM/BLOG
- WWW.LINKEDIN.COM/IN/MINDIROSSER
- @MINDIRROSSER
- WWW.FACEBOOK.COM/MINDIROSSERMARKETING
- Q WWW.QUORA.COM/PROFILE/MINDI-ROSSER

NICOLE BRASHEAR

SOCIAL MEDIA MARKETING AND STRATEGIST

HOW DO YOU DETERMINE THE EFFECTIVENESS OF A SOCIAL MEDIA MARKETING CAMPAIGN?

First, it's important to determine your goals and objectives. This is a very important part of the overall social media strategy. Don't just jump into each page and measure every single tweet, post, or comment. That will burn you out and put you in a tailspin. Determine what you are trying to accomplish or gain through your social channels. Do you want to spread awareness of your brand or do you want to introduce a new product and create conversion? Once you have decided on your goals and what channels are best for your objectives, you can start to use native channel analytics (e.g. Facebook Insights) or third-party metrics (e.g. Google Analytics) to measure awareness metrics like volume, reach, and exposure. How far is your message spreading? If your goal is to drive traffic to your website, then track URL shares, clicks, and conversions.

WHAT IS THE SINGLE MOST EFFECTIVE SOCIAL MEDIA MARKETING TACTIC YOU'VE LEARNED?

The most successful tactic I have learned for Social Media Marketing is using what I call "The Daily Workout." This is a strategic method I use to create organic communication, engagement, and brand awareness. We can't hide the fact that social media has become a pay-to-play channel, but we can use other tactics such as my Daily Workout to create engagement and relationships we would not have received otherwise.

The Daily Workout consists of taking thirty to forty minutes of your day to comb through your social media page(s) and:

1. Answer messages or comments.

2. Comment on seven other posts from pages you follow that are in your niche.

3. Update profiles to include a vanity (you can create in bit.ly) link to your website, blog or event.

4. Create two stories for your Instagram story.

5. Read updates on changes that may have occurred in social media so you can be sure to be current.

It is time consuming because you spend about thirty minutes on each channel networking the old fashioned way, in a sense. This method creates a system for you to get back to socializing rather than advertising. People like to be connected to a community, which is why this works.

IF YOU COULD CARRY ONLY FIVE TOOLS IN YOUR SOCIAL MEDIA MARKETING TOOLKIT, WHAT WOULD THEY BE?

A robust third-party social media management tool such as Hootsuite Pro, a photo editor such as the Photoshop app, a video editor like iMovie, a graphics editor template like Canva, and the Braintoss app that allows me to record my thoughts, ideas, and images in one space.

WHAT'S THE SINGLE BIGGEST MISTAKE YOU SEE PEOPLE MAKE IN SOCIAL MEDIA MARKETING?

This is an easy one. I see it all the time. People assume that posting a single post, tweet, snap, or gram will grow your business, create leads, or sell your products. It won't. It takes time to create a community or a following. It comes with constant communication and The Daily Workout.

WHAT ADVICE WOULD YOU GIVE TO PEOPLE WHO ARE LOOKING TO RUN SUCCESSFUL SOCIAL MEDIA MARKETING CAMPAIGNS?

As I mentioned earlier, creating goals and objectives are key to any successful campaign. I can help identify those goals and objectives, create a strategy, and implement them. It is also important to know that strategies and campaigns need to be fluid, meaning there is not a set winning combination. I wish there were! Every campaign is different and needs to be monitored so we are able to change the campaign while it is running to receive the best results. Being flexible is key.

HOW DO YOU THINK SOCIAL MEDIA MARKETING WILL CHANGE OVER THE NEXT FEW YEARS?

Social media will become less and less a vehicle to showcase your kids or family updates and instead will become a broadcast tool for news channels and companies. I also think we will see paid membership packages. So instead of FREE social media with advertisements and political nuances in your feed, you will be able to pay a fee to be rid of them once and for all. Lastly, video, video, video. Specifically, live video. Being able to see through other people's eyes in real-time has become and will continue to be a mighty source.

LEARN MORE ABOUT NICOLE

I have been in digital marketing for over twelve years and have implemented many successful marketing programs that have helped increase visibility, build customer loyalty, elevate brand awareness, and increase sales by using a strategic blend of social media, influencer outreach, Email Marketing, and SEO.

⊕ NICOLEBRASHEAR.COM
✉ HELLO@NICOLEBRASHEAR.COM
📷 @NICOLEBRASHEAR

RINA LIDDLE

SOCIAL MEDIA DIRECTOR

HOW DO YOU DETERMINE THE EFFECTIVENESS OF A SOCIAL MEDIA MARKETING CAMPAIGN?

Effectiveness is measured by conversion. But "conversion" can mean anything, so we need to start with clear goals and decide which metrics reflect that conversion most specifically. I think the campaigns that are most successful work toward getting clients, demonstrating social proof, articulating a strong brand, and, when appropriate, working toward increasing the organic SEO for the site.

WHAT IS THE SINGLE MOST EFFECTIVE SOCIAL MEDIA MARKETING TACTIC YOU'VE LEARNED?

Sending the right message out to the right audience quickly so that the campaign seems to have a life of its own. Millennials are fun to work with because they tag and have conversations in public spaces that older generations won't have. You'll especially see this on Facebook event pages. Instead of using the invite function, they will tag their friends. The first time this happened, I thought my event had been hacked. There were hundreds of tags with one- or two-word replies. We had two thousand people show up to an art opening at a gallery out in the suburbs that usually gets around fifty people.

IF YOU COULD CARRY ONLY FIVE TOOLS IN YOUR SOCIAL MEDIA MARKETING TOOLKIT, WHAT WOULD THEY BE?

Do I get to count my iPhone as one tool? I think I could pretty much settle with my iPhone, a good light source, endless power, and solid Wi-Fi, providing my iPhone gets to keep all my apps! Seriously, the apps and platforms I use change all the time, and quite frankly, I'm never satisfied with just one app for each platform. I use Hootsuite on my laptop to schedule posts in Twitter but prefer to monitor Twitter using the Twitter app on my phone. I like the Facebook Pages app to post on my own business page and the Facebook Groups app rather than using the Facebook platform. So it's better to be flexible and responsive than fixate on finding (and loving) the perfect tools.

WHAT'S THE SINGLE BIGGEST MISTAKE YOU SEE PEOPLE MAKE IN SOCIAL MEDIA MARKETING?

Again, because everything is changing all the time, it's hard to choose just one thing that will be relevant in a couple of months. And really, the only thing that will surely lead to disaster is to not schedule the time to perform social media tasks. Marketing relies on crafting the right message, getting the message in front of the right people, and repeating the process for optimal exposure. It's a lot of testing and tweaking; therefore, if efforts are not consistent, improvement will be difficult. When that happens, social media is nothing more than throwing a message out there and hoping for the best.

WHAT ADVICE WOULD YOU GIVE TO PEOPLE WHO ARE LOOKING TO RUN SUCCESSFUL SOCIAL MEDIA MARKETING CAMPAIGNS?

Plan well in advance. Make SMART goals. Create compelling content. Work with a professional graphic designer and copywriter. Have an ads budget. Use a PR team to help get your message out to the media. Know your audience and break them down to small groups and speak specifically to them by creating ads for each group. Occupy as much online real estate as you can. Make sure you have a solid email list. If you don't, then create small campaigns to build your email list.

HOW DO YOU THINK SOCIAL MEDIA MARKETING WILL CHANGE OVER THE NEXT FEW YEARS?

I worry that access to audiences will become prohibitive for small businesses and nonprofit organizations due to tiered internet access and big brand saturation. I'm hoping net neutrality will become a mainstream movement to prevent this from happening. I think social media platforms will continue to move in the direction of keeping people in the apps, which leaves referral website traffic up in the air. I'd be thrilled to see social media platforms become a VR experience, and then we can move through ads rather than read, listen to, and watch them.

LEARN MORE ABOUT RINA

I run a boutique digital agency specializing in social media located in Vancouver, Canada, where I work with small businesses and nonprofit organizations. I also offer corporate training in-house or virtually across North America. I've taught Communication Theory, Cultural Theory, Visual Language, and Social Media at Emily Carr University, University Canada West, and Brighton College. I am a practicing artist and have shown work internationally that utilizes technology and social media. In my spare time, I love to snowshoe, hike, run, and throw dinner parties.

- 🌐 LIDDLEWORKS.COM
- ✉ RINA@LIDDLEWORKS.COM
- 💼 WWW.LINKEDIN.COM/IN/RINALIDDLE
- 🐦 @LIDDLEWORKS
- 📘 WWW.FACEBOOK.COM/LIDDLEWORKS
- 📷 @LIDDLEWORKS

CHAPTER 5
CONTENT MARKETING

A SIMPLE EXPLANATION OF CONTENT MARKETING

Content Marketing is a marketing approach centered on creating, distributing, and assessing valuable and relevant content to attract, acquire, engage, and/or retain a clearly defined audience.

Often, the goal of Content Marketing is to drive a valuable conversion action such as a lead, sale, or sign-up.

Content Marketing is considered a pull-based marketing strategy; by providing valuable information to prospects and customers, you attract them to your business. This is in contrast to advertising, which is considered a push-based marketing strategy.

Content Marketing can be used to break though the clutter of advertising and company messaging by providing useful information to a customer.

By releasing content that is useful and informative to customers, organizations can build trust with their customers so that when it comes time for the customer to buy, trust has been established through the company's content.

Content Marketing is an opportunity for organizations to establish themselves as the go-to brand for their product or service. Often, this is done by answering specific questions a customer might have about a product or service or by providing valuable information that the customer can't find anywhere else.

Content is considered "owned media"—it's produced by and owned by the organization and can include but is not limited to blog posts, web pages, infographics, video, podcasts, white papers, and e-books.

Content Marketing is becoming an increasingly important part of a business's online marketing ecosystem; content can support SEO, PR, PPC, and social media efforts.

CONTENT MARKETING SPECIALISTS SOUND OFF

JASON ABRAHAMS

VP DIGITAL, ROOT3 MARKETING & BUSINESS DEVELOPMENT

HOW DO YOU DETERMINE THE EFFECTIVENESS OF A CONTENT MARKETING CAMPAIGN?

Like a sales funnel, Content Marketing campaign effectiveness can be viewed as a metric funnel with four levels: consumption, engagement, lead generation, and revenue. At the top level of the funnel, we look at consumption and engagement metrics like pageviews, time on site, referral clicks, and social engagement. In the middle of the funnel, we measure based on the number of leads being added to the funnel via new subscribers, demo requests, whitepaper downloads, phone calls, or contact form fills. At the bottom of the funnel, we can measure effectiveness by tracking how many people make a purchase after reading a blog post or sign a contract after downloading a whitepaper. By tracking both short-term and long-term metrics, you can get a true picture of the campaign success while optimizing throughout the process.

WHAT IS THE SINGLE MOST EFFECTIVE CONTENT MARKETING TACTIC YOU'VE LEARNED?

The single most effective Content Marketing tactic that I've learned involves the concept of atomization. It can also be referred to as the dandelion effect. The overall concept is that you can take one big content idea (the dandelion itself), which should be "planted" on your website (the stalk) and then broken down into a multitude of smaller content executions (the seeds of the dandelion). The smaller content executions can be spread far and wide via multiple owned, paid, and earned channels. For our small to midmarket B2B clients with limited budgets and resources, we focus on developing one big content idea per quarter and then maximize our efforts by making lots of small ideas out of it. The concept of "repurpose, reuse, and recycle" has a place in the content marketing world too.

IF YOU COULD CARRY ONLY FIVE TOOLS IN YOUR CONTENT MARKETING TOOLKIT, WHAT WOULD THEY BE?

In the digital age where content is king, understanding buyer personas and user journeys are imperative to strategically developing tailored content to the specific needs of each. Using an editorial calendar to organize content by channel and persona is also critical to the effectiveness of a content marketing campaign. Google Analytics and other data tracking tools, along with a customer relationship management (CRM) platform, are also necessary for monitoring and measuring campaign ROI, especially as it relates to business development and pipeline growth.

WHAT'S THE SINGLE BIGGEST MISTAKE YOU SEE PEOPLE MAKE IN CONTENT MARKETING?

One-size-fits-all, mass communication is outdated. Consumers are too smart and their attention span is too short for this blanket approach. Personalization is key to the success of any content marketing campaign. Marketers should be focused on developing content that is highly personalized for specific target personas that can be developed based on demographic and behavioral data. This personalized Content Marketing approach should build on itself by aligning content with your sales funnel. This will create a natural progression that teaches at the beginning, engages in the middle, and persuades at the end, helping move the consumer through their buyer journey more efficiently.

WHAT ADVICE WOULD YOU GIVE TO PEOPLE WHO ARE LOOKING TO RUN SUCCESSFUL CONTENT MARKETING CAMPAIGNS?

Marketers should develop multi-touch, multichannel content marketing campaigns to optimize results. Content should be disseminated to targeted audiences via distribution platforms categorized into three broad categories: earned, paid, and owned. While earned content placement via media publications and niche blog websites should be a priority due to enhancing awareness and third-party credibility, earned placement is less predictable and can take time to get traction. Immediate results can be garnered via distribution on owned platforms, including your website and social media channels, as well as through paid channels via publication syndication, search advertising, social boosting, and retargeting ads. Content on owned platforms should also be optimized for search results to drive organic web traffic.

HOW DO YOU THINK CONTENT MARKETING WILL CHANGE OVER THE NEXT FEW YEARS?

I believe Content Marketing will continue to shift to developing custom content that builds on itself and is highly personalized, relevant, entertaining, and informational based on where the consumer is in their path to purchase. The technology already exists for this to occur at a high level, but as we continue to gather more and more data on both known and unknown audiences, we can utilize this data to serve the most appropriate content to help move the consumer through their journey. I also expect the cost of this personalization technology to become more affordable for small and midmarket businesses.

LEARN MORE ABOUT JASON

Currently, I am Vice President of Marketing for Root3 Marketing & Business Development, a Chicago-based firm focused on developing long-term success strategies for high-growth businesses. Acting in many cases as an outsourced CMO for my clients, I develop and execute innovative digital marketing programs that improve the efficiency and effectiveness of the business development process. My team executes emerging and traditional marketing tactics to drive customer base growth, digital conversions, and overall brand development. Prior to joining Root3, I oversaw marketing strategy and execution for a variety of B2B businesses. I have also taught digital marketing courses and seminars at the Digital Professional Institute in Chicago.

⊕ WWW.ROOT3MARKETING.COM
🐦 @ROOT3MARKETING
📘 WWW.FACEBOOK.COM/ROOT3MARKETING

ROBERT DREW

SENIOR MARKETING MANAGER, ZIFF DAVIS

HOW DO YOU DETERMINE THE EFFECTIVENESS OF A CONTENT MARKETING CAMPAIGN?

We measure the success of a Content Marketing campaign at two or three levels, depending on the goals of the campaigns in which they're used: engagements, marketing qualified leads (MQLs), and opportunities opened/won. Leads are a given; if trackable, leads are a goal of all campaigns. MQLs are either put into nurture or, if qualified and hot, forwarded promptly as sales qualified leads. We match all leads to opportunities in our CRM. Engagement metrics—opens, clicks, shares, and interactions—are important for branding and awareness campaigns, such as those for which display and social media play a part. Typical leads are content downloads, webinar views, form completions, or inquiries. Leads reflect more proactive responses than those noted for engagement metrics.

WHAT IS THE SINGLE MOST EFFECTIVE CONTENT MARKETING TACTIC YOU'VE LEARNED?

The art of content extension, which means creating multiple content pieces in a variety of formats from one cornerstone content piece. For example, reports created from original research excel in SEO and active promotional channels. We put research findings into an e-book format. Then we publish a handful of articles on key findings from the report on our blog with links to the form-protected e-book. Then, how about an infographic with report charts/stats? You can take it further and have an industry influencer (with a social media following) comment on report findings in another article, create separate white papers and how-to sheets on findings, and even develop a webinar. You do not have to produce research to enjoy the fruits of a content extension strategy. Do this for your webinars, white papers, and e-books. Not only will you have more to promote, but you will enjoy Content Marketing economies of scale.

IF YOU COULD CARRY ONLY FIVE TOOLS IN YOUR CONTENT MARKETING TOOLKIT, WHAT WOULD THEY BE?

I consider one's website hosting platform (WordPress for us), CRM (Salesforce), and major social media platforms "givens," so I won't include those, though they're critical. Almost every company relies on versions of these. We use HubSpot for marketing automation. I've worked with Marketo and Pardot, and all have strengths and weaknesses. These systems help you increase your output volume and measure results. SEMrush is very helpful for selecting keywords, which help drive content creation, competitor content research, backlink analysis, and other data to improve our online presence. BuzzSumo helps us understand what content can succeed with our audience and stay on top of our space, from a new content perspective. Quip is a big help for managing content teams and multiparty content projects. Finally, LinkedIn Pulse helps us share effectively content on that network, an important one for B2B.

WHAT'S THE SINGLE BIGGEST MISTAKE YOU SEE PEOPLE MAKE IN CONTENT MARKETING?

Companies still too frequently err on the side of selling rather than educating through the buying cycle. On the B2B side, consumers of content want to learn about the issues they face as business decision-makers. In the classic AIDA model stages, to develop Awareness, companies frequently need to inform potential clients that they even have a problem. To begin building Interest, and more awareness, too, successful marketers frequently frame the issues among a set of possible solutions. Through both of these stages, potential decision-makers are not ready for sales pitches. Instead, marketers should maintain the focus on thought leadership: educating, informing, raising the knowledge level. To the smaller set of content consumers who have engaged enough to be potential prospects, they can gradually target more sales-oriented content, with Desire and Action as objectives. Content Marketing is like sales in that both require a relationship building process. Start slow.

WHAT ADVICE WOULD YOU GIVE TO PEOPLE WHO ARE LOOKING TO RUN SUCCESSFUL CONTENT MARKETING CAMPAIGNS?

In many respects, content distribution strategy—how to make these channels work well together—gets short shrift. Make it a priority to figure out where your audience goes to get information on issues for which you provide solutions. Then make your content as findable as possible. Host your content in a resources center on your site, optimize it for Google and Bing, and publish a regular stream of fresh content. This drives inbound traffic from prospects in research mode.

Don't forget active promotion. Your email house list can be golden. Grow it with fresh marketing-qualified leads and nurture them with your content. To really monetize your content: Syndicate it. Market to prospects beyond your reach. Develop partner relationships for this and work with quality syndication specialists. Those that have a need for your solutions will identify it through your content and identify you as the provider of choice.

HOW DO YOU THINK CONTENT MARKETING WILL CHANGE OVER THE NEXT FEW YEARS?

Decision-makers have significantly increased the range of sources used to research issues and solutions, and this trend is not slowing. This includes a wider range of social media platforms and online publishers. Content marketers need to ensure they have broad-based exposure and that they do not rely just on inbound traffic. As more marketers adopt the content methodology, we all will need to keep this top of mind. Time will tell which content types will get the attention of our audiences. Video adoption will increase, and we watch the impact of voice response technologies with great interest. But written content will always have a prominent place, since it is still ideal to let the time-challenged skim quickly to the most useful information.

LEARN MORE ABOUT ROBERT

For the past decade, I have served in marketing management in the B2B division of global digital media company Ziff Davis, starting in its subsidiary emedia and including the B2BSignals, Salesify, and IT Toolbox brands. Our division's brands provide demand generation services for solutions marketers. In short, I serve as the demand generator for a demand generation company. Content is the jet fuel for demand generation. Before Ziff Davis/emedia, I managed e-commerce launches and other new product development in the B2B space, including InStock Fasteners, an early online store for industrial and MRO hardware. I received a BS in business management and political science from Northern Illinois University and a master's in international business studies from the University of South Carolina. Based in Chicago, my wife Vita and I enjoy biking, travel, and exploring this fascinating city, and I try to go west for at least one ski vacation annually.

✉ RDREW31@YAHOO.COM

in WWW.LINKEDIN.COM/IN/ROBERT-A-DREW-B2B-MARKETER

HOLLY JOHNSON

CONTENT MARKETING MANAGER

HOW DO YOU DETERMINE THE EFFECTIVENESS OF A CONTENT MARKETING CAMPAIGN?

I determine the effectiveness of a Content Marketing campaign by how many qualified leads are generated and how long the content stays "evergreen" (up-to-date and relevant to the audience) in search engines.

WHAT IS THE SINGLE MOST EFFECTIVE CONTENT MARKETING TACTIC YOU'VE LEARNED?

The single most effective Content Marketing tactic I've learned is that you shouldn't be afraid to take risks in creating your content; tap into the ugly things that are true for your reader.

IF YOU COULD CARRY ONLY FIVE TOOLS IN YOUR CONTENT MARKETING TOOLKIT, WHAT WOULD THEY BE?

My five Content Marketing tools would be: a website with blog, marketing automation software, Canva for graphics, Google Analytics, and Answer the Public.

WHAT'S THE SINGLE BIGGEST MISTAKE YOU SEE PEOPLE MAKE IN CONTENT MARKETING?

The biggest mistake I see people make in Content Marketing is letting a conversation go to waste by having it in private. Turn sales conversations with prospects into marketing.

WHAT ADVICE WOULD YOU GIVE TO PEOPLE WHO ARE LOOKING TO RUN SUCCESSFUL CONTENT MARKETING CAMPAIGNS?

Focus on creating relevant, consistent content that provides the most value to your reader at each step of the conversion funnel.

HOW DO YOU THINK CONTENT MARKETING WILL CHANGE OVER THE NEXT FEW YEARS?

Content Marketing is about to get smarter as companies take advantage of emerging technologies like AI and Big Data.

LEARN MORE ABOUT HOLLY

I've been in the B2B technology marketing space for six years. My specialty is in content marketing, and I enjoy writing stories about innovations in new technology that drive social shares and results.

⊕ HOLLYCONTENTMARKETING.BLOG
in WWW.LINKEDIN.COM/IN/HOLLYCONNOR
🐦 @TROMATASTIC

ARNIE KUENN

CEO, VERTICAL MEASURES

HOW DO YOU DETERMINE THE EFFECTIVENESS OF A CONTENT MARKETING CAMPAIGN?

There are a lot of factors that can determine the effectiveness of a Content Marketing campaign, but at the highest level, traffic and leads will indicate the campaign's success. If you get more users on your site and those users turn into leads and those leads turn into customers, your Content Marketing campaign has been successful. This success happens by moving users through the customer journey from awareness to consideration, decision, and finally, advocacy. Measuring the number of users in each stage of the customer journey will indicate how well each stage is performing and can help identify bottlenecks that need more attention. Creating and maintaining a strong customer journey is integral to running an effective Content Marketing campaign.

WHAT IS THE SINGLE MOST EFFECTIVE CONTENT MARKETING TACTIC YOU'VE LEARNED?

In our experience, the hub and spoke model has been most efficient at building our audience and converting organic traffic. With the hub and spoke model, you'll research, produce, and publish a main piece of content (hub). Then you'll create many smaller articles (spokes) that relate back to that significant piece of content. The spokes should be optimized for search to drive as much organic traffic back to your website as possible. As you publish more spokes and organic traffic increases, you can send more visitors to the hub (which should be gated behind a lead-capture form) to build your contact list and/or generate conversions.

Think of it like a wagon wheel. The hub is located at the center and the spokes are all connected to the hub. As the wheel rolls forward, it gains traction and moves traffic from the spokes directly to the hub. By building our library of gated content and creating supporting "spokes," we can entice our visitors to provide a little bit of information (i.e., become a lead), so they can access our hub content.

IF YOU COULD CARRY ONLY FIVE TOOLS IN YOUR CONTENT MARKETING TOOLKIT, WHAT WOULD THEY BE?

1. A CMS. You can't be in the Content Marketing business without the ability to publish content. We use WordPress.

2. Inbound marketing and sales software. A strong CRM with additional marketing and sales features is nonnegotiable. We use HubSpot.

3. Content Marketing software. Good software replaces the need to constantly upload, download, and try to manage and track it all in email and spreadsheets. We use ClearVoice.

4. A keyword tool. There are numerous ones out there — Moz, SEMrush, Keywordtool.io, Keyword Planner, and Answer the Public are a few we use.

5. Google Analytics. The ability to measure and compare data is vital— otherwise, how will you know if you're successful?

WHAT'S THE SINGLE BIGGEST MISTAKE YOU SEE PEOPLE MAKE IN CONTENT MARKETING?

Without a doubt, the single biggest mistake I see in the Content Marketing world is lack of consistent execution. You can develop the right strategy, do the best research, fully understand SEO, and have a plan for amplifying your content, but if you do not create the content AND publish it on a frequent basis for at least one year, odds are you are going to fail. We have worked with more than a hundred clients over the years. We teach and preach the same to all of them. The difference between those that have huge successes and those that are frustrated always boils down to prioritization and execution.

WHAT ADVICE WOULD YOU GIVE TO PEOPLE WHO ARE LOOKING TO RUN SUCCESSFUL CONTENT MARKETING CAMPAIGNS?

Don't create content just for the sake of creating content. Be intentional with your efforts and set goals in your strategy. For example, if you are trying to generate leads, ensure that there are calls-to-action within your content that encourage prospects toward the next natural step in their customer journey. Also, think about what delivery channels you will use to reach your ideal audience, whether that be social advertising, email, or other distribution networks. My advice for content-driven campaigns is to set a clear goal, create content that serves the intent of that goal, and choose delivery channels that will get your content in front of the right audiences.

HOW DO YOU THINK CONTENT MARKETING WILL CHANGE OVER THE NEXT FEW YEARS?

As Content Marketing matures, I see the customer experience continuing to improve because customers will demand improvement from websites and brands. Two things are going to become paramount: speed and personalization. People are using mobile devices more and more ("Get me my answer fast"), and they're reading less and less ("Show me only what is relevant"). Google is trying to keep up with these demands by adopting a mobile-first index. I think in short order, Google is going to start prioritizing things like video and text snippets, as opposed to long, keyword-driven text pages that few people are actually reading. We see this shift happening already with things like answer boxes, but I think it will really accelerate in the coming years. The faster you can get the answer to your customers, the more you'll be rewarded.

LEARN MORE ABOUT ARNIE

In 2006 I founded Vertical Measures, a highly respected digital marketing agency. In 2008 I started the Arizona Interactive Marketing Association

(AZIMA). In 2014, I was honored as the Interactive Person of the Year in Arizona, and in 2015 I entered the Content Marketing Hall of Fame. In 2017, I was named Content Marketing Person of the Year in Arizona, and my proudest accomplishment was having Vertical Measures named a Best Places to Work in Arizona. I am also the co-author of *Content Marketing Works* and author of *Accelerate*. I speak to and train thousands of people every year all around the world.

🌐 WWW.VERTICALMEASURES.COM
🔗 WWW.LINKEDIN.COM/IN/ARNIEKUENN
🐦 @ARNIEK

JON DAVIS

MARKETING MANAGER, CUSHING

HOW DO YOU DETERMINE THE EFFECTIVENESS OF A CONTENT MARKETING CAMPAIGN?

Beyond clicks and conversions, does the content have life beyond our website? Did the customer share the story with their own network? Did they link to it? Can the content be repurposed for print collateral? Will our business development team share it with their existing clients and prospects? Does the content lead to an ongoing relationship with the customer for future articles? Lastly, when a customer uses an idea they found in our website content for their own project, that helps us know we are moving in the right direction.

WHAT IS THE SINGLE MOST EFFECTIVE CONTENT MARKETING TACTIC YOU'VE LEARNED?

Realizing Content Marketing efforts require a sales approach and not being afraid to use the phone for follow-up. Email, LinkedIn, and Twitter are great—there is no debate they have helped me connect with contacts and resources. However, I don't think we use the phone enough as marketers. My case study or blog is not the priority for customers—email and direct messages are easy to ignore. Phone calls break through the clutter. Yes, you need to deal with rejection, but making a call has led to valuable content opportunities that have created customers we would not have today.

IF YOU COULD CARRY ONLY FIVE TOOLS IN YOUR CONTENT MARKETING TOOLKIT, WHAT WOULD THEY BE?

Hemingway App, Lucky Orange, Google Analytics/Search Console, Canva, and Adobe Spark.

WHAT'S THE SINGLE BIGGEST MISTAKE YOU SEE
PEOPLE MAKE IN CONTENT MARKETING?

It all depends on the business. But I believe, in the B2B world, not proactively tapping into your business development and project teams for ideas and contacts. Think about it: each day they are on the front line working with prospects, quoting projects, or managing relationships. Don't expect them to put a bunch of names in a tidy email. You need to ask. They are simply too busy to let you know about ones that could be a good fit for your next blog post or social proof such as website testimonials. Customers are YOUR leads to improve marketing collateral, generate reviews, gather website feedback, or input and prospects for your next on-site event.

WHAT ADVICE WOULD YOU GIVE TO PEOPLE WHO ARE LOOKING
TO RUN SUCCESSFUL CONTENT MARKETING CAMPAIGNS?

Again, it comes down to your customer base and goals, Do your best to understand your company target prospects and vertical markets and how your company offering can grow their businesses. Don't be afraid to try something new, but don't do it just because it's trendy. When you move forward with a campaign—whether it is a client testimonial video or writing a client success story—have backups ready to go (this is specifically in reference to contacts who agree to participate in your content/story/idea, and then you never hear from them again).

HOW DO YOU THINK CONTENT MARKETING WILL
CHANGE OVER THE NEXT FEW YEARS?

Voice search encourages (forces?) customized website experiences driven by content to evolve. A generic FAQ page won't cut it—if that potential customer can't find your website in seconds after talking into Alexa or Siri, you need to understand their expectations and your content needs to deliver a personalized experience. Employer brand continues to be increasingly important as customers want to know more about your company history and employee stories and how your team makes you different from the competition. Client testimonials and positive reviews won't be enough. Your customer-facing teams and their genuine experiences working with customers, troubleshooting, and problem solving will play a larger role. It won't all be positive stories, but this will help your customer storytelling evolve. You'll seek out challenging stories for content opportunities because of questions they raise and solutions your company provided. You won't reach out only to happy customers; more marketers will use customer service experiences to help them enrich content.

LEARN MORE ABOUT JONATHAN

I'm the marketing manager of a display graphics company in Chicago called Cushing (sorry if you were expecting me to say that I'm the lead singer of Korn). I'm responsible for generating inbound leads, writing our email newsletter, developing the blog, link earning, booking speakers for our on-site lunch and learns, and looking like Ben Stiller (I get this all the time). Feel free to contact me!

⊕ WWW.JONRDAVIS.COM
⊕ WWW.CUSHINGCO.COM
🔗 WWW.LINKEDIN.COM/IN/JONRYANDAVIS

AMANDA ELLIOTT

BLOGGER, WINDY CITY COSMO

HOW DO YOU DETERMINE THE EFFECTIVENESS OF A CONTENT MARKETING CAMPAIGN?

When you're starting out, you are building an audience and expertise by creating a content hub around your specialization. Once you're established, you have loyal followers and the added benefit of referrals and exposure—this means you can run campaigns and quickly see if they are effective using KPIs like engagement, open rates, and click-throughs. For those just starting out, build an active audience and always test. Develop a strategy and build enough data points to where you can see trends. One or two posts with low engagement don't necessarily mean the post was bad. It could be because the tactics and strategy were not in place for success.

WHAT IS THE SINGLE MOST EFFECTIVE CONTENT MARKETING TACTIC YOU'VE LEARNED?

Don't stop because you think no one is interested/listening. No one will listen if (a) you don't have content and (b) you don't tell them about your content. People need reminders. They also need you to get their attention. There are thousands of Instagram models. So why do some become popular? If you read through social media marketers' and content creators' tactics, they will say your content should have a theme, be high-quality, and be unique to your brand. Those things are important, but even if you create great content, it doesn't mean that traffic will come.

I think collaboration and building awareness is vital. Content creation isn't about building an island of content. The key is gaining attention—tagging influencers in posts, writing guest posts, sending newsletter campaigns, sharing content with people who like similar content, and looking at a mix of paid and organic search. Let's go back to the basics: work well with others and do a good job.

IF YOU COULD CARRY ONLY FIVE TOOLS IN YOUR CONTENT MARKETING TOOLKIT, WHAT WOULD THEY BE?

My iPhone—it's my lifeline, navigator, and how I stay connected on social media. I also love Canva. It's an app that makes it easy to create perfectly formatted content for social media. I think Email Marketing tools are important, like MailChimp, Boomerang, or Yet Another Mail Merge. I also love the Grammarly app. It helps me proofread, especially when I'm working on a solo project. Lastly, content scheduling tools are important: Missinglettr, Buffer, or Hootsuite.

WHAT'S THE SINGLE BIGGEST MISTAKE YOU SEE PEOPLE MAKE IN CONTENT MARKETING?

Marketers grow audiences on various channels but often forget about growing an email list; email won't go away any time soon. Also, make sure you have all your contacts and data in one place.

WHAT ADVICE WOULD YOU GIVE TO PEOPLE WHO ARE LOOKING TO RUN SUCCESSFUL CONTENT MARKETING CAMPAIGNS?

Content Marketing is as much about creating as it is about engaging with followers and your target market. I think the people and organizations that win with content are those that truly care about making an impact and helping their followers. Stay active and listen to what people are saying about your brand and about trends in your industry. Respond to comments and be aware of your clients' needs. Set up Google alerts, read industry news, follow and comment on other people's content, and reply to your clients' comments. Also, make sure you're tracking your content. Google Analytics Campaign URL Builder is great for that. It allows you to really see where your traffic is coming from by setting up specialized links and then referring back to Google Analytics.

HOW DO YOU THINK CONTENT MARKETING WILL CHANGE OVER THE NEXT FEW YEARS?

The organizations that win have a distinct brand that tells a story. They stand for something. There's two ways to tell your story: short-form and long-form content. Depending on the platform and your audience, there's an outlet for more visual and concise content. For example, PR companies find influencers through Instagram, and they look for short captions and great graphics. However, there's also a need for long-form content and good research as opposed to endless clickbait or how-to advice columns. The more brands offer value via both high-quality content *and* succinct messaging, the more they will win on any platform.

LEARN MORE ABOUT AMANDA

I've been creating content since 2008. I primarily focus on using social media to connect with people and then emphasize the value of meeting people in person. My background is in writing and interviewing business owners, entrepreneurs, and creatives, as well as attending, promoting, and organizing events to build community. My recent projects include my lifestyle blog, *Windy City Cosmo*, where I help women live the ultimate cosmopolitan life by introducing them to entrepreneurs and venues to meet others and teaching them how to take advantage of city life to achieve their goals and build their businesses. I also started a dating and relationship podcast, *Ok Cool Podcast*, about a male and female's perspective on modern dating in the city.

- ⊕ WINDYCITYCOSMO.COM
- ✉ WINDYCITYCOSMO@GMAIL.COM
- 🔗 WWW.LINKEDIN.COM/IN/AMANDAJELLIOTT
- 🐦 @RATIONALIZATION
- 📷 @WINDYCITYCOSMO
- 🎙 ITUNES.APPLE.COM/US/PODCAST/OK-COOL-PODCAST/IDI333467437?MT=2

ASHLEY POYNTER

CEO, CONTENT REWIRED

HOW DO YOU DETERMINE THE EFFECTIVENESS OF A CONTENT MARKETING CAMPAIGN?

Content Marketing effectiveness really depends on the goals. If we are working on a lead generation campaign where we've created a premium content asset for download, we may track how many leads are actually generated. If we're running an inbound campaign to drive awareness, we may look at traffic metrics, along with average time on site and pages per visit. We may also want to look at new vs. returning visitors. And if we're tracking the effectiveness of Content Marketing on social, we'll likely look at a whole different set of metrics specific to each social platform. Effectiveness is subjective to your goals.

WHAT IS THE SINGLE MOST EFFECTIVE CONTENT MARKETING TACTIC YOU'VE LEARNED?

It's really hard to hone down to just one tactic, but email drip marketing ranks highly in terms of most effective Content Marketing tactics. When done well, email drip sequences are excellent for nurturing leads, building trust, and positioning a business as a thought leader. The recipe for the best drip emails includes a personalized note that addresses a known question or concern the recipient has, along with links to content the business has produced around that topic. The goal is to not sound pre-packaged but to be hyper-customized and personal.

IF YOU COULD CARRY ONLY FIVE TOOLS IN YOUR CONTENT MARKETING TOOLKIT, WHAT WOULD THEY BE?

If I could only bring five Content Marketing tools with me along for the ride, they would probably be Google Analytics, HubSpot, BuzzSumo, Hootsuite, and Outbrain.

WHAT'S THE SINGLE BIGGEST MISTAKE YOU SEE PEOPLE MAKE IN CONTENT MARKETING?

The biggest mistake I see in Content Marketing is not having a strategy. This is by far the best way to waste time and money on a Content Marketing program. Many businesses I talk to have tried producing content at varying degrees without any real aim. They go through fits and starts of content production and try to see what sticks. Unfortunately, without a game plan, almost none of it ever sticks. Great Content Marketing always starts with a strategy, even if it's a simple one. Map out your goals and reverse engineer your tactics from there. This way, you can measure and track effectiveness over time and tweak where needed to achieve better results.

WHAT ADVICE WOULD YOU GIVE TO PEOPLE WHO ARE LOOKING TO RUN SUCCESSFUL CONTENT MARKETING CAMPAIGNS?

Have a plan. Go into Content Marketing with some short- and long-term goals. Write those goals down. Map out tactics that will help you hit your goals. Get organized. Meet with your content teams bimonthly or monthly to ensure you're on the right track. Measure everything and test where you're not seeing the results you want. Don't be afraid to hire help. Working with a consultant or outside team of experts can ease the time and resource burden internally.

HOW DO YOU THINK CONTENT MARKETING WILL CHANGE OVER THE NEXT FEW YEARS?

I think we're going to see a lot of innovation in the realm of augmented reality/virtual reality. Rather than reading or watching a video about something, users are going to be able to experience it through virtual reality. It's a new media type that brands should embrace and adopt early. I also see interesting things happening at the intersection of artificial intelligence (AI)/machine learning and Content Marketing. We're already seeing strides in this department with AI-enhanced PPC advertising and AI-powered chatbots on websites. The ability to personalize to the nth degree will become more of a reality—and a requirement to stay top of mind with millennial consumers.

LEARN MORE ABOUT ASHLEY

I am Chief Storyteller at Content Rewired. I have been honing my craft of telling tales (the good kind) for the past fifteen years. As a trained journalist, I was drawn to Content Marketing to help companies craft, produce, and promote the most important stories about their brands, products, and services. I have worked with both B2C and B2B companies across a range of industries, including payments, SaaS, FinTech, FinServ, healthcare, health and wellness, retail, IT, and others. I believe in the power of storytelling to help organizations meet their business objectives and connect with their audiences in a meaningful, actionable way.

⊕ CONTENTREWIRED.COM

CATE CONROY

HOW DO YOU DETERMINE THE EFFECTIVENESS OF A CONTENT MARKETING CAMPAIGN?

Efficacy of a Content Marketing campaign is all about whether the campaign is moving you toward your goal. To measure progress, you have to first establish a clear goal and metrics. To determine the goal of your campaign, take a step back to the business objectives of the campaign. What is the purpose of this campaign? To increase brand awareness? Use social listening to measure brand mentions and sentiment. Is the purpose to increase leads? Measure the conversion rate. Ultimately, determining the efficacy of any content marketing campaign always comes back to how well you have tied the campaign to the business objectives and how you are measuring the work. As long as those two elements are in place, the campaign will result in an actionable set of metrics.

WHAT IS THE SINGLE MOST EFFECTIVE CONTENT MARKETING TACTIC YOU'VE LEARNED?

Content Marketing always comes back to one thing: information. That is why the single most important Content Marketing tactic is gathering information effectively. Being able to ask questions, research subjects, and uncover important information is the one content skill set I always rely on, no matter the project. As technology changes, content formats and distribution channels will come and go. But being able to gather information and craft a story is a timeless tactic that will always play an important role in content marketing.

IF YOU COULD CARRY ONLY FIVE TOOLS IN YOUR CONTENT MARKETING TOOLKIT, WHAT WOULD THEY BE?

If I could carry only five tools in my Content Marketing toolkit, they would be a pen, paper, dictionary, and thesaurus, and another content marketer for bouncing ideas off each other.

WHAT'S THE SINGLE BIGGEST MISTAKE YOU SEE PEOPLE MAKE IN CONTENT MARKETING?

The biggest mistake I see people making in Content Marketing is not being strategic in their work. Spinning up social channels and blogs just for the sake of Content Marketing is easy but ultimately ineffective without a strategy in place. Content Marketing should always include a strategy that addresses who the audience is, what the message is, and how to get the message in front of that audience.

WHAT ADVICE WOULD YOU GIVE TO PEOPLE WHO ARE LOOKING TO RUN SUCCESSFUL CONTENT MARKETING CAMPAIGNS?

I always say start with a plan, even if it is high level. To run an effective Content Marketing campaign, you have to lay out the basics: the campaign goal, the audience, the message, the place/time the message is being delivered to the audience, and how to measure progress towards the goal. Once you have these foundational pieces in place, the rest of your work becomes that much more effective.

HOW DO YOU THINK CONTENT MARKETING WILL CHANGE OVER THE NEXT FEW YEARS?

The biggest change to content over the next few years will occur within the distribution channels we're using. With the rise of new channels for information distribution like virtual reality, augmented reality, and voice, content will have to adapt. Content marketers will need to find ways to effectively reach audiences on new platforms while maintaining meaningful conversations on existing channels. This will require an understanding of how these formats work in order to produce content that can be consumed over these various channels. Content marketers will need to work hard to maintain an understanding of emerging technology platforms.

LEARN MORE ABOUT CATE

As a strategist with a background in journalism, I have over thirteen years' experience in communications, but I consider myself a lifelong storyteller. As a digital consultant, I've worked as a key partner to Fortune 500 executives on user experience projects across the digital landscape of content, social, search, and data.

⊕ WWW.CATECONROY.COM

BOB GIROLAMO

CEO, SORC'D

HOW DO YOU DETERMINE THE EFFECTIVENESS OF A CONTENT MARKETING CAMPAIGN?

Our Content Marketing goals revolve around engagement, registrations, and customer retention. Some of the metrics we use to measure our Content Marketing goals include: blog comments, social shares, inbound links, online sales, and renewal rates. What ultimately determines our effectiveness depends on what audience we want to reach. For example, if we are focusing on creating content for current customers, then we'll take a look at the intersection of engagement metrics and customer retention. If we're trying to engage new customers, we'll look at how engagement metrics compare with the number of registrations.

While this may seem like a fairly straightforward practice, it goes in opposition to the common situation of many companies that try to build a single Content Marketing campaign for numerous audience types. Without tailoring your content marketing efforts to one well-defined, highly specific audience at a time, it just doesn't work. By continually learning about what your audience likes and using that information to continually improve, you'll create more effective campaigns that success-fully drive your overall goals.

WHAT IS THE SINGLE MOST EFFECTIVE CONTENT MARKETING TACTIC YOU'VE LEARNED?

The single most effective Content Marketing tactic we've embraced involves creating content that is truly valuable to well-defined audience segments. In order to do this, we listen to our audience, pick quality over quantity, and invest the time it takes to become expertly knowledgeable about customer needs and industry trends.

IF YOU COULD CARRY ONLY FIVE TOOLS IN YOUR CONTENT MARKETING TOOLKIT, WHAT WOULD THEY BE?

UpContent: a content curation tool that helps companies find the most relevant articles worth sharing in their industry. Sorc'd: shameless self-plug, but our users have found it to be the easiest way to keep track of research—from brainstorming to editing. Sorc'd acts as the glue for our content creation process. Google Drive: the easiest way to collaborate with the team on various content marketing initiatives. Drip: an automated Email Marketing solution for delivering our content to registered users. nDash Marketing: an innovative freelance network where writers pitch article ideas—great for keeping us on track and on trend.

WHAT'S THE SINGLE BIGGEST MISTAKE YOU SEE PEOPLE MAKE IN CONTENT MARKETING?

The single biggest Content Marketing mistake is giving up! Creating content for thirty days is not enough time to determine whether or not resulting sales justify the cost of content creation. You have to think of content marketing as the marathon of advertising. To be successful, it's necessary to spend a significant amount of time training for a consistently paced journey—recovering from periodic trips and enjoying the downhill glide from time to time. The compounding effects will be worth the lengthy journey, but you'll never realize them without consistency and time.

WHAT ADVICE WOULD YOU GIVE TO PEOPLE WHO ARE LOOKING TO RUN SUCCESSFUL CONTENT MARKETING CAMPAIGNS?

Plan the plan and work the plan. Determine your audience and goals long before pumping out content. As with most marketing strategies, it's best to start by working backward. Once you establish goals, you can define the strategy required to reach them. There may be pivots along the way, but your goals should remain the same.

HOW DO YOU THINK CONTENT MARKETING WILL CHANGE OVER THE NEXT FEW YEARS?

We're already starting to see it, but in coming years, marketers will embrace micro audiences at a greater frequency. The need is evident, as we're starting to see mass marketing programs failing in traditional media TV, newspapers, and even on display ads. People expect a unique message or experience when interacting with brands. Creating specialized content really is powerful.

LEARN MORE ABOUT BOB

I drive the overall vision and strategy for empowering Sorc'd users to have their research accessible wherever they are creating content. Prior to Sorc'd, I was Managing Director of HelloWorld Mobile, providing SMS and mobile app development to companies like Abercrombie & Fitch and Autotrader. Other leadership roles include being the owner of a real estate management business RE+3, general manager of consumer destination site CoolSavings, and SVP of Media Group for digital advertising agency Q Interactive.

✉ BOB@SORCD.COM

🔗 WWW.LINKEDIN.COM/IN/BOBGIROLAMO

🔗 WWW.LINKEDIN.COM/COMPANY/3642199

🐦 @BOBGIROLAMO

🐦 @SORC_D

GREG MISCHIO

OWNER AND CHIEF STRATEGIST, WINBOUND

HOW DO YOU DETERMINE THE EFFECTIVENESS OF A CONTENT MARKETING CAMPAIGN?

Two things: traffic and leads. The more traffic we get, the more chance that someone will convert on an offer and become a lead. Within those two goals are a variety of metrics that increase the chance of success—keyword ranking, time on page, conversion rate—but it's leads and traffic that indicate true success. The tough part is we can't control whether those leads can be converted into customers—but working with sales, we can improve messaging and offers to make it happen.

WHAT IS THE SINGLE MOST EFFECTIVE CONTENT MARKETING TACTIC YOU'VE LEARNED?

We work with small marketing departments, so without a lot of resources we've been able to generate solid inbound links and access different social media audiences through collaborative content. That involves working with influencers, partners, and suppliers to create unique, informative content. On the conversion optimization side, the use of serial testing is essential for low-traffic websites with low conversion rates. We've observed some telltale behaviors through the use of heatmaps, and online surveys have revealed some valuable strategic insights.

IF YOU COULD CARRY ONLY FIVE TOOLS IN YOUR CONTENT MARKETING TOOLKIT, WHAT WOULD THEY BE?

A talented writer. A talented analytics person. A talented qualitative research analyst. A talented strategist. And SEMrush and Hotjar.

WHAT'S THE SINGLE BIGGEST MISTAKE YOU SEE PEOPLE MAKE IN CONTENT MARKETING?

Not understanding that the goal of Content Marketing is to create content that drives your SEO, and that all the traffic you drive is worthless unless you are optimizing and testing your site to improve conversion. Beyond that, you must always be refining and improving your offer to create higher conversion rates, not just engage in something like A/B testing (which for low-traffic, low-conversion sites won't be effective anyway).

WHAT ADVICE WOULD YOU GIVE TO PEOPLE WHO ARE LOOKING TO RUN SUCCESSFUL CONTENT MARKETING CAMPAIGNS?

Establish your cost per acquisition target out of the gate. Understand that keywords for your website's "buying" pages are different than keywords for your blog's "information" pages. Use social media to network, promote copy, and ultimately develop relationships that will lead to inbound links. Get your analytics established immediately. Focus more on success trends than random goals. Keep learning, keep pushing, keep networking. And most of all, never give up. The only way you lose is if you give up.

HOW DO YOU THINK CONTENT MARKETING WILL CHANGE OVER THE NEXT FEW YEARS?

I think Content Marketing will become more ubiquitous, but the methodology for how it's delivered will change in terms of format. I don't see the written word going away, but I do see it being packaged with video and audio. Everyone learns differently. Some read. Some watch video. Some listen. I think multi-format will become the norm. Conversion optimization will continue to improve and become more automated, but qualitative feedback will remain important. The dark horse in all of this is artificial intelligence. And I truly have no idea what happens when the machines take over. Hopefully they will hire us.

LEARN MORE ABOUT GREG

After working for years as a freelancer and for other companies, I decided to create Winbound. I had been doing content marketing for a small group of clients and seeing great success. I knew there was a great need among small marketing departments who struggle with resources and expertise in the complicated world of content marketing, SEO, and conversion optimization. I created Winbound, a team of specialists in each of these critical areas. Not only have we delivered exceptional results for our clients, we've become an intrinsic part of their marketing teams.

⊕ WWW.WINBOUND.COM

🔲 WWW.LINKEDIN.COM/IN/GREGMISCHIO

🔲 @GREGMISCHIO

JOSH HOFFMAN

HOW DO YOU DETERMINE THE EFFECTIVENESS OF A CONTENT MARKETING CAMPAIGN?

I determine the effectiveness of a campaign via engagement. While relevant reach is important, engagement tells me how much attention people are paying to a campaign and how interested they may be. In the digital and mobile age, attention is the number-one form of currency. Without it, you'll be hard-pressed to get someone's money and loyalty.

WHAT IS THE SINGLE MOST EFFECTIVE CONTENT MARKETING TACTIC YOU'VE LEARNED?

The single most effective Content Marketing tactic I've learned is to include as many relevant noncompeting businesses, organizations, and people in your content as possible. When you feature various noncompeting businesses, organizations, and people, you accomplish two things: (1) You have a built-in group that will share your content, which gives you direct access to their audience; and (2) these people will become advocates for your brand because you've taken the time and effort to spotlight them.

IF YOU COULD CARRY ONLY FIVE TOOLS IN YOUR CONTENT MARKETING TOOLKIT, WHAT WOULD THEY BE?

I would carry Google Drive, Asana, Canva, MailChimp and my iPhone.

WHAT'S THE SINGLE BIGGEST MISTAKE YOU SEE PEOPLE MAKE IN CONTENT MARKETING?

The single biggest mistake I see people make in Content Marketing is focusing their content too much on their products and services. The most successful brands online make the story bigger—that is, they create content about the themes and topics their products and services represent, which ultimately makes their content more interesting and engaging.

(Again, it's a game of attention—and if people are paying attention to your business, they can't pay attention to your competitors at the same time.)

WHAT ADVICE WOULD YOU GIVE TO PEOPLE WHO ARE LOOKING TO RUN SUCCESSFUL CONTENT MARKETING CAMPAIGNS?

Make the story bigger by focusing your content on the themes and topics your products and services represent.

HOW DO YOU THINK CONTENT MARKETING WILL CHANGE OVER THE NEXT FEW YEARS?

We will see more sophisticated, original multimedia content produced and distributed by brands ("direct-to-consumer"), and native advertising will become the most popular form of advertising.

LEARN MORE ABOUT JOSH

I'm an advisor to forward thinkers who want to maximize their inherent potential through digital marketing and personal branding.

⊕ WWW.JOSHOFFMAN.COM

MADDY OSMAN

SEO CONTENT STRATEGIST, THE BLOGSMITH

HOW DO YOU DETERMINE THE EFFECTIVENESS OF A CONTENT MARKETING CAMPAIGN?

You can't know that you're successful without measuring your efforts. An analytics tool like Google Analytics should be installed before you go about the process of promoting the content you've worked so hard to create. If you don't measure the results of your content creation and content promotion, you won't have any basis from which to define success. Ideally, you'll define some Content Marketing KPIs (like conversions, views, and shares) before promoting content in order to definitively be able to say whether your content served its purpose.

WHAT IS THE SINGLE MOST EFFECTIVE CONTENT MARKETING TACTIC YOU'VE LEARNED?

One of the best ways to get ahead with Content Marketing is by creating reciprocal relationships. On your end, you should expect to give, not get. If someone asks for your help or you see an opportunity to add value to them, spend a few minutes selflessly giving. "Giving" can be as simple as helping another content marketer share something they've recently published. Don't expect anything in return, but know that karma usually works out in the favor of those who are known for being helpful to others.

IF YOU COULD CARRY ONLY FIVE TOOLS IN YOUR CONTENT MARKETING TOOLKIT, WHAT WOULD THEY BE?

1. Moz, for complete site audits but also for specialty content functions like tracking backlinks (and the authority they contribute to the websites I write for), keyword research tools, and on-page optimization insights. SEMrush would also be a great tool for these purposes.

2. Trello for planning content editorial calendar style and keeping track of my pitches in an organized fashion so I never lose a good idea.

3. Google Docs/Drive for content collaboration among my contractors, my clients, and myself. It works flawlessly as a word processor, with a great built-in version tracking tool.

4. Google Analytics for measuring the effectiveness of content marketing efforts. It's free and easy to install on any website, so why not install it to track your efforts in the background? You can even set specific goals regarding desired conversion actions as a result of successful content consumption by members of your audience.

5. WordPress for delivering my content; it's one of the best content management systems out there, with built-in tools for SEO optimization (with additional content marketing tools available as plug-ins).

WHAT'S THE SINGLE BIGGEST MISTAKE YOU SEE PEOPLE MAKE IN CONTENT MARKETING?

The single biggest mistake when it comes to Content Marketing relates to a focus on quantity instead of quality. When it comes to creating content, people sometimes focus on churning out tons of articles at set word lengths, likely to adhere to a directive given by someone higher up who doesn't understand that creating content for content's sake is a waste of time. Similarly, modern content marketers focus on aggregating backlinks, again with a focus on quantity over quality. But not all backlinks can help to boost the authority (and search ranking) of a piece of content. High-quality backlinks must be relevant and high-authority (measured by domain authority). In general with regard to content marketing efforts, more is not always better. Your efforts are best spent focusing on a limited amount of high-quality inputs and their resulting outputs.

WHAT ADVICE WOULD YOU GIVE TO PEOPLE WHO ARE LOOKING TO RUN SUCCESSFUL CONTENT MARKETING CAMPAIGNS?

Think in terms of the Pareto Principal: 20 percent of your time should be focused on content creation, while 80 percent of your time should be spent on content promotion. If this proportion leans more heavily in content creation, it may never reach the desired target audience and your efforts will be for nothing. So use all of your available resources and content promotion channels and consider paid tactics to reach even more people in your target audience.

HOW DO YOU THINK CONTENT MARKETING WILL CHANGE OVER THE NEXT FEW YEARS?

I think Content Marketing will continue to expand to involve new mediums and make content more interactive and personalized. Right now, the primary focus in Content Marketing is on the written word, but more and more we'll see the inclusion of photos, video, and infographics. Perhaps new forms of media will be invented and included in content marketing. Regardless of how it changes, it's fair to say that Content Marketing is here to stay.

LEARN MORE ABOUT MADDY

Website design eventually led to content marketing, and the intersection between my two passions also involves a focus on SEO. After a move from Chicago to Denver, I've involved myself in the local community by volunteering to organize WordCamp Denver, to run social media for BMA Colorado, and to organize meetings for Freelancers Union. I currently write for clients like *Search Engine Journal*, Sprout Social, GoDaddy, WPMU DEV, and many more.

- ⊕ WWW.THE-BLOGSMITH.COM
- ▥ WWW.LINKEDIN/IN/MADELINEOSMAN
- ▢ @MADDYOSMAN

BRIAN SLY

HOW DO YOU DETERMINE THE EFFECTIVENESS OF A CONTENT MARKETING CAMPAIGN?

When viewers are engaging with a brand, whether it's following a call-to-action, commenting, or sharing the content and generating leads, that's a win. We don't look to just increase views or likes. Views and likes are only passive ways of supporting a brand without really furthering communication. But when you have comments, questions, follow-ups, click-throughs, or purposeful sharing, your engagement level rises. That creates an opportunity for direct contact and gets you in the door for furthering conversations with actual warm leads.

WHAT IS THE SINGLE MOST EFFECTIVE CONTENT MARKETING TACTIC YOU'VE LEARNED?

The most effective way we've discovered to increase our audience interaction level is to make our content emotional. "Storytelling" is a buzzword that's loosely thrown around, like the word "marketing." Without a plan, it's most likely ineffective. Sure, you can tell a story about how your brand has been around for three or four generations, but try to dig deeper into what the brand has meant during that time. Have the values or morals changed? Are you still doing your core business the exact same way as your great-grandparents? What's the essence of the business? What's the core emotional connection that would make someone HAVE to go to your business? If your story leads with "why" you do what you do, you have a much better chance of reaching the audience's heart zones and connecting emotionally. People buy through their emotions.

IF YOU COULD CARRY ONLY FIVE TOOLS IN YOUR CONTENT MARKETING TOOLKIT, WHAT WOULD THEY BE?

The five tools I would carry are video, audio, imagery, humor, and empathy. Each of these tools plays a vital role in connecting with someone inside and outside your brand. When storytelling, you'll want to reach your potential customer emotionally, and each person reacts differently. Humor and empathy are keys to connecting. As a good sales friend of mine once said, "If you can make a person laugh, you can make them buy." With laughter, you talk as if you're friends and start to build trust. With empathy, the person knows you understand them. You understand their wants, their needs, and most importantly, their fears. Using video, audio, and imagery strategically allows you to connect subconsciously with different learning styles. Video is the future of marketing, but audio and imagery play a key role, as well.

WHAT'S THE SINGLE BIGGEST MISTAKE YOU SEE PEOPLE MAKE IN CONTENT MARKETING?

The biggest mistake I see brands make is actually twofold: they don't have a full strategy with goals, and more specifically, they don't have a video strategy with goals. We get a lot of calls from companies who need a video the following week. When we explain they're probably wasting their money rushing into a video without a plan, the answer we get most often is "but we just need a video." And that's where the problem is. "Just a video" isn't well thought out and won't yield many results. It's not part of a larger strategy. Why not break up that one video into multiple videos with a single mission and a single call-to-action each? Videos in a series will always add brand awareness without diluting your messaging. While you may spend more up front, you're actually headed for a ROI.

WHAT ADVICE WOULD YOU GIVE TO PEOPLE WHO ARE LOOKING TO RUN SUCCESSFUL CONTENT MARKETING CAMPAIGNS?

My advice to anyone looking to run a successful interactive content campaign is to put others first. Content doesn't always have to be about what you do or promoting your next great product or service. Try offering free advice or commenting on other companies' blogs or videos. The more you put out in the world to help someone else, the more it will come back to you. There's a reason that blogs with "Top 7" lists work so well. Those authors are writing from the customers' point of view. They are seeing their pain points and offering ways to help them for free. Sure, there might be a sign-up form or other CTA on there, but there isn't a hard sell associated with it. By putting other people first, you're guaranteeing people see you as someone invested in them—and not just their money.

HOW DO YOU THINK CONTENT MARKETING WILL CHANGE OVER THE NEXT FEW YEARS?

I think as technology continues to evolve, interactive content is going to become more hands-on. Right now, we're seeing communities online, but eventually people will miss the hands-on approach. Much like bookstores, some people need to have something physical they can touch. So if you have only an online presence, you're going to have to find a way to physically reach your customers. Look at what Amazon is doing. They're opening up retail stores at the same time other retailers are closing. Why? Because they have their community built—and now to keep them, they are working to solve their customers' biggest need: getting their orders as fast as possible. For anyone creating content of any kind, look for ways to make it truly interactive. Create games, go experiential, or find new ways to develop the other senses outside of sight and sound.

LEARN MORE ABOUT BRIAN

I started off in the video production world, like so many other professionals. But over time, I knew I didn't want to just run another video company. I wanted us to tell stories no one else was telling. I wanted to make content fun again—and interactive. I wanted to help more brands. Most importantly, I wanted brands to know they didn't have to figure this out on their own. Over the years, my team went through a lot of trial and error, following what was working, analyzing what wasn't, and building connections between the content people loved most. What we discovered was interactive content fell into four categories and by designing your content to fit within one (or more) of these categories, you have a much higher chance of reaching your audience emotionally. We'd love the opportunity to look at your brand and help guide content that sticks in the minds and hearts of your audience.

🌐 EMBLEMMEDIAINC.COM

SCOTT A. ROGERSON

FOUNDER AND CEO, UPCONTENT

HOW DO YOU DETERMINE THE EFFECTIVENESS OF A CONTENT MARKETING CAMPAIGN?

Top of funnel: inform your site's visitors by showcasing your perspective on their problem, saving the them time and prompting them to continue their research process. Key metrics include decrease in bounce rate and increased pages per session. Middle of funnel: reinforce your position within original content and/or contrast your differences. Curated content in this context helps build trust, comfort, and credibility with your reader. You are looking for longer session durations on this content and increased micro conversions by traffic that visits this content. Bottom of funnel: cut out the "just checking in" emails and leverage curated content as a sales enablement tool to keep yourself top of mind while continuing to provide value to your prospect, furthering your relationship. Increased response rates and, ultimately, higher close rates can help inform effectiveness.

WHAT IS THE SINGLE MOST EFFECTIVE CONTENT MARKETING TACTIC YOU'VE LEARNED?

While conventional wisdom often has marketers flocking to the most popular articles in their industry, the use of "underground content" (effective content that people have not yet seen) has been shown to drive the greatest amount of value to my audience, resulting in a far higher rate of new relationships formed/furthered.

IF YOU COULD CARRY ONLY FIVE TOOLS IN YOUR CONTENT MARKETING TOOLKIT, WHAT WOULD THEY BE?

Hootsuite: quickly schedule, monitor, and analyze the performance of your curated posts in sparking/progressing conversations. Sniply: leverage custom calls-to-action on curated content to direct traffic to your conversion points. Unbounce: easily create and experiment with landing pages to drive conversions. Google Analytics: understand how the traffic created by your curated social media posts and newsletter content interacts with your site, where they leave, and what friction exists in the qualification and conversion process. UpContent: content discovery engine that integrates with Hootsuite and Sniply, helping me find and act on the best underground content (but I am a bit biased).

WHAT'S THE SINGLE BIGGEST MISTAKE YOU SEE PEOPLE MAKE IN CONTENT MARKETING?

We often fall into the trap of leveraging an ad hoc process for stumbling upon great articles: we frequent the same handful of publishers we know and trust and rely on popularity scores in determining what content to share. While these measures will certainly get you the volume of sharing needed, checking the box, you ultimately provide little value to your audience, as they have likely already seen this content elsewhere.

WHAT ADVICE WOULD YOU GIVE TO PEOPLE WHO ARE LOOKING TO RUN SUCCESSFUL CONTENT MARKETING CAMPAIGNS?

As with your larger Content Marketing strategy, it is important to spend time upfront and strategically determine the areas in which you want to be a resource for your audience. From there, you can create a process for efficiently and effectively sourcing these articles (using a variety of methods) and consistently bring this insight to your audience.

HOW DO YOU THINK CONTENT MARKETING WILL CHANGE OVER THE NEXT FEW YEARS?

Since we began our work in content discovery in early 2015, we have witnessed this task evolve from being an ancillary or "filler" activity to one that is critical for driving overall marketing spend ROI. We expect this trend to continue as both the number and locations in which great content can be sourced continue to grow exponentially. Original content will continue to be the "closer" in the inbound journey, but curated articles that help inform the audience—providing context within which the organization's unique perspective can shine—will be crucial in cutting through the noisy (and getting noisier) world in which we operate.

LEARN MORE ABOUT SCOTT

I am the Founder and CEO of UpContent, a leading intelligent content discovery technology that helps you drive new, more meaningful conversations with your audience. I was previously CEO of Cosmitto, a digital marketing services company that focuses on the day-to-day execution of marketing strategies. UpContent was born from the pain our Cosmitto team experienced in manually scouring the internet for great content. I also have experience in private equity as the Managing Director of search fund Oakhill Equity, as well as nonprofit and for-profit consulting. I am always open to swapping war stories and sharing notes.

⊕ UPCONTENT.COM
🖸 @SCOTTAROGERSON

SYDNEY DELOACH

CONTENT AND SOCIAL MEDIA MANAGER, S. DELOACH MARKETING

HOW DO YOU DETERMINE THE EFFECTIVENESS OF A CONTENT MARKETING CAMPAIGN?

As society carousels toward a more digitally inclined atmosphere, metrics for measurement that were once very successful are now added to a much larger formula for determining the effectiveness of a campaign. However, I focus primarily on three topics that I use to gauge how successful a campaign was: (1) Lead growth and nurturing. An effective and successful campaign will introduce new marketing qualified leads (MQLs) while converting previous MQLs to sales qualified leads (SQLs). In a sense, this measures how engaging your content is to possible customers. (2) Shareability within social media. Successful content campaigns are easy to read, flow nicely, and are something that your target audience would want to share. (3) Low bounce rate. The direct opposite of a high time on page rate is a high bounce rate, meaning that customers visited your site, saw your content, and immediately bounced off to another site.

WHAT IS THE SINGLE MOST EFFECTIVE CONTENT MARKETING TACTIC YOU'VE LEARNED?

From my experience, the single most effective tactic when it comes to Content Marketing is to write down a well-defined strategy and commit to it. This includes goals, demographics of your target audience, method for getting your content out there, and notes close by that describe how you have grown from unsuccessful campaigns. Many digital marketers who are starting out forgo this step, but I think it is an absolute must. Your content will be aligned from day to day and give off a more clear voice for your client.

IF YOU COULD CARRY ONLY FIVE TOOLS IN YOUR CONTENT MARKETING TOOLKIT, WHAT WOULD THEY BE?

First, I must always have Hootsuite. I'm slightly in love with it. It provides such an easy way to share my content and obtain analytics on campaigns. I also really enjoy working with Klout to help define my strategy, see what is working for other niches similar to my clients', and track engagement from my campaigns. Hemingway Editor is another tool that I depend greatly on. This source grades your readability and notifies you of edits that you'll need to make to a "T." I avoid a lot of mistakes by using this, which helps my campaigns be spot-on before they go live. As far as organization and working with my clients, the tool I'd need most would be Trello. Lastly and most importantly, I'd never make it a single day without coffee.

WHAT'S THE SINGLE BIGGEST MISTAKE YOU SEE PEOPLE MAKE IN CONTENT MARKETING?

The biggest and most deadly mistake that I see others make in the field of Content Marketing is thinking that content equates to blog posts and blog posts only. This is so not true. Don't get me wrong: blogs are amazing and a great way to launch campaigns, but content marketing goes so much farther than just a blog. Think about the viral things you see on social media. More specifically, think of the viral memes you've seen. Who says content marketing can't take the form of a quirky, funny photo that is directed at an audience and portrays a message? You have to take into consideration what would appeal to your target audience. Don't be afraid to think outside the box.

WHAT ADVICE WOULD YOU GIVE TO PEOPLE WHO ARE LOOKING TO RUN SUCCESSFUL CONTENT MARKETING CAMPAIGNS?

I highly advise focusing your efforts within your campaign on areas that are specific to the interests of your target audience. This may seem like a no-brainer, but novice marketers and seasoned experts make this mistake. Sometimes we get lost in what is trendy or successful at the moment or divert from our strategy and see campaigns fail because they weren't directly aligned with the demographics of the audience. Always ask your-self, "If I were in this target audience, what would I want to see?" Get your feet wet, do research, take a look back at past mistakes or successes, and tweak your campaigns accordingly.

HOW DO YOU THINK CONTENT MARKETING WILL CHANGE OVER THE NEXT FEW YEARS?

I think content marketers are already starting to see a big change in our area of expertise. The shift in recent years was toward blogging and social media but still incorporating offline methods like newspapers ads, cold calls, infomercials, and the like. Now, and in the future, I think we will see the shift towards online marketing continue, but including a more lax, casual version of Content Marketing—especially as millennials and centennials become an even more dominant part of our society.

LEARN MORE ABOUT SYDNEY

I'm a content and Social Media Marketing manager and consultant located in south Georgia. I have been working in this field for a little over five years now and truly have a passion for helping my clients and their businesses grow through successful creative marketing strategies. In my spare time, I enjoy binge watching Netflix shows, drinking hot tea, and doing yoga. I'm so thankful to be a part of this project, and I'd love to hear from you!

✉ SDELOACHMARKETING@GMAIL.COM

MATTHEW JONAS

HOW DO YOU DETERMINE THE EFFECTIVENESS OF A CONTENT MARKETING CAMPAIGN?

Content strategy is a lot like Public Relations, as far as determining effectiveness. If you are doing a good job, your customers are going to tell you. They are going to use your language to talk about your products and services. They are going to generate word-of-mouth influence and you'll hear "So and so was going on and on about you. I just had to see for myself." An effective content strategy helps to shape the conversation and the perception of the brand. It will supply the adjectives in the testimonial. It will cite the benefits and outcomes described in reviews. In a more technical sense, you'll also see a clear uptick in shares, retweets, likes, backlinks, click-through rate, and conversions. An effective content strategy shows itself, really.

WHAT IS THE SINGLE MOST EFFECTIVE CONTENT MARKETING TACTIC YOU'VE LEARNED?

I think the most effective tactic in developing a sound content strategy is situational awareness. For example, when we're pushing a content strategy across social media, we consider what our target audience is seeing in their feed. If we're targeting mothers of young children, we need to stand out as different or interesting. Are they looking for a break from the norm or more of the same or something similar but unique? What will make our audience take notice and follow our diversion? With blogging, what is our audience searching for and why? Are they doing primary research, in-depth research, or last-minute comparisons and evaluation? Content strategy is all about understanding humans and their behavior and being able to coerce a particular course of action. Understanding the environment and circumstances helps to control the variables.

IF YOU COULD CARRY ONLY FIVE TOOLS IN YOUR CONTENT MARKETING TOOLKIT, WHAT WOULD THEY BE?

When I'm working with our content strategists, I tell them they need just a few things to succeed. First, you need Google. Second, you need Facebook. Third, you need Twitter. Fourth, you need a tireless curiosity. And, finally, you need common sense. Use your curiosity to research on Google, observe on Facebook, and to listen on Twitter. Then, use your common sense to put together a simple outline of relevant information that comes up again and again, that stokes people's emotions or interest, and make sure you know what you're talking about. With those five tools, it's possible to craft an effective content strategy.

WHAT'S THE SINGLE BIGGEST MISTAKE YOU SEE PEOPLE MAKE IN CONTENT MARKETING?

The biggest mistake in content strategy is having the wrong perspective/being uninformed. These are two different facets of the same problem, which is brands writing about themselves and not writing for their audience. Marketing is all about connecting with an audience and positioning a product or service as the answer to a core need or desire. A brand's content strategy needs to be relevant to the reader and provide value. If you don't fully understand your audience, or why you are—or should be—relevant to them, and you aren't reflecting this to your audience, you've got it all wrong. When I see brands focusing on themselves more than their audience, they are missing an opportunity to form a bond with a potential customer.

WHAT ADVICE WOULD YOU GIVE TO PEOPLE WHO ARE LOOKING TO RUN SUCCESSFUL CONTENT MARKETING CAMPAIGNS?

In order to execute a successful content campaign, it's necessary to perform due diligence. It's necessary to clearly understand the brand and the product/service, to fully explore the marketplace, to get to know all of the competitors (and the alternatives), and to thoroughly understand the motivations and behaviors of the audience. We do a lot of persona development and behavioral role-playing to understand how, why, and when prospects take action. Consumers can see through hollow content, they don't have time for fluff, and they understand their options. The more a brand can reflect that same understanding and cut through the noise, the better your chances at success.

HOW DO YOU THINK CONTENT MARKETING WILL CHANGE OVER THE NEXT FEW YEARS?

I think we're just beginning to move beyond clickbait and as a society (hopefully) beginning to mature in the ways we engage with others online. I think content strategists and writers are going to have to dial it in more and more in the years ahead. I also think the emergence of voice search and its impact on findability will continue to influence content strategy moving forward. In the way mobile devices changed "near me" searches and required writers to adapt content for proximity, voice search will require writers to further understand the nuances of natural language search queries. All together, this likely means more personalization and more concentration on value and far fewer gimmicks and cheap manipulations of readers.

LEARN MORE ABOUT MATTHEW

I am President and Co-founder of TopFire Media. As TopFire Media's brand steward, I work to define high-impact digital PR and marketing strategies for an impressive cache of consumer and franchise-based clientele. I am a seasoned marketer and highly respected franchise marketing expert and have built my twenty-year career dedicated to delivering outcomes and results through an integrated and strategy-based approach. As a product of the dot-com era, I built my marketing expertise during digital media's infancy, something I continue to refine today. With a distinct understanding and expertise of digital strategies and a persistent dedication to our craft, my team and I have successfully guided clients through the ever-evolving environment of the online media world.

⊕ WWW.TOPFIREMEDIA.COM
📞 708-249-1090
🐦 @TOPFIREMEDIA
📘 WWW.FACEBOOK.COM/TOPFIREMEDIA

CHARLENE PETERS

MARKETING & PR MANAGER, VISIT CALISTOGA

HOW DO YOU DETERMINE THE EFFECTIVENESS OF A CONTENT MARKETING CAMPAIGN?

The effectiveness of a digital campaign can be measured by engagement. In Calistoga, the chamber of commerce hosts an annual signature event, Calistoga Harvest Table. My role in marketing is to create a desire for guests to want a seat at the table. Last year's event, which marked the fourth Calistoga Harvest Table, was a sellout in thirty-nine minutes. At the Calistoga Welcome Center, we receive regular telephone requests throughout the year from attendees who want to know when tickets will be available for sale and when the next event will be held. I consider the marketing campaign effective when engagement is elevated—and in this case, the buzz to get tickets is not only rising, but competitive among ticket holders who boast their talents on acquiring tickets within the first five minutes of ticket sales.

WHAT IS THE SINGLE MOST EFFECTIVE CONTENT MARKETING TACTIC YOU'VE LEARNED?

To create content that incorporates commentary from expert sources on pop culture. For example, in creating a blog post to promote Calistoga wineries, I utilize Oscar-nominated films and ask wineries to send me their pick of wine that pairs best with one of the films and explain why. An example of a response from Fairwinds Estate Winery was that its 2013 inky black petit verdot will pair perfectly with *The Darkest Hour*. On a separate occasion, I took advantage of Girl Scout cookie season by creating an infographic of various Girl Scout cookies and again reaching out to wineries for pairing suggestions. I took this campaign a bit further to create an event of Girl Scout cookies and wine tasting at the Calistoga Welcome Center. It was a hit!

IF YOU COULD CARRY ONLY FIVE TOOLS IN YOUR CONTENT MARKETING TOOLKIT, WHAT WOULD THEY BE?

My laptop and a good internet connection, because you cannot produce digital marketing without either (cell phones are possible, but not the easiest platform). The third tool would be WordPress for creating a website and blog. I like WordPress because it offers so many plug-ins, and it has proven its worthiness in my marketing needs. My fourth tool is a subscription to Canva, which is an essential tool that enables full control in my creative. Canva is easy to use and offers templates for social media, flyers, presentations, and more. Additionally, you can plug in your Pantone brand colors, fonts, and logos to keep separately for easy access. My final tool would be the use of Later.com so I can schedule Instagram posts ahead of time and manage content months in advance.

WHAT'S THE SINGLE BIGGEST MISTAKE YOU SEE PEOPLE MAKE IN CONTENT MARKETING?

Not connecting all digital portals is a missed opportunity for marketing and promotion. For instance, if you have created a blog post on mud baths and mineral springs pools in Calistoga and a journalist published a great piece on the same subject, why not link the article to your blog? Furthermore, share the blog on social media channels and keep checking back to link within other blog posts on similar touch points. Good SEO practices are often overlooked due to lack of staff resources. And when creating blog posts, be sure to use Pinterest-size images with branded text to drive traffic back to your website.

WHAT ADVICE WOULD YOU GIVE TO PEOPLE WHO ARE LOOKING TO RUN SUCCESSFUL CONTENT MARKETING CAMPAIGNS?

If you want to be successful, begin with a strategy. You'll want to work with a small group to brainstorm words associated with whatever it is you want to market. For example, Calistoga Lighted Tractor Parade is known throughout the United States as a "quirky" Calistoga event that draws in a crowd of fifteen thousand to watch sixty decorated trucks and tractors parade down the main street. "Quirky" goes a long way to promote ancillary products such as Tractor Parade ornaments sold on the day of the parade, as well as sweatshirts with the Tractor Parade logo and year of the parade, making them collectibles.

HOW DO YOU THINK CONTENT MARKETING WILL CHANGE OVER THE NEXT FEW YEARS?

In respect to destination marketing, I believe cluster branding will become more essential in successfully marketing entire regions that will work together as opposed to competitively, especially in the digital realm. Geo-targeted digital display ads and use of video is quickly becoming more widespread within the marketing communities. In a globalized world catering more and more to millennials, why not work with your neighbors and/or regional businesses to create the desire to return time and time again, and create a multichannel campaign to meet the demands for an authentic experience? Smart itineraries are interactive and offer guests the chance to engage, ultimately creating their dream trips.

LEARN MORE ABOUT CHARLENE

As a destination marketing professional, I create the desire for potential guests to travel. With my background working as a special features editor, and education in branding, marketing, and international public relations, I can confidently say I am well versed in how to tell a story and effectively sell a destination. My cutting-edge masters degree education in global communications from the American University of Paris has brought me back to the United States armed with an arsenal of tools to propel a brand to its highest success. In between working full-time, I pen a syndicated travel/food column, Taste of Travel.

- WWW.SPAVALOUS.COM
- SIPTRIPPER.COM
- CHARLENEPETERS@COMCAST.NET
- @SPAVALOUS
- @SIPTRIPPER

CHAPTER 6
PUBLIC RELATIONS (PR)

A SIMPLE EXPLANATION OF PUBLIC RELATIONS

Public Relations (PR) is managing the way companies and organizations interact with the public and media.

PR is all about influencing, engaging, and building relationships to shape the public perception of a company or organization.

A PR specialist communicates with their target market through the media, with the goal of creating and maintaining a strong positive relationship with their audience.

A PR specialist's responsibilities can be varied and may include analyzing public opinion, counseling management in an organization with regard to course of action or policy, setting objectives and managing resources to protect the reputation of an organization, and overseeing campaigns to shape the perception of an organization.

Common tools used by PR specialists are press releases, newsletters, and statements to the media, along with in-person channels like events and conferences.

PR specialists establish relationships with relevant trade media and opinion leaders in order to publish content through those people and their publications. Often, a PR specialist will "pitch" suggested story ideas to journalists with the hope of getting media coverage for their company's product or service.

At times, PR specialists are called in to put out company "fires." When something happens at a company that casts it in a negative light to the public, a PR specialist is called in to get control of the situation and protect their client's reputation.

Now that PR specialists can communicate with their target audience over the Internet via blogging, social media, and Content Marketing, PR specialists are increasingly turning to digital and social media to improve the effectiveness of their communication with the public.

PUBLIC RELATIONS SPECIALISTS SOUND OFF

NIKKI NARDICK

FOUNDER, KNACK PUBLIC RELATIONS

HOW DO YOU DETERMINE THE EFFECTIVENESS OF A PR CAMPAIGN?

By reputation, Public Relations is challenging to measure. However, if a campaign is working, you will certainly know it. People will be talking about the creative campaign you just successfully executed, and your client will feel the love. If your press outreach truly worked, your client will be known for this specific campaign for years to come, and their customers will expect you to execute more campaigns of the same caliber. No pressure. Besides word-of-mouth buzz, there are the usual measurement suspects, such as social media shares, publication readership, article engagement, and quality of press placements.

After executing many effective campaigns, I discovered other nontraditional ways to measure PR success. In the days following a noteworthy press placement, track foot traffic, sales, page views, franchise applications, or whatever measurable item you're trying to boost. Compare it to the prior weeks and weeks to come. Measure the direct correlation between run items and these measurable numbers, and suddenly it doesn't seem so tricky to prove the effectiveness of PR campaigns. Learn what works and do more of it!

WHAT IS THE SINGLE MOST EFFECTIVE PR TACTIC YOU'VE LEARNED?

News pegging! What the heck is news pegging? Piggybacking on major headlines. You don't always need your own news to make noise. Coming up with your own calendar of announcements is important, too, but it can be extra effective to add a strategic talking point to the current conversation. Reporters are always looking for more tidbits to add to their stories that follow a timely, evolving headline. Some of my favorite news pegging campaigns that I led piggybacked on major brands' headlines. Remember when Chipotle closed its doors for a systemwide food safety meeting? I worked with my client to offer 50 percent off of their Mexican-inspired menu items on that fateful day.

Another memorable moment with that same fast-casual client: writing an open letter to the CEO of McDonald's after a poor earnings call, suggesting that fast food and fresh food could coexist. Both campaigns attracted more new franchise applications than the restaurant concept had experienced in its history. News pegging works. Don't be afraid to play with the big dogs.

IF YOU COULD CARRY ONLY FIVE TOOLS IN YOUR PR TOOLKIT, WHAT WOULD THEY BE?

1. A knack for strategic storytelling

2. Patience

3. Curiosity

4. The ability to craft intriguing subject lines that lead to memorable headlines

5. Cision (every PR pro's job is made possible by this magical database)

WHAT'S THE SINGLE BIGGEST MISTAKE YOU SEE PEOPLE MAKE IN PR?

Too often, companies stray from their mission. A company's brand mission is the North Star for every campaign a PR person executes. That means that every pitch a publicist pushes out should drive the brand mission forward. Be creative, but don't lose sight of your strategy.

WHAT ADVICE WOULD YOU GIVE TO PEOPLE WHO ARE LOOKING TO RUN SUCCESSFUL PR CAMPAIGNS?

Dive into your client's DNA. Once you become fluent in their voice and digest their competitive landscape, you can create a custom PR strategy with compelling campaign ideas. Couple that with custom media outreach, and you have yourself a cover story. The ability to generate memorable media coverage for your client is dependent on your press outreach. For the love of PR professionals everywhere, please do not spam the media. Read the published work of the reporters you are pitching to make sure your suggestion is aligned with their area of coverage. The reward? A large database of contacts who want to hear from you.

HOW DO YOU THINK PR WILL CHANGE OVER THE NEXT FEW YEARS?

Public Relations has come a long way from the dinosaur days of sending pitches to press via fax machines. One day not so far from now, PR professionals might pitch the media via Alexa or virtual reality (mind blown!). Nowadays, instead of pitching glossy magazines, radio shows, and community newspapers, the key targets are social media influencers, podcasts, and newsletters. (Heart you, theSkimm!) As PR becomes more dependent on digital and less on print, one thing remains the same: a commitment to storytelling. No matter the medium that each generation uses to seek its news, PR will always be about building brand awareness and helping a company achieve its strategic goals.

LEARN MORE ABOUT NIKKI

I have been surrounded by entrepreneurs my entire life and worked for them throughout my career. I utilize Public Relations to build their brands. From start-ups to salads, I have excelled at securing ink across countless industries. I am always actively listening to seek out stories and craft the perfect pitch to deliver to the press. I created Knack PR to work with brands I admire and entrepreneurs I believe in. Are you creating something you're passionate about? Tell me all about it.

✉ NIKKI@KNACKPR.COM

MAEVE CLOHERTY

**LEAD MARKETING AND EVENTS SPECIALIST,
JOBSPRING PARTNERS AND TECH IN MOTION**

HOW DO YOU DETERMINE THE EFFECTIVENESS OF A PR CAMPAIGN?

We determine the effectiveness of our PR campaigns using multiple tools, including HubSpot, Brand24, Google Analytics, and a digital engagement dashboard my team built using Google Data Studio. With these tools, we're able to track our audience's engagement with our brands based on the number of features, mentions, bylines, and blogs within digital and print media.

WHAT IS THE SINGLE MOST EFFECTIVE PR TACTIC YOU'VE LEARNED?

The most important PR tactic I've learned is providing your audiences the materials they need to become your brand's number-one advocates. As a small team, we knew creating and distributing press kits to the companies and individuals involved in Tech in Motion's annual awards ceremony, The Timmy Awards, would result in increased media coverage. The kits include precrafted press releases, digital and print promotional items, and social media copy and images. We provided more than 350 finalists and 35 winners these materials to generate a 300 percent increase in our overall media coverage from 2015/2016 to 2017.

IF YOU COULD CARRY ONLY FIVE TOOLS IN YOUR PR TOOLKIT, WHAT WOULD THEY BE?

The most important tool in my toolkit is community building through events. Tech in Motion, a tech-focused event series created by my company, Jobspring Partners, is our best community relations tool. It brings my company face to face with the people who make up local tech communities to meet, learn, and innovate together. Also, no other recruiting agency has built a similar community to the scale and reach of Tech in Motion. In addition to Tech in Motion, the other tools that are crucial to be an effective PR specialist include employee relations, media relations/partnerships, social media, and a passionate, driven team.

WHAT'S THE SINGLE BIGGEST MISTAKE YOU SEE PEOPLE MAKE IN PR?

The biggest mistake I've seen in PR is not utilizing all media relationships, no matter the size of a writer's following. When conducting media outreach, think local and be specific to your message and audiences. It's more likely that a writer, blogger, or podcast creator for a local or industry-specific publication would be willing to share your story. Once they do, the larger media outlets will take notice. Most members of the media are sent pitches for stories daily, and yours may get thrown in the no pile with the rest of them if you don't have a tailored pitch—which is far easier to start with in your home turf.

WHAT ADVICE WOULD YOU GIVE TO PEOPLE WHO ARE LOOKING TO RUN SUCCESSFUL PR CAMPAIGNS?

Learn to work with what you have. Throughout my career, I've worked with small, close-knit teams who are passionate about the work they do. Even if most of your team members are not PR experts, when you provide them the right tools and resources you can empower them to become one.

HOW DO YOU THINK PR WILL CHANGE OVER THE NEXT FEW YEARS?

There will be more tools than you can imagine helping you as a PR professional, but not all of them will be suitable for how your company and team runs. Make sure to try before you buy. Trial runs can help your team test if the software will positively impact your business, team goals, and efficiency. It will also prevent you from making the mistake of spending part of your budget on software when you can use only half of its capabilities or it's not the right tool for the job, as cool as it may sound.

LEARN MORE ABOUT MAEVE

I'm a Lead Marketing Specialist for an IT recruiting agency, Jobspring Partners, and a Lead Events Specialist for our tech-focused event series, Tech in Motion. Jobspring Partners and its sister recruiting agency, Workbridge Associates, created Tech in Motion in 2011 to give back to local tech communities. Tech in Motion now has more than ninety-five thousand members and counting across eleven North American cities. With my passion and excitement for PR, I now help lead our social, content and PR Team with a focus on Tech in Motion and its annual award ceremony, the Timmy Awards.

⊕ TECHINMOTIONEVENTS.COM
🔲 WWW.LINKEDIN.COM/IN/MAEVE-CLOHERTY
🔲 @MAEVE92JSPRINGP

ALEXANDRA BROWN

PR MANAGER, HEIDRICK & STRUGGLES

HOW DO YOU DETERMINE THE EFFECTIVENESS OF A PR CAMPAIGN?

I look at the number of media placements secured in top tier business media (think *The Wall Street Journal*, *Fortune*, HBR, etc.) to ensure that we're reaching our audience—c-suite and senior-level executives. Of course, it is difficult to measure the effectiveness of Public Relations. Ultimately, my goal is to make sure that my company remains top of mind for current and prospective clients and that they think of our consultants whenever they have a leadership, talent, or culture problem that needs solving. More than anything, earned tier 1 media is a huge driver of reputation and brand awareness.

WHAT IS THE SINGLE MOST EFFECTIVE PR TACTIC YOU'VE LEARNED?

It's super old school, but the embargo tactic does work wonders in getting media's attention. Offering a select handful of high-impact publications the opportunity to preview research or news has proven extremely effective in getting results and fostering relationships with reporters. The embargo offers an air of "white glove treatment" and exclusivity that really resonates, and it enables us to target several publications to work a story in advance rather than aiming for one exclusive.

IF YOU COULD CARRY ONLY FIVE TOOLS IN YOUR PR TOOLKIT, WHAT WOULD THEY BE?

iPhone, coffee, laptop, coffee, and coffee.

WHAT'S THE SINGLE BIGGEST MISTAKE YOU SEE PEOPLE MAKE IN PR?

Sometimes you need to slow down to speed up. Working in a fast-paced field like Public Relations makes it easy to overlook the details in an effort to move quickly, but the wrong error can have longstanding effects on your reputation.

WHAT ADVICE WOULD YOU GIVE TO PEOPLE WHO ARE LOOKING TO RUN SUCCESSFUL PR CAMPAIGNS?

It's good to be aspirational, but staying grounded in your objective is key. I've seen plenty of pros fall into a creative trap that strayed way too far from the goal of the campaign or needs of the client. Creativity is good but needs to be rooted in strategy.

HOW DO YOU THINK PR WILL CHANGE OVER THE NEXT FEW YEARS?

While we can anticipate the pace of the news cycle to get even faster and the digitalization of media to intensify, I think both journalists and PR practitioners are going to go back to their roots in some ways. More and more, I'm finding that organizations are trying to bridge the gap between the digital and physical world to create communities, and I think that will apply to PR, too. Despite technological advances, in-person human interactions will be key to deepening relationships with journalists, influencers, and other key stakeholders.

LEARN MORE ABOUT ALEXANDRA

I'm the PR Manager at Heidrick & Struggles and am responsible for driving our media strategy globally, counseling and prepping our partners for interview opportunities, and collaborating closely with the broader marketing team to further position the firm as a top advisor in talent, leadership, and culture. Outside of my 9-to-5, I focus my energy toward empowering women to achieve their goals through my role on the associate board of the Girl Scouts of Greater Chicago and Northwest Indiana.

WWW.LINKEDIN.COM/IN/ALEXANDRA-BROWN-405657IA
@ALEXZBROWN

MEGAN MARTIN

HOW DO YOU DETERMINE THE EFFECTIVENESS OF A PR CAMPAIGN?

I think a successful campaign has to include a 360-degree approach to marketing. You can't just do Public Relations and expect to see direct sales results. As a PR agency, we insist on working closely with the marketing and sales team to ensure everything is concise and consistent (that includes media relations, events, partnerships, social media, and marketing). Working together and creating a bigger buzz creates a stronger awareness and in turn will lead to sales.

WHAT IS THE SINGLE MOST EFFECTIVE PR TACTIC YOU'VE LEARNED?

Fully understanding what you are representing. We really dive into the brands and learn everything we can to become an extension of their brand. I think that is so important to understand the various angles and story ideas that can be pitched to the media.

IF YOU COULD CARRY ONLY FIVE TOOLS IN YOUR PR TOOLKIT, WHAT WOULD THEY BE?

Cision to build media lists, Talkwalker for monitoring press mentions, Help a Reporter Out (HARO) to assist with generating press leads for clients, Google Drive to provide clients and employees access to documents, and Excel for media lists and recap reports.

WHAT'S THE SINGLE BIGGEST MISTAKE YOU SEE PEOPLE MAKE IN PR?

I think publicists sometimes do not understand who they are pitching and end up pitching the wrong journalist. A good publicist researches each journalist prior to sending the pitch to make sure it's an appropriate fit and that it would make sense for the client they are pitching. Too many publicists rely on mass pitching. That is a huge mistake as most journalist won't be covering the same story. You need to craft each pitch and make it unique to the journalist and the publication.

WHAT ADVICE WOULD YOU GIVE TO PEOPLE WHO ARE LOOKING TO RUN SUCCESSFUL PR CAMPAIGNS?

I recommend working closely with the client's marketing and sales departments to ensure everyone is working together to get the same end result. It is important to make sure all communication and sales and marketing tactics are seamless and all messaging is consistent. You cannot have a successful campaign working individually -- everyone has to work together!

HOW DO YOU THINK PR WILL CHANGE OVER THE NEXT FEW YEARS?

I think Public Relations is changing rapidly. The media landscape is changing and we have to look beyond just media relations and also look to partnerships, social media and influencer marketing. Besides just traditional media outreach, we now create influencer marketing programs, we look at various local and national partnerships, we create events to get media interested. We need to work closely with the social media teams to make sure they are communicating press hits and sharing related stories on their channels.

LEARN MORE ABOUT MEGAN

I am the founding principal of Page One Public Relations based in Chicago, Illinois. I use my strong relationships with local and national media to effectively promote my clients' strategic marketing agendas. I work closely with my clients to not only assist in developing a comprehensive plan but also make suggestions on tactics and messaging that will be most effective with individual outlets. This collaborative process produces a results-oriented strategy that focuses on achieving the objectives of each client. Page One has been named as one of the top twenty PR firms in Chicago for two years in a row (2017 and 2018).

WWW.FACEBOOK.COM/PAGEONEPUBLICRELATIONS
@PAGEONEPR

CHRISTINE PIETRYLA WETZLER

OWNER, PIETRYLA PR & MARKETING

HOW DO YOU DETERMINE THE EFFECTIVENESS OF A PR CAMPAIGN?

Strategically, everything we do to build credibility with PR is assigned to an automation or SEM tactic so that we can measure effectiveness. For example, we use landing pages and automation during media pitching to determine who is responding to each part of our media pitch. Conversely, when we market, we also look for ways to bring third-party credibility into the discussion. You can have a perfect marketing plan, but without credibility it falls flat.

WHAT IS THE SINGLE MOST EFFECTIVE PR TACTIC YOU'VE LEARNED?

PR is about creating relationships with the media. Automation allows us to personalize multiple conversations, learn more about our individual targets, and maximize the potential of each interaction. And it allows us to do this en masse without being disrespectful of each reporter's time.

IF YOU COULD CARRY ONLY FIVE TOOLS IN YOUR PR TOOLKIT, WHAT WOULD THEY BE?

Google Analytics, Google AdWords, Infusionsoft, Cision, and Boomerang.

WHAT'S THE SINGLE BIGGEST MISTAKE YOU SEE PEOPLE MAKE IN PR?

They forget that at its core, media relations is about forging reciprocal relationships with reporters who speak to your target audience. I have a client that hired a huge agency that achieved a handful of minor placements over three months before they were fired. We got them one hit in our local business trade, and it catapulted their fundraising and sales efforts. The agency focused on number of placements; we focused on quality of placements and were, therefore, able to help them achieve their stated business goals.

WHAT ADVICE WOULD YOU GIVE TO PEOPLE WHO ARE LOOKING TO RUN SUCCESSFUL PR CAMPAIGNS?

Understand the playing field. Don't do something just because that's how it's always been done or that's how your competitor is doing it; understand what you need to accomplish and what tactics will help move the needle. If you need help, get it, but you can't get good advice if you don't know what you're trying to achieve. Similarly, understand how the tools work. Just *having* Google Analytics doesn't make you an awesome webmaster. You have to know how and why to use it.

HOW DO YOU THINK PR WILL CHANGE OVER THE NEXT FEW YEARS?

Technology is going to make it easier for people who do it right to do it very well without breaking the bank. The operative word there is "right."

LEARN MORE ABOUT CHRISTINE

I help companies develop core messaging and create marketing automation plans designed to preserve brand equity and curate influencer groups. I've assisted many clients by serving as lead strategist, company spokesperson, and primary communications counsel. Clients often hire me as an interim CMO during early growth stages or during a watershed moment like an acquisition or a new product launch. My specialty is developing great strategy and mapping automation to achieve specific business goals. I graduated from the University of Florida College of Journalism and proudly serve on its PR Department Advisory Board.

🌐 WWW.PIETRYLAPR.COM

✉ CHRISTINE@PIETRYLAPR.COM

in WWW.LINKEDIN.COM/IN/CHRISTINEPIETRYLA

CAROLYN S. FRASER

PRINCIPAL & FOUNDER, THE PR SHOPPE

HOW DO YOU DETERMINE THE EFFECTIVENESS OF A PR CAMPAIGN?

Meeting and exceeding key performance indicators, such as the amount of secured media coverage, strategic partnerships, relationships, endorsements, speaking opportunities, meaningful introductions, and, of course, anything resulting in ROI, sales, and brand awareness and engagement.

WHAT IS THE SINGLE MOST EFFECTIVE PR TACTIC YOU'VE LEARNED?

Although we are able to publish "news" on behalf of our clients, thanks to digital/social media, I've found that fostering meaningful relationships with our media contacts (both traditional and digital) is the most effective way for us to achieve our PR/media relations goals. Anyone can write and pitch a great story, but having an edge on the competition because your media contact trusts your work and actually likes you is priceless! Get to know your media contacts. After all, they are people too. Acknowledgment goes a long way.

IF YOU COULD CARRY ONLY FIVE TOOLS IN YOUR PR TOOLKIT, WHAT WOULD THEY BE?

1. A marketing budget; it takes money to grow brands.

2. A robust and updated media contact database for outreach.

3. A graphic/web designer and content creator.

4. My trusty laptop.

5. My phone, of course.

WHAT'S THE SINGLE BIGGEST MISTAKE YOU SEE PEOPLE MAKE IN PR?

Lack of follow up/persistence when pitching for media coverage. People often get discouraged and fall off the bandwagon because of laziness, disappointment, and rejection. Don't take the media not responding personally . . . success is in the follow-up!

WHAT ADVICE WOULD YOU GIVE TO PEOPLE WHO ARE LOOKING TO RUN SUCCESSFUL PR CAMPAIGNS?

Be clear on client objectives and stay in constant communication with them, as strategies—and budgets—may change. Ensure client objectives align with their target audience's desires and interests. Organization and planning goes a long way. Establish key performance indicators and exceed them. Be open to feedback and don't take things personally. Lastly, work in excellence—people notice more than you realize.

HOW DO YOU THINK PR WILL CHANGE OVER THE NEXT FEW YEARS?

PR has already shifted from traditional media to digital media, which has an expansive yet targeted reach and is constantly evolving. The great thing about this shift is that brands can now create "news" and directly target and engage their audiences without having to spend big advertising dollars. Publicists are able to leverage this opportunity by taking the reins of digital marketing, especially social media—creating strategies and opportunities for brands that want to play in this space. We must become expert content creators and storytellers for our clients in order to remain competitive and be successful in this space.

LEARN MORE ABOUT CAROLYN

I love developing and implementing effective Public Relations and marketing strategies for brands and helping them transform messaging and objectives into measurable results. My agency offers strategic integrated marketing and Public Relations services to brands in beauty, health and wellness, and lifestyle industries across all markets. I've been fortunate to have been worked on amazing PR campaigns for top agencies such as Ogilvy and FleishmanHillard and major brands like Tylenol, Revlon, Visa, BET Networks, CURLS, and Maytag. I truly enjoy being a goal achiever and miracle worker for my clients.

⊕ WWW.THEPRSHOPPE.BIZ
✉ INFO@THEPRSHOPPE.BIZ
ⓛ WWW.LINKEDIN.COM/IN/CAROLYNSFRASER

🐦 @THEPRSHOPPEPR

📘 WWW.FACEBOOK.COM/THEPRSHOPPEPR

📷 @THEPRSHOPPEPR

ANDREW NUNO

SOCIAL MEDIA MANAGER, FANFOOD

HOW DO YOU DETERMINE THE EFFECTIVENESS OF A PR CAMPAIGN?

Especially for start-ups like FanFood, it is very easy to get caught up in the game of solid metrics to determine the effectiveness of a Public Relations campaign. However, I have found that the effectiveness of these kind of campaigns is truly about the conversation you're creating with customers. When FanFood was about to launch at Formula One in Austin Texas, there was a lot of pressure on our PR campaign to succeed. Thus, for weeks beforehand, we were creating flyers, putting up ads, and trying to get on radio stations to let people know about FanFood.

However, when FanFood was at Formula One over the three-day period, we found that the effectiveness of the campaign was seen in the conversations people were having. Whether it was their experience with the app or the ease they had getting the food, all of this played a huge role in making our PR campaign effective. The work we did beforehand sparked the interest of a few people who ordered off the app, had a great experience, and not only ordered again but also told others. This led to us making $40,000 in revenue in three days.

WHAT IS THE SINGLE MOST EFFECTIVE PR TACTIC YOU'VE LEARNED?

The single most effective Public Relations tactic I've learned is that people love to have a face to put to a brand. During my time at FanFood, I began organizing weekly Facebook Live Sessions, and it was amazing to see the reception it has garnered. When we premiered these sessions, it was the week our CEO went to meet Daymond John of Shark Tank fame. Even so, our initial Facebook Live session garnered more engagement than the Daymond John post we made. And one week, I had the topic of the session be "valuing your employees," and our CEO got a bit emotional discussing the sacrifices our employees have made in order to make FanFood happen. As soon as he got emotional, the viewership of our session spiked. People love having a hero to root for. At the end of the day, that's exactly what my job is about: taking the FanFood story and making it more transparent to others.

IF YOU COULD CARRY ONLY FIVE TOOLS IN YOUR PR TOOLKIT, WHAT WOULD THEY BE?

The first tool I would carry in my Public Relations toolkit is Google Alerts. Google Alerts is my lifesaver when it comes to tuning into what the competition is up to and ensuring that we are maintaining an edge. The second tool I would carry in my Public Relations toolkit is social media. Social media plays such a gigantic role in helping us communicate with our audience, and it is a tool that people often take for granted.

The third tool I would carry in my PR toolkit is my video assets. There is a reason that videos are more likely to be engaged with than any other kind of visual asset: videos are the key to communication. They help you get your message across to an audience. The fourth tool I would carry is the power of e-mail newsletters. As great as social media is, email mailing lists carry a much stronger meaning in the fact that your mailing list is full of people who are letting you into a world more sacred than their news feed: their inbox. That means a lot, and you can do a lot with that power.

The fifth and final tool I would carry in my toolkit is the ability to write copy within the brand voice. People often underestimate the effectiveness that a consistent brand voice can have, but I've learned the power that it holds, especially during my time with FanFood. As PR professionals go from company to company, they have to learn a company's brand voice. Some are much easier to grasp than others, but the ability to quickly grasp the voice of a company is something that truly cannot be valued enough.

WHAT'S THE SINGLE BIGGEST MISTAKE YOU SEE PEOPLE MAKE IN PR?

Hands down, the biggest mistake that I see people making in PR is that they often think too much inside the box. Public Relations is constantly changing, and it is an absolute necessity for people in PR to always be on the edge of what is new. Even on a month-by-month basis, there is so much going on, whether it be new additions to social media platforms, actions your competitors are taking, or a change in public opinion influenced by current events. While there is the saying "If it ain't broke, don't fix it," I would amend that for Public Relations to be instead "If it ain't broke, revise it anyway." Constantly thinking outside of the box not only keeps your Public Relations efforts fresh, but it also helps you find new methods that you would not have considered before.

WHAT ADVICE WOULD YOU GIVE TO PEOPLE WHO ARE LOOKING TO RUN SUCCESSFUL PR CAMPAIGNS?

Find your story. It's cheesy, but it's true. The most successful PR campaigns remember that at the end of the day, people want a story to be drawn into. Whether it is the story of your product or the story of your company's founders, a narrative does a great job of drawing people in and keeping them engaged. It's the reason budding companies prepare elevator pitches for investors. It's the reason the best commercials are like short films. Story is king. That's the rule in filmmaking, and it is very much the rule with PR.

HOW DO YOU THINK PR WILL CHANGE OVER THE NEXT FEW YEARS?

Perhaps the biggest challenge facing Public Relations now is that it is incredibly difficult to measure ROI. While there are some stats that provide a picture of how posts are doing in regard to engagement, there still is a strong lack of the kind of information that can help measure a return on investment. However, I believe that in the next few years, there will be tools that will come about that will make it easier than ever to measure ROI.

LEARN MORE ABOUT ANDREW

I am currently a Social Media Manager at FanFood, a mobile technology start-up in Chicago, Illinois. I have experience working in over five different industries that include sustainability, sales, film, theater, pharmaceuticals and now the start-up sector, doing everything from rebranding to creating and implementing digital awareness campaigns. Aside from my marketing and Public Relations work, I am also an award-winning filmmaker who is currently finishing up my short film *Little Things*, which was made in cooperation with the National Alliance on Mental Illness.

✉ ANDREWNUNO16@GMAIL.COM
🐦 @ANDREWNUNO
📷 @ANDREWTHENUNOTWIN

LINA KHALIL

FETCH PR CO-OWNER

HOW DO YOU DETERMINE THE EFFECTIVENESS OF A PR CAMPAIGN?

Thanks to the variety of digital products available today, results reporting has become more tangible and robust. Our PR strategy has evolved because we're now able to obtain these quantifiable results, present them to our clients, and show them how our efforts have directly impacted their business. We are no longer beholden to vague numbers like media impressions and comparisons to advertising dollars. While press hits are still important to PR campaigns, we're able to implement a much more data-driven strategy thanks to the accessibility of social media and Google Analytics.

WHAT IS THE SINGLE MOST EFFECTIVE PR TACTIC YOU'VE LEARNED?

We continue to develop our media relations strategy of reaching out to individual reporters who cover our specific clients' industries. While wanting to be on television will never go out of style, we are able to get more traction out of digital outlets, such as podcasts and popular online magazines. Media don't want to receive phone calls anymore. (Not that they ever loved our follow-up calls!) A quick, targeted email to an important freelancer is the new media pitch. Twitter is also a great way to reach out to media if you know they're looking to speak with someone on a certain topic or issue.

IF YOU COULD CARRY ONLY FIVE TOOLS IN YOUR PR TOOLKIT, WHAT WOULD THEY BE?

Cision is essential when building your contact list of journalists who write about a specific industry or topic. You can also manage and optimize your media lists within the platform, making media outreach easier and more effective. We use Hootsuite for our daily social media management, as well as monitoring online chatter and reaching out to target audiences with specially crafted messages. For Email Marketing, we prefer Constant Contact because it's extremely user friendly. The dashboard makes it easy to organize contacts, create targeted email lists, and design branded templates. Trello is our go-to for project management and internal communications. And HARO is an ideal supplement for our proactive media relations efforts.

WHAT'S THE SINGLE BIGGEST MISTAKE YOU SEE PEOPLE MAKE IN PR?

A big mistake is lack of transparency. Whether it's selling to a prospective client, pitching a reporter, or communicating within the company, it is vital to be honest and transparent with anyone you come across. For example, when we have a proposal presentation with a prospective client, the first thing we tell them is our price. We know this is the question on our audience's mind, so we get it out of the way first to get to the meat of the presentation. The prospect responds positively to this candor and instantly feels at ease for the duration of our meeting.

WHAT ADVICE WOULD YOU GIVE TO PEOPLE WHO ARE LOOKING TO RUN SUCCESSFUL PR CAMPAIGNS?

It's important to develop a consistent, branded voice for each campaign. This sets your brand apart from others in the same industry and allows your brand to be more recognizable to customers. This type of familiarity can provide a sense of comfort to customers, similar to how we feel when we're with our friends. Additionally, this voice should permeate every type of content you produce (social media posts, blogs, and pitches) in order to maintain its consistency.

HOW DO YOU THINK PR WILL CHANGE OVER THE NEXT FEW YEARS?

Influencer marketing is definitely going to dominate the Public Relations game for the next few years. Influencer marketing is not just asking celebrities to help sell product; it's also forging relationships with social media influencers and their thousands of followers. This type of marketing has allowed brands to sell directly to their desired audience and obtain quality exposure. With that being said, an influencer marketing campaign is more than just picking someone on social media with a million followers. You really need to know your audience and find an influencer who reflects that; otherwise, your campaign won't be as successful.

LEARN MORE ABOUT LINA

For the last decade, I have applied my networking and communication skills in the fields of publicity and marketing, promoting noteworthy brands like Playboy, Elie Tahari, Red Bull USA, Michelob Ultra, Bacardi Silver, and Baskin-Robbins. This unparalleled experience led my business partner, Erryn Cobb, and me to start our own firm, Fetch PR, in Chicago. At Fetch PR, we represent small to mid-sized businesses in the Chicago area. Our invaluable skills in branding, content/direct marketing, and media relations have made us a prominent player in the PR industry. We look forward to entering our eighth year in business and continuing our success.

🌐 WWW.FETCH-PR.COM
✉ 411@FETCH-PR.COM
📞 312-554-5023
🔗 WWW.LINKEDIN.COM/COMPANY/718097
🐦 @FETCHPR
📘 WWW.FACEBOOK.COM/FETCHPR
📷 @FETCHPUBLICRELATIONS

BARBARA ROZGONYI

CEO, CORYWEST MEDIA LLC
FOUNDER, SOCIAL MEDIA CLUB CHICAGO

HOW DO YOU DETERMINE THE EFFECTIVENESS OF A PR CAMPAIGN?

Lots of factors can go into measuring PR success, including media mentions, social media activity, search engine ranking, and even attendance at events. When you know what you want to measure at the start, you can build out the campaign to hit your targets along the way.

WHAT IS THE SINGLE MOST EFFECTIVE PR TACTIC YOU'VE LEARNED?

Storytelling is key. Think in words and pictures to convey a compelling story with interesting characters who inspire action. Become a producer and step into creating a series of stories over a season to build momentum and attract a loyal following.

IF YOU COULD CARRY ONLY FIVE TOOLS IN YOUR
PR TOOLKIT, WHAT WOULD THEY BE?

The WIRED system is our multipurpose tool. It goes like this:

- **W**ords: Keywords for SEO
- **I**ntentions: Who, What, When, Where, Why?
  Goals for you and your client
- **R**outes: GPS for messaging to deliver and connect with
  key communities
- **E**xperiences: Storytelling all along the customer experience journey 3D
- **D**esign: How will the campaign story play out digitally, directly,
  and dynamically?

WHAT'S THE SINGLE BIGGEST MISTAKE YOU SEE PEOPLE MAKE IN PR?

Ignoring the impact PR [Personality + Reputation—a philosophy I teach] can have on everything and everyone.

WHAT ADVICE WOULD YOU GIVE TO PEOPLE WHO ARE LOOKING TO RUN SUCCESSFUL PR CAMPAIGNS?

Take a tip from Google. They built the Chrome browser based on a press release the engineers wrote about what they wanted people to say—in 2008.

HOW DO YOU THINK PR WILL CHANGE OVER THE NEXT FEW YEARS?

By 2020 PR, as an industry, will fully fuse into digital and social. The people and companies who understand the importance of Personality + Reputation as a fluid field will stand out and be sought out.

LEARN MORE ABOUT BARBARA

Hello there! I'm a digital pioneer who loves forging new communications frontiers. You can get tips on how to get new media to work for you at my blog, which I started in June 2006. I create marketing and sales programs that attract attention, build brands, and connect communities in 3D.

🌐 WWW.BARBARAROZGONYI.COM
🐦 WIREDPRWORKS.COM

MICHELLE CHIERA

HOW DO YOU DETERMINE THE EFFECTIVENESS OF A PR CAMPAIGN?

An effective PR life or cycle is defined not only by the quantity of publications your story is featured in, but also by the impact each publication has. For our product-based clients, one CNN article is worth more than five "Bob's Gadgets."

WHAT IS THE SINGLE MOST EFFECTIVE PR TACTIC YOU'VE LEARNED?

I've learned that in this field, communication is the strongest skill set and the best tool I have for the client, for my team, and ultimately for a strong campaign. Setting clear expectations and being a trustworthy team member to your clients, and not just yes-men/women, is the best thing you can do for all parties.

IF YOU COULD CARRY ONLY FIVE TOOLS IN YOUR PR TOOLKIT, WHAT WOULD THEY BE?

This job is all about connections, and to be frank, some of the best tools for PR are free. Twitter and Slack are best for communication between writers and the team. Services like TrendKite and Cision are best for strategy and client management.

WHAT'S THE SINGLE BIGGEST MISTAKE YOU SEE PEOPLE MAKE IN PR?

PR professionals have a reputation among writers and advertisers for BS-ing and making big promises on little information. And rightfully so. A lot of people—including start-ups who choose to handle their own PR—oversell and use the wrong terminology and tools in reaching relevant writers. Even if the news is bad and unfavorable to your client, feedback on UI, glitches, design, etc., can only help in returning with a stronger response and a better product down the line.

WHAT ADVICE WOULD YOU GIVE TO PEOPLE WHO ARE LOOKING TO RUN SUCCESSFUL PR CAMPAIGNS?

Always, always, always, we ask people: What makes you unique? Be honest and open with your marketing team, PR agency, and consultants. Sometimes being so close to a product or an idea, people tend to miss things that, from a digital marketing perspective, are relevant and exciting. Additionally, patience and time are key. Businesses aren't created overnight and neither are stories. People need patience when pitching, when writing, and when publishing. The biggest mistake people make is to try to rush a lot of good stories out like a roadside diner. You don't want to be the diner of products and news; you want to be a Michelin 3-star restaurant, and to get there takes time and a PR agency that can back up what they promise.

HOW DO YOU THINK PR WILL CHANGE OVER THE NEXT FEW YEARS?

We're already seeing it more and more within our agency—PR and social media are becoming even more connected. I think that with people looking to go viral and go big quickly, PR will have to adapt some social tactics. Social media experts will have to position themselves as more than just likes and shares but as a substantial force in PR.

LEARN MORE ABOUT MICHELLE

I am a PR Supervisor at Blonde 2.0, an international PR agency based in Boston and Tel Aviv. From successful crowdfunding campaigns to API launches and product development, I create the messaging for technology, lifestyle, AdTech, FinTech, and crypto companies for international media.

WWW.LINKEDIN.COM/IN/MICHELLE-CHIERA-05455089
@LOSTKRAVITZ
WWW.FACEBOOK.COM/MICH.CHIERA

BOB SPOERL

PRESIDENT, BEAR ICEBOX COMMUNICATIONS

HOW DO YOU DETERMINE THE EFFECTIVENESS OF A PR CAMPAIGN?

B2B Public Relations campaigns are all about influencing a specific audience of people who stand to benefit most from your product or service. B2B PR campaigns influence key decision-makers within companies and organizations who are likely to use your product or service to take some sort of action. Some of the most effective ways to measure results from these campaigns are: through web traffic; through downloads of e-books or case studies highlighting your offering; through lead flow (PR can have both a short-term and long-term sort of umbrella impact on interest and leads); and, most ideally, through an increase in sales and revenue.

WHAT IS THE SINGLE MOST EFFECTIVE PR TACTIC YOU'VE LEARNED?

Case studies can really have an incredible impact in a B2B PR campaign. We've used case studies to illustrate how clients of ours are helping the businesses they serve—telling that story, especially to relevant trade publications and outlets, can influence companies in that same industry to take action. It's the idea that, if it worked for their company and increased their revenue by 30 percent, we want that same magic tool that is going to help us, as well. Proving your product or service through success stories of clients is sort of a timeless way to influence target audiences and create a compelling B2B PR campaign.

IF YOU COULD CARRY ONLY FIVE TOOLS IN YOUR PR TOOLKIT, WHAT WOULD THEY BE?

If I could choose only five tools for my B2B PR toolkit, I would choose: Computer: this probably goes without saying, but just about everything I do is done through my laptop. It's essential. iPhone: when I'm not by my computer, I'm typically catching up on emails or news or texting/calling/emailing clients or media sources. Cision: it's the global media database we subscribe to that helps us monitor media contacts and ensure that we're staying abreast of the industry. Slack: this is how we stay connected with most of our clients. B2B PR can get tricky—we're typically working with clients who are in niche markets and have complex stories to tell. Having an open line of communication, a kind of two-way street, is incredibly important. Slack helps us communicate with our B2B clients around the globe instantaneously. *The Wall Street Journal* subscription: when it comes to B2B PR news sources, I think WSJ is the best. It offers a quick snapshot into the economy as a whole and allows me to be on top of any trending items/stories that may impact or benefit my clients.

WHAT'S THE SINGLE BIGGEST MISTAKE YOU SEE PEOPLE MAKE IN PR?

One of the biggest mistakes a novice B2B PR professional will make is treating it as if it is consumer-facing Public Relations. While there is overlap, the two are different animals with totally different types of target audiences. For example, if you're selling directly to consumers, a placement on a local TV network may drive an incredible amount of traffic to your website and increase e-sales. A placement on a local TV network for a SaaS company selling around the world? Not going to offer a whole lot other than a nice clip to add to the news section of your website. B2B clients are going to demand PR experts to know their product or service and take a deep dive into the industry. They need to become thought leaders to sell their sophisticated solutions, and they are going to want/ need their PR leaders to do the same.

WHAT ADVICE WOULD YOU GIVE TO PEOPLE WHO ARE LOOKING TO RUN SUCCESSFUL PR CAMPAIGNS?

Anyone looking to run a successful B2B PR campaigns needs to do the following: First, know your client's ideal customer profile and create a campaign around that audience. When it comes to media outreach for these campaigns, target media outlets who are either going to speak directly to that audience (typically, these will be trade publications focused on a particular industry) or so big (e.g., TechCrunch, *The Wall Street Journal*,

CNBC) that a placement in the outlet is going to have a kind of universal, far-reaching positive impact for the client.

Next, create assets that are going to support your client and its sales propositions. For example, if you represent a client with fantastic internal data, work with them to develop a data study or industry trend report you can share with media contacts as a data-focused pitch. Or, focus on a couple of client success stories and create relevant case studies you can use in your media outreach.

And finally, perhaps most important, be disciplined and systematic in your PR outreach. Find the right media outlets and create personalized pitches to specific editors and reporters there. Beyond traditional media, find blogs or businesses in which you can cross-promote, offering your client as a thought leader to create a byline or be a Q&A expert source on a complementary website.

HOW DO YOU THINK PR WILL CHANGE OVER THE NEXT FEW YEARS?

In the same way we're seeing a rise in the use of AI to make sales and marketing more efficient, I think we will see a similar approach to making PR and influencer outreach more efficient, meaningful, and targeted. Perhaps tools integrated with AI features will help make the life of a PR professional a bit easier, offering a way to better learn and understand outlets and media to target and combing the web—and then offering customized feedback—to the B2B PR person seeking further clarity.

LEARN MORE ABOUT BOB

Whether it is communicating with clients or talking to reporters, I strive to be a "PRo" as the president of Bear Icebox Communications, a global B2B-focused Public Relations and Content Marketing agency in the Chicago area. With a knack for getting clients in the news and a passion for helping the underdog win, I have helped clients land coverage on and in *The Wall Street Journal*, *The New York Times*, CNBC, Fox Business, and the *Chicago Tribune*, to name a few. My professional background is focused on B2B clients working in a variety of sectors: from tech start-ups to franchises to healthcare companies to restaurants and retail concepts. I hold degrees in journalism from Northwestern University and English and Philosophy from Loyola University Chicago. When I'm not busy turning clients into sources, I'm probably spending time with my wife and two kids.

🌐 BICOMGLOBAL.COM
▢ @BOBSPOERL

CHAPTER 7
AFFILIATE MARKETING

A SIMPLE EXPLANATION OF AFFILIATE MARKETING

Affiliate Marketing is a way for a company to sell its products by signing up individuals or companies ("affiliates") who market the company's products for a commission.

Affiliate Marketing is considered "performance-based" marketing—businesses reward affiliates for the customers they bring to their company.

There are typically three parties involved in an Affiliate Marketing relationship: the advertiser, the publisher, and the customer.

The advertiser is the organization looking to sell a product or service. The publisher promotes the products or services, gaining commissions on their successes from the advertiser. The customer performs the desired action, such as purchasing a product.

The affiliate process typically looks like this: the affiliate (publisher) owns a website. The publisher markets the advertiser's products on their website, often in the form of banner or text ads, links, or phone numbers. Once the customer clicks on the advertiser's ad or link on the publisher's website and/or performs the desired action, the publisher is paid a commission for bringing that customer to the advertiser.

An affiliate's performance is often tied to a specific goal, such as website traffic generated by the affiliate, leads generated by the affiliate, or sales generated by the affiliate.

There are multiple Affiliate Marketing platforms, such as CJ Affiliate (formerly Commission Junction), that allow for the Affiliate Marketing transaction to take place. The platform does the legwork of ensuring customers are properly tracked from the publisher's properties to the advertiser, along with tracking the desired on-site actions such as purchases or lead form completions.

AFFILIATE MARKETING SPECIALISTS SOUND OFF

JULIA HOCHSTEIN

AFFILIATE MANAGER

HOW DO YOU DETERMINE THE EFFECTIVENESS OF AN AFFILIATE MARKETING CAMPAIGN?

Affiliate Marketing is effective because it is flexible in its ability to help contribute to a variety of goals. There are publishers that can help with a myriad of company goals, including new customer acquisition, product launches and reviews, search, price comparison, top line revenue growth, influencer/Content Marketing, and many others. With this diversity in mind, it's important for an affiliate manager to first determine what place her program has in the company's overall goals. Once that decision is made, an affiliate manager can benchmark against those goals. Once we've established the KPI that affiliate is best at supporting, my goal is to drill down to the publisher level and invest more time and energy with the ones that are showing the most promise in that area. If a publisher isn't able to help drive toward program goals, we may have to reevaluate the other positives they bring to the relationship. If we can't find a good fit, we may determine it best to end the relationship.

WHAT IS THE SINGLE MOST EFFECTIVE AFFILIATE MARKETING TACTIC YOU'VE LEARNED?

Be the consultant. I always tell people that while I'm glad to no longer be in a sales position, I was grateful for my time in sales. Learning consultative sales tactics out of school gave me a framework of how to best approach business partnerships. Whether you are speaking with an internal business partner or a publisher, it's always a good idea to learn about their business, goals, and aspirations. When you know what they are trying to achieve, you can give your best recommendations for how you align with their strategy. Understanding your partner's goals and pain points can help you recommend solutions that position your channel in a positive fashion.

Working with a blogger who has too many emails? Perhaps you recommend connecting via their favorite social media and creating a private group for program alerts. Have a product team internally that is launching a new product? Ask them what they are still struggling to get from other channels, in terms of support, and see if you have the publisher who can do that.

IF YOU COULD CARRY ONLY FIVE TOOLS IN YOUR AFFILIATE MARKETING TOOLKIT, WHAT WOULD THEY BE?

Access to good data and a good affiliate network are the first two tools that are vital, for obvious reasons. I also would not trade my phone for anything. I'm a firm believer that a good phone call is more effective than a series of emails. Along those lines, find a system for keeping track of publisher conversations. It may be a formal CRM or maybe it's a collection of notes in a notebook. As you move through your affiliate career, it's helpful to have a reference of what publishers can and can't do, even if you can't immediately work with them.

Finally, a good mentor/friend in the space is another wonderful tool. If you are running your own program internally, you may be fairly isolated. Share stories, vent your frustrations, and soundboard ideas. Some of my best ideas come after regular lunches with a friend who is in the space.

WHAT'S THE SINGLE BIGGEST MISTAKE YOU SEE PEOPLE MAKE IN AFFILIATE MARKETING?

One of the most frustrating experiences as an affiliate manager is seeing publishers who are impacted by merchants lowering commissions (even as low as 0 percent) because they've run out of budget. Of course, this is also done primarily in Q4, giving publishers fodder to believe that affiliate managers have no heart, are trying to pull one over on them, or are just misers on the level of Ebenezer Scrooge. And I see their point, in a channel where most payments are typically made only when a sale has been referred to the merchant; it's got to be hard to believe that there are people who set budgets for the channel without understanding how it works. But it can happen, even to the best, especially when affiliate managers are not getting a seat at the table when budgets are created.

Many finance teams assume affiliate operates similar to other paid channels and can be turned off at a moment's notice with no harm done. Get a seat at that table. Come prepared to walk them through the financials. They may be experts in finance, but you are the expert of your channel.

WHAT ADVICE WOULD YOU GIVE TO PEOPLE WHO ARE LOOKING TO RUN SUCCESSFUL AFFILIATE MARKETING CAMPAIGNS?

The most successful programs are ones where the affiliate manager is actively pursuing relationships with the publishers in the program and looking for ways to continually create beneficial opportunities. Because many of our publishers started as one-person operations, there is still a very personal component to it. If you have to make a decision for your program that negatively impacts a publisher, it's much easier to do so when you have an honest relationship already established. And the same goes for the good conversations. When a publisher is invested in your program, you are able to brainstorm and come up with new ideas that help achieve your program's goals. I have a handful of publishers I can present a business problem to and get sound advice on how they can help alleviate that issue. It's definitely an invaluable resource and a key to success.

HOW DO YOU THINK AFFILIATE MARKETING WILL CHANGE OVER THE NEXT FEW YEARS?

My hope is that affiliate will see the need to become better at providing rich data points and follow up with ways to act on that data. As a channel, we are significantly behind our counterparts working in other paid channels where data is more easily extrapolated and shared. The diversity of affiliate publishers is a downfall, in this case. Small publishers who wish to hold on in a world where data is ever increasing will need to look to tools that can help them better understand their audience and deliver that understanding to the affiliate managers.

It's easier to justify spending more with a publisher that can take a more surgical approach and gain quality customers than it is for a broad net approach that may not fit the intended customer profile. Even when paid search is technically less efficient from a cost perspective, the story is considered more interesting and more actionable than affiliate because they can hone in on demographics, like customer groups and other customer identifiers, that are better aligned to business needs.

LEARN MORE ABOUT JULIA

I am an eight-year affiliate industry expert with experience launching, migrating, and growing programs of varying sizes and goals across multiple verticals. I've had experience working in-house and at an affiliate network, as well as leading my own program for the last four years. When I'm not knee-deep in Affiliate Marketing concepts, I can be found drinking wine and enjoying time with my husband and daughter. If you liked what I said or would like to discuss more, I'd love to hear from you.

in WWW.LINKEDIN.COM/IN/JULIA-KOZUCK-HOCHSTEIN

ADAM MANKOFF

AFFILIATE MARKETING EXPERT, CONSULTANT

HOW DO YOU DETERMINE THE EFFECTIVENESS OF AN AFFILIATE MARKETING CAMPAIGN?

When evaluating the effectiveness of an Affiliate Marketing campaign, there are multiple factors typically tied to specific goals of each company utilizing performance marketing. Effectiveness is usually determined by a lift in sales revenue, incremental revenue, and new customer acquisition. Other success metrics can include a lift in conversion rate, average order value, clicks or website traffic, or impressions. It's important to set goals and align the proper strategy to achieve them and then execute accordingly.

WHAT IS THE SINGLE MOST EFFECTIVE AFFILIATE MARKETING TACTIC YOU'VE LEARNED?

Having a win-win approach to the affiliate space is key in achieving success. It sounds like common sense, but more often than not, both the advertiser and publisher site focus on what's best for them. For example, many advertisers deliberately underpay or take advantage of what a publisher can offer. Inversely, publishers may accept funding for paid placements knowing that the return on spend is highly unlikely. Building toward goals together as a team will drive true success.

IF YOU COULD CARRY ONLY FIVE TOOLS IN YOUR AFFILIATE MARKETING TOOLKIT, WHAT WOULD THEY BE?

The five tools needed to thrive in Affiliate Marketing include email, access to affiliate network reporting, Rolodex, suitcase for travel, and phone. The reporting piece provides the data necessary to make decisions and run successful Affiliate Marketing campaigns. The other four tools have one thing in common: their importance in the communication process. Having the right relationships and then growing and optimizing them is essential to any performance marketing strategy. Email, phone, and quality face time are just a few of the key tools needed.

WHAT'S THE SINGLE BIGGEST MISTAKE YOU SEE PEOPLE MAKE IN AFFILIATE MARKETING?

The single biggest mistake made in the affiliate space is not making data-driven decisions. It's easy to go with your gut, work with a partner because you like the look of their site, give your business to a colleague because you get along well, adjust affiliate payouts to help drive more sales, or buy a paid placement because it's a visually appealing spot. But the reality is that without data, you're taking a shot in the dark. Let the data be your guide and you'll end up making more right decisions than not.

WHAT ADVICE WOULD YOU GIVE TO PEOPLE WHO ARE LOOKING TO RUN SUCCESSFUL AFFILIATE MARKETING CAMPAIGNS?

Always use attribution analytics to determine the true value of your Affiliate Marketing strategy. Having transparency into your own business will help you determine the incremental value of performance marketing. For example, you may be driving strong revenue with a new Affiliate Marketing strategy. However, this revenue may not be incremental. Instead, you're just shifting dollars from another internal marketing channel, such as email or paid search, into the affiliate channel. Attribution can paint the whole picture and tie other marketing channel data into one.

HOW DO YOU THINK AFFILIATE MARKETING WILL CHANGE OVER THE NEXT FEW YEARS?

Over the next few years, expect the Affiliate Marketing industry to become much more transparent. This will improve relationships between advertisers, publishers, and networks and allow everyone to work smarter together. Historically there has been a lot of gray area in the affiliate space combined with negative preconceptions about the value of the channel. The truth is the affiliate space does have a lot of value to offer, and the shift towards greater transparency will help to highlight it.

LEARN MORE ABOUT ADAM

I am a passionate affiliate marketer with ten well-rounded years in the performance marketing space. I've worked extensively on the network/ agency, advertiser, and publisher sides, respectively. From Amazon to Walgreens, I've been hands-on with hundreds of affiliate programs and continue to be a leader/innovator in the space. I specialize in building affiliate programs from the ground up and bringing explosive growth to existing ones.

in WWW.LINKEDIN.COM/IN/ADAMMANKOFF

IGOR ONYSHCHENKO

SENIOR AFFILIATE MANAGER, NETFUSION MEDIA INC.

HOW DO YOU DETERMINE THE EFFECTIVENESS OF AN AFFILIATE MARKETING CAMPAIGN?

In my opinion, the only thing that can be determined as campaign effectiveness is profit. ROI is the main KPI for marketers. Typically, business owners don't care as much about clicks, impressions, or conversions as they do about the difference between money spent and money generated.

WHAT IS THE SINGLE MOST EFFECTIVE AFFILIATE MARKETING TACTIC YOU'VE LEARNED?

The more effective tactic I've learned is paying only for a result. My favorite format is CPA because you pay for a particular action—not view, click, or mille. People may say that different formats have different aims, but I'm speaking from the point of view of profit as the most important KPI.

IF YOU COULD CARRY ONLY FIVE TOOLS IN YOUR AFFILIATE MARKETING TOOLKIT, WHAT WOULD THEY BE?

The CAKE tracking platform is enough for me :)

WHAT'S THE SINGLE BIGGEST MISTAKE YOU SEE PEOPLE MAKE IN AFFILIATE MARKETING?

From the point of publishers: a lot of people try to compete with huge companies in tough verticals. This leads to wasted budget, as an individual cannot spend as much for testing as a large company can. From the point of view of advertisers: buying any advertising that's not results-based advertising is a big mistake.

WHAT ADVICE WOULD YOU GIVE TO PEOPLE WHO ARE LOOKING TO RUN SUCCESSFUL AFFILIATE MARKETING CAMPAIGNS?

Creativity is the best skill here. I have seen a lot of case studies for out-dated verticals that were really successful because of their creativity. Do not limit your creativity to the creative only (yeah, that sounds tautological), but think about the traffic source, the ad text, the pre-lander, and all other elements.

HOW DO YOU THINK AFFILIATE MARKETING WILL CHANGE OVER THE NEXT FEW YEARS?

I think the role of big companies will be increasing constantly. Based on my experience, I can say that even several years ago, you could just create a website and start earning money and see the potential quickly. Nowadays it has become really tough to compete with huge corporations for traffic.

LEARN MORE ABOUT IGOR

I started my online job track record with an internship in a big internet marketing agency that led to a department head position in a couple of years. I have solid experience in everything connected with online marketing and creating/managing web projects. Currently I'm working with NetFusion Media, and I'm running several of my own projects.

in WWW.LINKEDIN.COM/IN/DANNKO

CHANTAL DALTON

DIGITAL AND AFFILIATE MARKETER

HOW DO YOU DETERMINE THE EFFECTIVENESS OF AN AFFILIATE MARKETING CAMPAIGN?

To determine whether an Affiliate Marketing campaign is effective, check the number of qualified leads that come in from each affiliate. The secret sauce of any great marketing campaign is, "Did the campaign meet the goal?" Be sure to have goals for every marketing program, including affiliates. At times, it can feel hard to set a goal because you are relying on a third party to help you generate leads and sales. To ensure any affiliate campaign is effective, you need to share your expectation/goal with the affiliate and ask for their expectation/goal in partnering with you, as well. If you two are in alignment, then the affiliate campaign is going to be successful.

WHAT IS THE SINGLE MOST EFFECTIVE AFFILIATE MARKETING TACTIC YOU'VE LEARNED?

The most successful Affiliate Marketing tactic is the onboarding of the affiliate. If that affiliate buys into your brand, you have an engaged affiliate. A lot of times, the affiliate needs more understanding of what your company or product does so they can appropriately promote you. Too often, companies sign up affiliates, send them marketing material, and say, "Go for it! Start promoting us," only to not get the results they hoped for—or worse, an disengaged affiliate. By effectively onboarding new affiliates— such as making sure they have the right marketing material to promote you, understand the company's goal, know the sales process, know how to submit leads, and know how they are going to be informed about products and company updates—you will have an incredibly engaged partner who will generate quality leads and help you close deals faster.

IF YOU COULD CARRY ONLY FIVE TOOLS IN YOUR AFFILIATE MARKETING TOOLKIT, WHAT WOULD THEY BE?

If I could have only five tools for an Affiliate Marketing toolkit, it would include: a through recruiting and onboarding process, a well-designed website, affiliate banner/badge and landing page, engaging content for the affiliate to use, and a referral portal. Bottom line is, Affiliate Marketing's job is to make it easy for the affiliate to promote you and send you the qualified leads.

WHAT'S THE SINGLE BIGGEST MISTAKE YOU SEE PEOPLE MAKE IN AFFILIATE MARKETING?

The biggest mistake I see being made with Affiliate Marketing is signing up affiliates without any understanding of the affiliate's business. Too many times, affiliate managers just sign up all new affiliates, thinking "the more the merrier." While that approach will yield some hits, it will usually yield just as many misses. A more detailed, focused approach will have more hits and fewer misses.

You need to find the right type of affiliate, see that it is working, and then make it scalable. This starts by ensuring the affiliate has the same target market as your company or product. Then ask the affiliate the right questions about their business, such as, "How do you currently attract clients to your website?" or "How many new and returning visitors are coming to your blog?" or "What are the marketing tactics you use to get new clients?" Understanding the basic information about your affiliates will set you up for success and minimize bringing on the wrong affiliate.

WHAT ADVICE WOULD YOU GIVE TO PEOPLE WHO ARE LOOKING TO RUN SUCCESSFUL AFFILIATE MARKETING CAMPAIGNS?

My advice for running a successful Affiliate Marketing campaign is to start with having the right affiliates and ensuring they have the right tools to promote you. Also, to keep your affiliates engaged; have regular check-ins with them to let them know the quality of their leads and see what you can do to help their business. Remember, at the end of the day this is a partnership, and you want your top affiliates happy. Anything you can do to reciprocate will benefit you in the long run.

HOW DO YOU THINK AFFILIATE MARKETING WILL CHANGE OVER THE NEXT FEW YEARS?

You will continue to see Affiliate Marketing grow in prominence in the next few years, particularly around having better developed onboarding programs, adding influencer marketing to the Affiliate Marketing mix, and going more mobile. Again, you have to think of it like this: the more ways you can get your brand out to your target audience in an authentic way, the better for your business and your affiliates.

LEARN MORE ABOUT CHANTAL

I am sassy, a master at networking, and a marketing ninja! I love working and marketing for brands that I think are there to make people's lives easier. With over twelve years of marketing and leadership experience in B2B tech, telecom, and SaaS, I have a vast array of knowledge in digital, affiliate, event, and partner marketing.

✉ CHDALTON35@GMAIL.COM
in LINKEDIN.COM/IN/CHANTALDALTON

TODD WEITZMAN

AFFILIATE MANAGER, TWOPM

HOW DO YOU DETERMINE THE EFFECTIVENESS OF AN AFFILIATE MARKETING CAMPAIGN?

Affiliate Marketing is referral marketing, so if you have a product or service with unique traits and selling points that are proven, you should absolutely consider Affiliate Marketing. If your product isn't being shared enough, that's a surefire sign that your affiliate program may not have enough of a following.

WHAT IS THE SINGLE MOST EFFECTIVE AFFILIATE MARKETING TACTIC YOU'VE LEARNED?

Hidden opportunities yield the best results. Most affiliate programs aren't started until it's too late. If there's a business that can gain traction through referrals or value propositions like coupon codes, Affiliate Marketing should be there. It just so happens that many companies have started an affiliate program in their infancy but never fully grew them. These are the opportunities that blogs, coupon sites, and others can take advantage of with these hidden (underutilized) affiliate programs!

IF YOU COULD CARRY ONLY FIVE TOOLS IN YOUR AFFILIATE MARKETING TOOLKIT, WHAT WOULD THEY BE?

ahrefs.com for competitor analysis, LinkedIn Premium for new messaging opportunities, Affiliate Summit passes for relationship networking, access to restricted affiliate programs, and marketing manager approvals.

WHAT'S THE SINGLE BIGGEST MISTAKE YOU SEE PEOPLE MAKE IN AFFILIATE MARKETING?

Being too reliant on one publisher (blog or website pushing offers) or one advertiser (one business hosting the offers). Having worked on all sides of affiliate management, being too focused on your proven revenue opportunities is a death knell in the affiliate world. Why? Wheels are always turning.

I worked for one company that was insistent on working only with the top ten revenue producing websites. Turns out the top producer decided to run another offer elsewhere, and the company had a major drop-off in revenue production. Blogs or websites don't need to be loyal to an advertiser if they see more money elsewhere. Affiliate marketing is about pursuing multiple opportunities and making sure you cover all of your bases; keep the wheel turning and bringing in new opportunities and value propositions.

WHAT ADVICE WOULD YOU GIVE TO PEOPLE WHO ARE LOOKING TO RUN SUCCESSFUL AFFILIATE MARKETING CAMPAIGNS?

If you are a publisher running an affiliate campaign, have an alternative (like I mentioned before about not being too reliant), negotiate with the campaign manager for more commission should you bring in the traffic, and keep building content that relates to your revenue producing audience.

HOW DO YOU THINK AFFILIATE MARKETING WILL CHANGE OVER THE NEXT FEW YEARS?

I've seen a growth in online to offline affiliate relationships. What that means is that you can choose offers online and then redeem a purchase in person. Affiliate coupon-related websites are oversaturated, and I think there will be a drop off in the quantity of these types of websites. Content sources like blogs still have an opportunity to build a loyal audience and refer them to great affiliate programs.

LEARN MORE ABOUT TODD

I have been in the affiliate industry for several years, starting out working with a cash-back website and building my skills and knowledge there. Once I dug deeper into the affiliate space, I saw the opportunity to grow and expand my career, and now I operate my own performance marketing agency and personal finance website.

⊕ TWOPM.NET
⊕ MONEYHAX.COM

JESSIE FENTON

HOW DO YOU DETERMINE THE EFFECTIVENESS OF AN AFFILIATE MARKETING CAMPAIGN?

Like most marketing initiatives, the end goal and continual purpose of an affiliate program are conversions and ROI. A close runner-up is your affiliate count—active affiliates, that is. Whether a small operation or large corporation, your affiliates are an extension of your business, and quality exceeds quantity.

For example, more than five hundred affiliates sounds great, but if only 3 percent are actively promoting your company or product, your campaign is not as effective as an affiliate army of eighty with over 50 percent active. Active affiliates are promoting your product or company daily or weekly (depending on your model) and acquiring new users to your site, which equates to more purchases and overall traffic. If you can maintain that at least 25 percent of your affiliates are active, your ROI is competitive to your other marketing channels and you're continuing to increase your conversion rate—you are doing it right.

WHAT IS THE SINGLE MOST EFFECTIVE AFFILIATE MARKETING TACTIC YOU'VE LEARNED?

Be a person, not an automated email. Congratulate your affiliates when they hit a new milestone; show them how to best use your website or third-party platform. The more educated they are, the more likely they are to use your links and assets. Not to mention, more commissions for them means more conversions for you. It's that simple. The added personalization and incentives not only set you apart from competitors, but also help with your word-of-mouth marketing. Bloggers and influencers talk. Make your program desirable. Competitive commissions and additional perks can only intrigue so much. A great user experience is gold.

IF YOU COULD CARRY ONLY FIVE TOOLS IN YOUR AFFILIATE MARKETING TOOLKIT, WHAT WOULD THEY BE?

My Affiliate Marketing toolkit would be filled with elements for the user, my affiliates, and my company. To start, custom creative assets for my affiliates to use on their social media platforms and websites, outside of the traditional links and product carousels. Specific commission structure based off of new users, existing users, and special campaigns. An affiliate CPS network—ShareASale, CJ, Affiliate Window, or Rakuten, to name a few.

A third-party platform makes conversions and tracking much easier and are more user-friendly for your affiliates. A welcome package, including an introduction to your business model, what you are offering, where all of your assets live, and why their followers should love you. And lastly, data. Not only to track your trends but to analyze any curious findings, such as fraudulent charges or spam-worthy websites. These tools equip you for a successful affiliate program.

WHAT'S THE SINGLE BIGGEST MISTAKE YOU SEE PEOPLE MAKE IN AFFILIATE MARKETING?

The biggest mistake I see in Affiliate Marketing is solely looking through the lens of a merchant, not an affiliate. Knowing what other merchants, not just your competitors, are offering and understanding what entices your affiliates to post your assets to their websites. Solve a problem for them. Whether it be added income for a stay-at-home mom or boosting a start-up's website traffic, explain why this partnership is a great fit for the both of you, not just your commission structure. Affiliate Marketing is not a "set it and forget it" marketing initiative; it's a living, breathing marketing channel that can blossom if groomed properly.

WHAT ADVICE WOULD YOU GIVE TO PEOPLE WHO ARE LOOKING TO RUN SUCCESSFUL AFFILIATE MARKETING CAMPAIGNS?

Be exclusive. Don't accept every affiliate or ambassador into your program.

Seek those that fit your business model and audience type. Dedicate some time to finding the right affiliates. Finding those big fish with the ideal following is a huge long-term win. Do your research. Wow them. Loyalty goes both ways. They will be loyal when your competitors come knocking at their door. Offer them weekly, monthly, or seasonal incentives that are exclusive to your affiliates. Set them apart from their competition, as well.

HOW DO YOU THINK AFFILIATE MARKETING WILL CHANGE OVER THE NEXT FEW YEARS?

It will continue to become a competitive platform where companies must compete for the best benefits, commissions, and assets to acquire great affiliates. People can use their affiliates links almost anywhere. As technology and social platforms continue to evolve, Affiliate Marketing will have to do the same.

LEARN MORE ABOUT JESSIE

I'm an always evolving marketing maven who loves to give handmade gifts and surprises. Living the hectic Chicago lifestyle as a marketer, wife, and soon-to-be mama. Starting my adventures at the second largest PR firm in the world to an in-house marketer for a start-up, I've experienced many different shades of marketing and facets in my years in the industry. As the Digital Marketing Manager at Built In, I focus my efforts on brand awareness and informing talented, quality candidates about the amazing start-ups that are hiring in their nearby city using Content Marketing to lead the charge.

✉ JESSIE.FENTON@BUILTIN.COM

DORINE MOONEY

HOW DO YOU DETERMINE THE EFFECTIVENESS OF AN AFFILIATE MARKETING CAMPAIGN?

I determine effectiveness by looking at whether or not the goals set for that campaign have been achieved. For example, different campaigns have different end goals: Is it the sale, is it new customer acquisition, is it a sign up for a service, or is it a combination of various goals? Having clear goals and a clear strategy helps to create the wins that make the program successful. I have seen so many programs fail due to no clear goals or the constant changing of the goals without any sort thought behind it.

WHAT IS THE SINGLE MOST EFFECTIVE AFFILIATE MARKETING TACTIC YOU'VE LEARNED?

The single most effective tactic is communication, hands down. It is so important to keep communication open with your affiliates; what is working and what is not and feedback for the affiliates is crucial. Communicating and keeping the affiliate engaged and delivering effective results helps with optimization and the overall success of the campaign.

IF YOU COULD CARRY ONLY FIVE TOOLS IN YOUR AFFILIATE MARKETING TOOLKIT, WHAT WOULD THEY BE?

I feel the five tools that I need for the success of any program are a great research tool to help identify relevant affiliates for a program, an affiliate platform that is intuitive as well as innovative, strong affiliate relationships in a variety of classifications, a good relationship with a developer/engineer, and a good analytics platform.

WHAT'S THE SINGLE BIGGEST MISTAKE YOU SEE PEOPLE MAKE IN AFFILIATE MARKETING?

The single biggest mistake I see is not being flexible with a program.

I am a firm believer in testing. I have seen so many programs that are too rigid and have too many restrictions. Really, any program is like a living breathing being that needs to consistently diversify or it will get boxed in and hit a ceiling. You need to always stay innovative and ahead of the curve to achieve the growth a program needs to succeed.

WHAT ADVICE WOULD YOU GIVE TO PEOPLE WHO ARE LOOKING TO RUN SUCCESSFUL AFFILIATE MARKETING CAMPAIGNS?

The best advice I have is to go into any program with an open mind and listen to the feedback given by affiliates. Flexibility and communication is key—I cannot stress that enough. Attribution is also very important to the success of any program.

HOW DO YOU THINK AFFILIATE MARKETING WILL CHANGE OVER THE NEXT FEW YEARS?

I think there are many changes going to happen in the next few years, with traditional retail shifting to online and influencers becoming more integral in affiliate. Also, video is becoming increasingly important. I believe platforms will evolve and programs will need more attention than a "set it and leave it" attitude.

LEARN MORE ABOUT DORINE

In the past thirteen years, I have developed, managed, and optimized Affiliate Marketing programs in a variety of verticals. After starting my career managing lead generation campaigns for EDU, pharmaceutical, and automotive industries, I went on to work in e-commerce, managing programs in tech fashion, jewelry, home decor, and office supplies.

✉ DORINE.MOONEY@GRACELOCKINDUSTRIES.COM
🔗 WWW.LINKEDIN.COM/IN/DORINEMOONEYCA

NICK OSWALD

AFFILIATE MARKETING MANAGER, CLEVERBRIDGE

HOW DO YOU DETERMINE THE EFFECTIVENESS OF AN AFFILIATE MARKETING CAMPAIGN?

Return on ad spend (ROAS) is always my primary focus when reflecting a campaign's success. However, I don't just tabulate ROAS on a month-to-month basis; instead, I look ahead to year two and year three. When selling subscription-based products, losing a little bit on margin after affiliate commissions in the current year will still pay big dividends over a customer's lifetime. This even works with physical goods, as well, if you have the tools to measure new customers incoming from your affiliate partners. If I can prove to a merchant that affiliates bring in more new customers and those customers are going to keep coming back, I've not only just made their month, I've made their next few years.

WHAT IS THE SINGLE MOST EFFECTIVE AFFILIATE MARKETING TACTIC YOU'VE LEARNED?

Affiliates are human beings with tight schedules and overloaded inboxes, just like the rest of us. Digital marketing generalists tend to treat affiliates like the rest of their marketing channels. They assume affiliates can go live with their next marketing campaign with the same instantaneous output like executing a new paid search ad or uploading a new image. It doesn't work like that. You're not the only gig in town for any given affiliate. Communicate with affiliates early and often. Give special treatment to your high performers. Be friendly and generous, and the humans on the other end will return the favor.

IF YOU COULD CARRY ONLY FIVE TOOLS IN YOUR AFFILIATE MARKETING TOOLKIT, WHAT WOULD THEY BE?

I can't live without my HTTP redirect trackers (HttpFox or Fiddler). Those are always my first line of defense for figuring out why an affiliate isn't getting paid and then quickly rectifying the problem. I'll give the obvious answer and list Excel. I live for pivot tables! You won't be effective in Excel without a comprehensive performance-reporting tool. Every affiliate network has its own flavor, so be sure to go with one from which you're comfortable pulling reports. You're going to be doing it all the time.

I hate email. Most of the time it's work about work, rather than proactive, revenue-generating work. I don't have a great tool for this per se, but I couldn't function without a coherent triage system in place to respond to more urgent messages first, save more extended responses for later, and ignore the meaningless junk. Last but not least: two monitors. Life is too short to be squinting over a tiny laptop screen. Spread out your windows!

WHAT'S THE SINGLE BIGGEST MISTAKE YOU SEE PEOPLE MAKE IN AFFILIATE MARKETING?

The single biggest mistake I see affiliate managers doing is not speaking up against bad strategies. Don't be afraid to push back on your clients when their plan for an affiliate campaign is misguided. Your clients have hired you because you're the expert and most likely they know little to nothing about Affiliate Marketing. If you're constantly sprinting in a new direction every day, you're never going to achieve holistic, years-long goals; you'll only be living in the short term. Push back and stick to your expertise.

WHAT ADVICE WOULD YOU GIVE TO PEOPLE WHO ARE LOOKING TO RUN SUCCESSFUL AFFILIATE MARKETING CAMPAIGNS?

Set expectations. Go for the long haul. Affiliate programs generate steady, performance-based revenue, but it doesn't happen right when you launch. You can expect four to six months of hard work before seeing any notable results on your new program. Set your merchants', team's, and boss's expectations knowing that fact. Stay consistent. Once your program gets a good amount of conversions coming in, plan your new campaigns months in advance and stick to the plan with only minor variations based on performance. You can't stay successful in the long run if you're changing your direction every week. Take time to reflect.

Affiliate Marketing can seem like an endless grind with no real beginning and end. So manufacture a beginning and end for yourself, whether that be months, quarters, or holiday seasons. Stop what you're doing and ask yourself what worked and what didn't. Make changes to your strategy. Then begin again. Make your next plan having learned from your last one. This is the surefire way to avoid burnout.

HOW DO YOU THINK AFFILIATE MARKETING WILL CHANGE OVER THE NEXT FEW YEARS?

More and more, the word "affiliate" is getting a negative connotation. Set up a Google Alerts for "Affiliate Marketing" and chances are you'll get articles about tech support fraud and diet pills. These are real problems with which the rest of the industry is getting lumped together. Because of this, I foresee the term "performance marketing" becoming much more prevalent in the United States, though it is already big in the United Kingdom. This branding shift is even more useful than image control. Performance marketing encompasses more than just the traditional affiliate-gets-a-percentage model, and it will allow marketers to focus on new ways of thinking and promoting.

Influencer marketing is a big example of this shift. It turns the cookie stuffing, gray hat SEO employing affiliate image on its head and recognizes the importance of having another voice out there talking about your brand. Performance marketing isn't just one channel; it's all of your channels being carried out by other influential voices who may have more of a sway over your target market than your brand does. Your SEM, display, and retargeting are all communicating positive brand messages, but consumers expect you to say nice things about your brand. Invite other marketers into the fold to help you spread that message.

LEARN MORE ABOUT NICK

I am the US Affiliate Marketing Manager at cleverbridge, a provider of flexible commerce solutions for monetizing digital goods, online services, and SaaS. In my role, I manage unconventional merchant and affiliate verticals. With a keen eye turned to tracking and attribution and the other eye on partner relationships, I employ a balanced, strategic approach to affiliate management. I strive to expand top line revenue for clients but not at the expense of understanding the incremental value of affiliate partnerships. Prior to cleverbridge, I worked at CJ Affiliate by Conversant (formerly Commission Junction), servicing clients ranging from boutique apparel to consumer electronics to automotive. When not managing affiliate programs, I enjoy writing and podcasting about *Star Wars*, going to metal shows, and frequenting Disney World with my high school sweetheart wife, Jenny.

- WWW.CLEVERBRIDGE.COM/CORPORATE/AFFILIATE-PROGRAMS
- WWW.LINKEDIN.COM/IN/NOSWALD
- @NICK_OSWALD
- WWW.STARWARSLOOSECANON.COM

DIRK MIETH

12+ YEAR AFFILIATE INDUSTRY VETERAN & ADVISOR

HOW DO YOU DETERMINE THE EFFECTIVENESS OF AN AFFILIATE MARKETING CAMPAIGN?

Answering from a publisher's perspective: As a publisher, there are always several factors to consider when gauging campaign effectiveness. You must consider effectiveness of the site's user experience, the merchant experience, and overall publisher and merchant revenue goals. Sustainable publishers develop a loyal following and truly understand their audience. They focus on delivering content that resonates with their core audience. If offers or content aren't relevant, users leave the platform. From this perspective, effective campaigns must deliver relevant content.

Merchants expect certain levels of performance in exchange for increased commissions, exclusives, or media buys. If goals aren't met, it's tough to go back to the well. As a publisher, you need to be realistic and up front with the merchant. While hard to predict, revenue goals generally help define a successful campaign. It's important for all parties to agree to reasonable terms and that all parties have a stake in attaining those goals. In any case, I believe its always important to debrief with all parties post campaign to determine what worked and didn't and how to improve in the future.

WHAT IS THE SINGLE MOST EFFECTIVE AFFILIATE MARKETING TACTIC YOU'VE LEARNED?

From the publisher's perspective: networking. The affiliate space is such a tight-knit community; generally, I find there are fewer than three layers of separation between you and anyone in the space. If your promotional methods are aboveboard and you're looking to grow your affiliate business, attending industry events has become a very efficient way to accelerate growth. Conferences are a great opportunity to quickly share your story among a targeted group of industry professionals and gather candid feedback on your approach. You'll find that many affiliate professionals readily offer help and suggestions when asked and can become invaluable business partners, mentors, and friends. Success in affiliate is truly tied to who you know, and conferences are a great way to start meaningful relationships. I generally attend over eight affiliate events per year, both US and international, and will continue to invest heavily in this area.

IF YOU COULD CARRY ONLY FIVE TOOLS IN YOUR AFFILIATE MARKETING TOOLKIT, WHAT WOULD THEY BE?

From the publisher's perspective: know your clients. A flexible third-party CRM system that allows you to track all of your clients, contacts, and opportunities is invaluable. If you're a coupon/deal/loyalty site working with thousands of merchants, you'll need this to keep track of everything and keep your business moving forward. CRM also makes your actions more tangible and repeatable. I prefer Salesforce.com and have leveraged their solution with every affiliate company I've worked with. Mediarails is another great affiliate-specific CRM solution that has gained in recent popularity.

You need to have a firm handle on your numbers. This becomes exponentially more difficult as you increase your merchant count across multiple networks. Manual reporting can become a real time suck when working with over ten networks and hundreds or even thousands of partners. Invest in a good network/merchant affiliate data consolidation and visualization tool, like Trackonomics.net. This can literally save you hours a day, per employee, in reporting and keep you abreast of the latest key metric trends via tangible data.

I've seen many companies try to piece together their own internal data consolidation solutions, but the end results tend to be costly and consistently lacking in data integrity. Third-party vendors in the affiliate data consolidation space are still relatively new, but many large publishers and agencies have adopted these tools. I believe the affiliate data consolidation approach by many publishers to build vs. buy will go in the same direction as similar build vs. buy CRM conversations went ten years ago. Why waste time and money building and maintaining a system when best-in-class tools like Trackonomics.net are available off the shelf?

Mass communication is key. While one-off emails will always be necessary, leveraging Email Marketing services like MailChimp, among many others, is a necessary tool for making your affiliate team more efficient and getting your message out there. Leverage group communication platforms like Slack. Having a centralized repository to communicate and collaborate will save lots of time and help spread best practices among your team. Tools like this really help new employees ramp and help lessen the knowledge gap between your star and struggling performers.

WHAT'S THE SINGLE BIGGEST MISTAKE YOU SEE PEOPLE MAKE IN AFFILIATE MARKETING?

Don't ignore long-tail affiliate opportunities. As a publisher, the big payoffs still reside with the largest merchant partnerships . . . but so does the competition's. Don't neglect the big merchant partnerships, but always be willing to test with the new merchants on the block. There's usually a steady stream of new merchants flowing into the affiliate channel; publishers willing to continually test these new partnerships tend to reap first mover advantages. If you're among the first new merchant program adopters and grow sales at a steady rate, you will be given right of first refusal on exclusives and have leverage to negotiate stronger terms than your competitors.

I observe the same trends on the merchant side of the business. Many merchants say they want to diversify publisher business model distribution but decline to test with smaller publishers or emerging market publishers because it generally does require more initial hand-holding. In my experience, some long-tail opportunities can become your most profitable partnerships if you're willing to invest in the future and test frequently and early in their program lifecycle.

WHAT ADVICE WOULD YOU GIVE TO PEOPLE WHO ARE LOOKING TO RUN SUCCESSFUL AFFILIATE MARKETING CAMPAIGNS?

Be willing to test. The beauty of affiliate is that it's all based around miti-gating risk through pay-for-performance modeling and third-party net-work quality oversights provided by reputable networks. You can always expire relationships if things don't run as expected. Use tests to collect data, vet potential partners, and stay on top of industry trends. Be sure to set clear goals and deadlines and benchmark against your goals on regular intervals.

HOW DO YOU THINK AFFILIATE MARKETING WILL CHANGE OVER THE NEXT FEW YEARS?

I've seen an evolving trend of increased globalization within the perfor-mance marketing channel and believe this will evolve further over the coming years. I've found in many cases merchants don't even realize they have cross-border equity, but consumers from various global markets are purchasing cross-border from their sites. In many cases, these are US market focused merchants who haven't adopted any infrastructure changes to better target various global markets.

Consumers from these emerging markets like China are figuring out resourceful ways around merchants without international shipping and payment methods. Chinese cross-border shoppers commonly use US-based freight forwarders to receive their US purchases, repack them, complete international shipping forms, and then send those products to their final international destinations. In these instances, US merchants don't even realize these orders are shipping to China but instead attribute them domestic sales because all they see is a US ship-to address from their warehouse. This just proves that cross-border shoppers are resourceful, and in China's case, consumers are dipping outside their core markets to purchase authentic products and take advantage of better pricing on brand name goods due to lower US sales tax and better brand product selection.

The affiliate channel offers a really low-risk way to go global, just by identifying publishers with global reach and pushing a CPA offer. There are many more best practices around this strategy, but the point is that most US companies are probably already selling globally, and they don't require any infrastructure changes in order to take advantage of the initial opportunity. Once the cross-border opportunity is recognized, there are many ways to optimize the experience for specific cross-border shoppers.

Also, attribution will become more relevant, and networks will be forced to adopt attribution standards to better meet the needs of merchants. It's common knowledge that more than 70 percent of US affiliate distribution still falls into the coupon/deal/loyalty bucket. If networks and merchants truly want to attract more top of funnel distribution (content/influencer publishers), attribution modeling will require significant adoption. I believe the long-term outlook for healthy publisher distribution rests on the shoulders of effective attribution modeling, and the first network to truly adopt this will reap significant benefits.

LEARN MORE ABOUT DIRK

I've been in the affiliate space for over twelve years and have had the unique opportunity to witness its evolution firsthand and help shape the industry through involvement and visible positions at CJ.com and various domestic and global publishers and in working with most large merchants in the industry. I love the industry and always enjoy talking and learning about emerging trends, as well as meeting new people.

in WWW.LINKEDIN.COM/IN/AFFILIATEMARKETINGDIGITALMEDIA

CHAPTER 8
EMAIL MARKETING

A SIMPLE EXPLANATION OF EMAIL MARKETING

Email Marketing is a form of direct marketing that uses email as a means of communicating commercial messages to an audience.

In a typical Email Marketing scenario, an organization builds an email list and then uses an Email Marketing platform called an email service provider (ESP) to send email messages to that list.

Often, a key responsibility of an Email Marketing specialist is to build, curate, and segment a list of people's emails for use in Email Marketing campaigns.

Email Marketing is commonly used to promote new products, acquire new customers, and gain exposure to company sales material and content, as well as a means to upsell current customers. Email newsletters can be an effective method for keeping an organization's client base informed about products or services.

Email allows marketers to reach out to consumers with personalized, relevant, dynamic messages.

Email Marketing can also be used as a means of continuously "touching" a customer—keeping them aware of what's happening with a brand and notifying them of updates in the business.

An Email Marketing message's content can come in many shapes and forms, from simple text and HTML to rich media and video. As Internet media has evolved, Email Marketing has evolved along with it, and email messages now feature increasingly interactive and engaging messaging.

EMAIL MARKETING SPECIALISTS SOUND OFF

ILONA ABRAMOVA

EMAIL MARKETING MANAGER, APPSUMO

HOW DO YOU DETERMINE THE EFFECTIVENESS OF AN EMAIL MARKETING CAMPAIGN?

When it comes to Email Marketing, you're always hearing that you're supposed to grow your list—which is definitely true, but having engaged subscribers is more important than having a giant list of people who aren't opening or clicking through to your content. Open rates and click-through rates are the main metric, but I also consider how each campaign affects the size of my most engaged segment.

WHAT IS THE SINGLE MOST EFFECTIVE EMAIL MARKETING TACTIC YOU'VE LEARNED?

When it comes to sending good emails, striking the balance between entertainment and information is what I've found to be most effective for AppSumo. We write in a fun and engaging way about software tools that we're excited about because we want our readers to be excited too!

IF YOU COULD CARRY ONLY FIVE TOOLS IN YOUR EMAIL MARKETING TOOLKIT, WHAT WOULD THEY BE?

A design tool like Stencil, a copy editing tool like Grammarly, a project management tool like Plutio, a subject line tester like Send Check It, and a strong data analytics platform—we use Klaviyo, which tracks the performance of each campaign and allows me to create and edit segments of our list based on behavior triggers.

WHAT'S THE SINGLE BIGGEST MISTAKE YOU SEE PEOPLE MAKE IN EMAIL MARKETING?

Trying to optimize too early. It's more important to focus on the big wins, like getting an engaged subscriber base, having quality content, and directing to a product or service that people actually want. Too many people try to personalize their emails and segment before they build a strong foundation.

WHAT ADVICE WOULD YOU GIVE TO PEOPLE WHO ARE LOOKING TO RUN SUCCESSFUL EMAIL MARKETING CAMPAIGNS?

Write to a single person. Every time I start writing copy, I write the name of a person I actually know who would be interested in what I have to say. It sounds silly and childish, but the amount of clarity and focus it gives me is hard to exaggerate. It brings everything from the macro (focusing on selling to everyone) to the micro (trying to persuade a single friend).

HOW DO YOU THINK EMAIL MARKETING WILL CHANGE OVER THE NEXT FEW YEARS?

My position at AppSumo, because of the focus of our business, gives me a watchtower view of the software tech industry. Software is figuring out how to handle the personalization, automation, and segmentation aspects of Email Marketing, which makes it even more important to be able to focus on the big things like writing compelling copy, getting quality designs, and understanding your ideal audience.

LEARN MORE ABOUT ILONA

Hey y'all! I manage Email Marketing at AppSumo, the online store for entrepreneurs. I love good copy and sending emails that people are excited to read. I'm currently working to build the entire Email Marketing platform for our newest company, Briefcase by AppSumo. Happy to connect and talk some email!

🌐 BRIEFCASEHQ.COM

💼 WWW.LINKEDIN.COM/IN/ILONA-ABRAMOVA

BEN MEYER

HOW DO YOU DETERMINE THE EFFECTIVENESS OF AN EMAIL MARKETING CAMPAIGN?

I'm a data nerd. Data doesn't only involve your subscribers but also includes reporting metrics. If you are not using customer engagement like opens and clicks to segment your subscribers, then if this is the only thing you read, please implement that strategy. You won't be disappointed with the return. Benchmarking and reporting are two of the essential aspects of Email Marketing. Understanding historical data and campaign performance is vital to maintaining an Email Marketing strategy. Also, reporting needs to be a part of the campaign's build-out.

While scoping out your campaign requirements, it is imperative to factor in the reporting metrics needed to show the performance of the email program. Having the right reporting in place will allow you to optimize all aspects of your email program. The primary metrics I monitor are:

- Open rate. This is the metric that shows how your subscribers initially engage with your brand or email. These are what I call "the envelope." Open rates help you determine what "from name," send time, and cadences help drive higher engagement.

- Click-through rate (CTR). A true metric that shows you how a subscriber engages with the email layout and content.

- Click to open rate (CTOR). This is my favorite metric and is often overlooked. CTOR shows you overall how the email you worked on performed among the targets you sent emails to. Establishing CTORs for specific email campaigns allows you the opportunity to identify areas for improvement. You can track your performance over time. Then, based on all your efforts, update the emails and/or campaigns.

- Conversion rate and return per email sent. This is the most important metric to your clients. Remember, a client can be anyone—a boss or an organization. ROI helps determine whether all your efforts were worth it.

WHAT IS THE SINGLE MOST EFFECTIVE EMAIL MARKETING TACTIC YOU'VE LEARNED?

Segmenting! Refining your subscribers is something I am very passionate about. I love data. I've been working in Email Marketing for eight years now; early on, the approach to Email Marketing was to send as many emails as you could. I now call this "old school" Email Marketing. Now, to have a high-performing email program, you need to create a 1:1 subscriber experience. Obviously, you need the right data in place, but it's the way you segment your data that defines your email experience. Companies are starting to focus on customer lifetime value more and more. To succeed in retaining your customers, you will need to focus on the individual. Sending timely, relevant content starts with the data and segments you are creating.

IF YOU COULD CARRY ONLY FIVE TOOLS IN YOUR EMAIL MARKETING TOOLKIT, WHAT WOULD THEY BE?

- Return Path, Deliverability needs to be a part of all Email Marketing strategies. Finding an excellent platform like Return Path to monitor sender reputation helps to build relationships with ISPs and ensure your emails are sent to your subscribers' inboxes.

- Litmus. This tool doubles as a great team collaboration tool and an excellent coding platform. Litmus helps make sure your design is rendering correctly for all mobile devices, ISPs, and browsers.

- Really Good Emails. Email design is continuously changing. Sometimes it's good to get a little inspiration. Really Good Emails is a collection of design-focused emails. They even provide code inspiration.

- Google Analytics. It is essential to track the performance of your email campaign. It is even more important to tie all your online marketing efforts together. Implementing an attribution model is important to monitor successful touchpoints and make sure you are spending your money in the right spots.

- Email service provider (ESP). This is the most important tool in all Email Marketing programs. ESPs offer a lot of different features and capabilities. That is why it is important to research the ESPs that match your needs. If you are just starting an Email Marketing program, I would go with a solution like MailChimp that offers a lot of great features at an affordable cost. If you're an enterprise-level company and looking for an ESP, I would recommend Salesforce Marketing Cloud (ExactTarget).

WHAT'S THE SINGLE BIGGEST MISTAKE YOU SEE PEOPLE MAKE IN EMAIL MARKETING?

Lousy list hygiene . . . gross! Email Marketing is a great channel to create 1:1 relationships while still sending to a higher volume of contacts. It's a hard thing for a marketer to admit that a customer is no longer interested in the brand, but it happens. An important item that is commonly left out of Email Marketing strategies is simple list hygiene practices. Would you skip taking a shower? No, it's gross. Keep your database clean and focused on the subscribers that are engaging with your emails.

Here's a few list hygiene tactics: Create a suppression list of hard and specific block bounce reasons. Implement a double opt-in process to reduce fake email addresses, increase sender reputation, and increase engagement metrics. Incorporate validation functionality into your signup forms or data feeds. Run an automated reengagement campaign every six months to see if subscribers still want to receive your emails. Remember, an unsubscribe is a lot better than receiving spam complaints, which could hurt your relationships with ISPs.

WHAT ADVICE WOULD YOU GIVE TO PEOPLE WHO ARE LOOKING TO RUN SUCCESSFUL EMAIL MARKETING CAMPAIGNS?

Don't try to implement (or change) too much at one time. Email Marketing is the game of tracking performance and gathering insights to increase engagement. If you make too many changes to your email campaigns, you won't know what changes affected the test. Which brings me to my next point: you should always be testing. Everyone would like to increase opens or clicks, but guess what? The only way to do that is by testing. Work with an ESP that allows you to automate your testing ideas. Remember, you have a limited time to grab your subscriber's attention. Start simple with your email design and content. Work to find a creative subject line and compelling email content.

Another mistake people make when it comes to Email Marketing is relying too much on images to drive the design of the emails. New subscribers are not comfortable with your emails yet and may not allow images to render. It's a hard game to rely on alt tags to convey your full message.

HOW DO YOU THINK EMAIL MARKETING WILL CHANGE OVER THE NEXT FEW YEARS?

Every year I hear marketers talk about the "death" of Email Marketing. I disagree. Over the years, Email Marketing has proven to be the most valuable channel for customer engagement and revenue return. Email Marketing is not dying; it is merely evolving. Over the next couple of years, I believe Email Marketing will genuinely become a 1:1 based communication.

Companies will (and should) incorporate more advocacy-based campaigns. Advocacy asks the customers to provide feedback on their brand or product experience. Advocacy is a big step toward a multichannel online marketing approach. Asking the customer to write reviews or create videos of their experience on social media channels turns existing customers into a micro sales team. Let the customer promote your brand and convince others that this is a product or service they need. Email

Marketing is the most relationship building online marketing channel. In the next couple of years, companies will need to focus on more personalization and dynamic content to present more relevant content that is appealing to customers.

LEARN MORE ABOUT BEN

I am a passionate professional when it comes to all things marketing. I studied advertising all through college. I am fortunate to enhance my skills and challenge myself for many years now at cleverbridge. In my younger years, my favorite hobby was to draw and play sports. I knew at a young age that I want to move into a career that allowed me to be creative and expand my abilities as an individual. Online marketing has given me the opportunities to keep my childhood dream to be creative and focus on new things. I love what I do, and I try to put my passion into my work and life! Please get in contact with me if you are interested about setting up an Email Marketing program or want to know my thoughts on life or anything at all.

🌐 CLEVERBRIDGE.COM
✉ BENJAMIN.M.MEYER@GMAIL.COM
🐦 @BENMMEYER

JOE SLEPSKI

EMAIL MARKETING MANAGER, GAMEFLY INC.

HOW DO YOU DETERMINE THE EFFECTIVENESS OF AN EMAIL MARKETING CAMPAIGN?

There are many layers to determining the success of an email program. I always consider an email as the extension of any kind of sales proposition. Your online identity and mailing reputation is the cold call. Your subject line is the opening value proposition. The body of your email is the first meeting you have with a client where they get to know who you are. The click is them agreeing to a price quote. When they land on your page, that's passing them off to your internal sales team to complete the buy. All those pieces are measurable and can be compared to see your effectiveness.

WHAT IS THE SINGLE MOST EFFECTIVE EMAIL MARKETING TACTIC YOU'VE LEARNED?

Gone are the days of people being impressed that you've personalized their email with their first name. It's all about product desires. The more you can tailor your email to match the items the reader is searching for or needs, the better—that is the only personalization that matters.

IF YOU COULD CARRY ONLY FIVE TOOLS IN YOUR EMAIL MARKETING TOOLKIT, WHAT WOULD THEY BE?

1. A clean email list, rid of old and unresponsive names

2. Compelling content

3. Robust reporting so you can understand your programs

WHAT'S THE SINGLE BIGGEST MISTAKE YOU SEE PEOPLE MAKE IN EMAIL MARKETING?

Clinging to old names for the sake of boasting a larger email file. If they're not responding, drop them, but not before learning WHY they're not responding.

WHAT ADVICE WOULD YOU GIVE TO PEOPLE WHO ARE LOOKING TO RUN SUCCESSFUL EMAIL MARKETING CAMPAIGNS?

Keep it simple. One idea at a time. When you include too many items in an email, you're going to lose a lot of eyeballs. Find one good reason to send them the email and focus on that.

HOW DO YOU THINK EMAIL MARKETING WILL CHANGE OVER THE NEXT FEW YEARS?

Email is getting more and more regulated and harder to get into personal inboxes. Because of this, the ones that you are getting into are going to be very activated. Take care of those readers and your overall list will grow. When you aim for the field, you'll miss the target.

LEARN MORE ABOUT JOE

I've been in the Email Marketing field for over fifteen years. I've worked with all aspects of email programs, from editorial to HTML to list management, and I've seen every angle of the industry. In my free time, I run the *Joe on Joe* podcast, and I'm happily married with two dogs in Los Angeles.

WWW.LINKEDIN.COM/IN/JOE-SLEPSKI-5A46A85
@JOEONJOEPOD

KYLE HENDERICK

SR. DIRECTOR OF CLIENT SERVICES, YES LIFECYCLE MARKETING

HOW DO YOU DETERMINE THE EFFECTIVENESS OF AN EMAIL MARKETING CAMPAIGN?

I research industry and past program benchmarks by audience segment and campaign type to establish a baseline for future measurement. For every campaign, I look at the following in this order: revenue (or conversion), customer retention, user experience, and engagement metrics. My recommendation is to look at each of these areas individually and allow it to tell its own story in effectiveness. Whether it be a success or failure, there are learnings that will fuel future program growth. One of my favorite client case studies is a design enhancement that on the surface appeared to lower email-attributed revenue and engagement. However, after digging deeper into the data, it turned out that the design's user experience enhancement led to customers in the test group spending twice the amount of money in comparison to the control group!

WHAT IS THE SINGLE MOST EFFECTIVE EMAIL MARKETING TACTIC YOU'VE LEARNED?

Review EVERY piece of data you are collecting and figure out how to use as much as you can. Currently, many marketers are STILL scared of using data for personalization or segmentation due to the potential "inaccuracy" of it. In my experience, the results of using new data in these scenarios tend to win out nine out of ten times and break even in the "failure" moments. As an added benefit, the customer complaints/failure moments that come in help you prioritize cleaning up your data. It's a win/win.

IF YOU COULD CARRY ONLY FIVE TOOLS IN YOUR EMAIL MARKETING TOOLKIT, WHAT WOULD THEY BE?

1.   Email service provider with segmentation and analytics—uploading

lists is painful, and not being able to report on specific audiences is even more so.

2. Deliverability inboxing—if emails are not hitting the inbox at a minimum percent, KPIs will suffer.

3. Responsive template/render checking—mobile devices and ISPs like Gmail, Yahoo, and Hotmail keep evolving. KPIs are hurt if email design becomes flawed, especially with the growing mobile audience.

4. QA Checklist—a wrong image, alt text, or link could lead to a catastrophic loss in performance.

5. Click Map—emails are more scrollable than ever, so the ability to understand which pieces of content drive website traffic is important.

WHAT'S THE SINGLE BIGGEST MISTAKE YOU SEE PEOPLE MAKE IN EMAIL MARKETING?

I'm a big fan of the English-adapted version of a quote by Voltaire: "Perfect is the enemy of good." In my experience, innovation slows and programs suffer when fear of imperfection is prevalent. Don't let perfectionism slow down progress; fail fast and course correct to ensure you're driving innovation.

WHAT ADVICE WOULD YOU GIVE TO PEOPLE WHO ARE LOOKING TO RUN SUCCESSFUL EMAIL MARKETING CAMPAIGNS?

It takes discipline to test. Every campaign should be testing something. Whether it is confirming what you believe or testing into something new, with the aggressive change in consumer, every campaign should have a percent of the audience dedicated to testing a new idea or reconfirming an old one.

HOW DO YOU THINK EMAIL MARKETING WILL CHANGE OVER THE NEXT FEW YEARS?

Email will continue to bridge the gap from inbox to website experience, overtaking more of the interactivity and purchase process—replacing website behavior. It has the potential to become the primary key for identifying the handle of the person behind it, with its only competition being the mobile phone number.

LEARN MORE ABOUT KYLE

I'm Sr. Director of Client Services at Yes Lifecycle Marketing, a solution provider who delivers relevant communications across all channels for mid and enterprise-sized companies. I'm responsible for helping major clients implement new programs, processes, and data-driven strategies to create campaigns that truly drive revenue. I have a passion for technology implementation and a background in database, email, web, and social media marketing. When I'm not being a marketing nerd, I enjoy traveling, trying any food that does not include raw onions, and wearing my heart on my sleeve for any & all Chicago-based sports teams. And yes, that means rooting for BOTH the Sox and Cubs!

WWW.LINKEDIN.COM/IN/KYLEHENDERICK
@KHENDERICK

GEOFF ANDERSON

EMAIL MARKETING MANAGER, COLUMBIA COLLEGE CHICAGO;
CEO/FOUNDER, GLIMMER APP

HOW DO YOU DETERMINE THE EFFECTIVENESS OF AN EMAIL MARKETING CAMPAIGN?

The standard metrics include delivery rate, open rate, click-through rates, revenue per email, and conversion rates. Personally, I like to dig a little deeper to measure engagement. In both higher ed and tech, I find it necessary to create individual landing pages for all of my campaigns and incorporate Google Analytics to track user behavior. By using all of these metrics, we can examine how the user interacted with the campaign from start to finish, from opening the email to time spent on the landing page to conversion.

WHAT IS THE SINGLE MOST EFFECTIVE EMAIL MARKETING TACTIC YOU'VE LEARNED?

The most effective thing—and this goes for all marketing—is telling a story about your brand, connecting that with your product, and connecting everything back to your customer. With Email Marketing, this means knowing who your core audience is and building a narrative through evocative, personalized images and clever, concise copy. Some of the best email campaigns I've seen have begun with piquing the recipient's curiosity in the subject line and then delivering a powerful image.

IF YOU COULD CARRY ONLY FIVE TOOLS IN YOUR EMAIL MARKETING TOOLKIT, WHAT WOULD THEY BE?

Your imagination, first and foremost. Sure, your product could be a bachelor's degree in film or a specialized social application, like mine are, but why are those important and what makes what you are offering different or better than your competition? Get creative. The other things that are important: being able to say more with less, a familiarity with minimalist design, gorgeous photography, and a clean list of clients.

WHAT'S THE SINGLE BIGGEST MISTAKE YOU SEE PEOPLE MAKE IN EMAIL MARKETING?

It's tough to pick one: (1) Not delivering on your promise. This means using a subject line that is irrelevant to your product or brand. (2) Too much copy. Keep your campaigns as short and simple as possible. The average person receives 121 business emails each day, not to mention hundreds of personal emails. That means competition is fierce and attention is scarce. Make it count!

WHAT ADVICE WOULD YOU GIVE TO PEOPLE WHO ARE LOOKING TO RUN SUCCESSFUL EMAIL MARKETING CAMPAIGNS?

Make sure you have all the necessary tools in place to track your campaigns from start to finish. You can improve your current performance only if you know what mistakes are being made. The more specific you get in targeting your audience, the better the results will be. This means segmentation. Finally, integrate all of your social channels into your campaigns. I can't stress how helpful this can be in building an audience. Your hard work shouldn't go unnoticed, and chances are your audience will want to share it with others they think will enjoy it or find it useful. Nothing is more cheaper, faster, or more persuasive than social sharing. It's difficult to control, but if your work is honest, thoughtful, and different, your chances are that much greater.

HOW DO YOU THINK EMAIL MARKETING WILL CHANGE OVER THE NEXT FEW YEARS?

I think we are absolutely going to see more video integrated into email. Many email service providers do not currently support video content, which makes its use risky. However, the power of video is undeniable, so look for a lot of the email giants to start to allow this capability and then witness another shift in the power of Email Marketing. I also think we will continue to see a rise in personalized and interactive design or malleable microsites. When users are receiving targeted campaigns based on their prior behavior and are afforded the ability to interact with campaigns inside of their inbox, purchases become faster and easier.

LEARN MORE ABOUT GEOFF

I have over a decade of experience as a digital marketing specialist. I have worked in several industries from entertainment to nonprofits. Currently, I am Email Marketing Manager at Columbia College Chicago, with a focus on strategy. In addition, I am the co-founder of the Glimmer App, available for free download in both the Google Play and App stores. Launched in January 2017, Glimmer is the first social and dating application designed to be inclusive for people with disabilities. To date, we have tens of thousands of downloads from all parts of the world and have been featured in Buzzfeed, *The Chicago Tribune*, Newsy, Fox32 Chicago, and more.

⊕ WWW.GLIMMERINDUSTRIES.COM
🔲 WWW.LINKEDIN.COM/IN/GEOFF-ANDERSON-MBA-25307921
🟦 WWW.FACEBOOK.COM/GLIMMERLIFEAPP

WILHELM ONG

EMAIL MARKETING MANAGER

HOW DO YOU DETERMINE THE EFFECTIVENESS OF AN EMAIL MARKETING CAMPAIGN?

An effective Email Marketing campaign is determined based on performance metrics—specifically opens, unsubscribes, and most important, clicks. Regardless of your industry, your goal should always be focused on driving customers to click your email. Opens and unsubscribes are important indicators of a customer's interest; however, clicks are a truer sign of overall customer engagement.

WHAT IS THE SINGLE MOST EFFECTIVE EMAIL MARKETING TACTIC YOU'VE LEARNED?

Testing is one of the most effective tactics I've learned in Email Marketing. Whether you decide to test your "From" name or address, subject line and body copy (content, length), image, CTA button placement, email design/layout (long vs. short), or date/time of email send (morning vs. evening), testing provides valuable data to make informed decisions that will allow you to improve future email campaigns.

IF YOU COULD CARRY ONLY FIVE TOOLS IN YOUR EMAIL MARKETING TOOLKIT, WHAT WOULD THEY BE?

If I could carry only five tools in my Email Marketing toolkit, it would include the following: Litmus to run email quality assurance and make sure an email is rendering properly across all major email service providers. Sublime Text to edit and review email HTML. Adobe Creative Cloud (formerly Adobe Creative Suite) to edit and review email creative assets and files. G Suite and Trello to organize, manage, and record email operational tasks related to specific campaigns.

WHAT'S THE SINGLE BIGGEST MISTAKE YOU SEE PEOPLE MAKE IN EMAIL MARKETING?

The single biggest mistake that I see people make in Email Marketing is their lack of testing campaigns. Email trends do exist, but that does not necessarily mean it applies to all companies and industries. What may work for one company may not necessarily work for the other. Companies should constantly test to gather valuable data in order to have a better understanding of their audience. The more contextual and relevant the email is to your customer, the better.

WHAT ADVICE WOULD YOU GIVE TO PEOPLE WHO ARE LOOKING TO RUN SUCCESSFUL EMAIL MARKETING CAMPAIGNS?

Always look at the bigger picture, not just the individual campaign. Remember, trust has been built between a company and its customer. It is the company's responsibility to deliver engaging and relevant content. If a customer unsubscribes from an email, the opportunity to communicate is lost.

HOW DO YOU THINK EMAIL MARKETING WILL CHANGE OVER THE NEXT FEW YEARS?

In an age of short attention spans and the rise of virtual reality, voice assistants, and mobile technology, I think Email Marketing will become more visual and interactive in the next few years. Customers may be able to interact with their inbox through motion or touch, like click and drag or click and preview for mobile devices and virtual reality or by command for voice assistants. Companies may be forced to design emails around these up and coming channels.

LEARN MORE ABOUT WILHELM

I currently reside in the city of Oakland, California. For the last year, I've been working at Twitter as an Email Marketing Manager, where I manage consumer-facing email campaigns from start to finish. Aside from my professional experience, I enjoy taking photos and drinking an occasional craft beer, and I have an unusual obsession with green onions.

- WWW.LINKEDIN.COM/IN/WILHELMONG
- @WLHLMNG
- @WILHELMONG

BRETT SWENSEN

EMAIL & MARKETING AUTOMATION, PURPLE

HOW DO YOU DETERMINE THE EFFECTIVENESS OF AN EMAIL MARKETING CAMPAIGN?

I think this depends on the end goal of your business. For me it comes down to overall revenue most of the time, but I also look at smaller metrics of each email (unique open rate, CTR, unsubscribes) to determine how successful it was. I also measure the success of people moving to the next part of the funnel so I can understand whether customers are taking the path I anticipated or perhaps another path I hadn't thought about.

WHAT IS THE SINGLE MOST EFFECTIVE EMAIL MARKETING TACTIC YOU'VE LEARNED?

Understanding the buyer's journey and marketing funnel and being able to capture how people move through that funnel is by far the most important thing to learn. It allows you to understand when and where to insert yourself and deliver a personalized piece of content.

IF YOU COULD CARRY ONLY FIVE TOOLS IN YOUR EMAIL MARKETING TOOLKIT, WHAT WOULD THEY BE?

Marketing automation platform, email list scrubber, analytics software, Photoshop, and access to freelancers.

WHAT'S THE SINGLE BIGGEST MISTAKE YOU SEE PEOPLE MAKE IN EMAIL MARKETING?

Most of the time, I see brands interacting with their audience as if they were all the same. People want to feel like they're unique and that you know them. It's important to know how they've interacted with you in the past and then pick up where they left off. I think most brands are too lazy to set up the proper data sources, and if they do, they don't know what to do with the data.

WHAT ADVICE WOULD YOU GIVE TO PEOPLE WHO ARE LOOKING TO RUN SUCCESSFUL EMAIL MARKETING CAMPAIGNS?

Make sure you understand your audience thoroughly and personalize each touch you have with them as much as you can. Invest in learning about them and gathering the data. You'll see a much higher success rate if you can speak to the specific needs of your audience.

HOW DO YOU THINK EMAIL MARKETING WILL CHANGE OVER THE NEXT FEW YEARS?

I think email and marketing automation will continue to become more personal, and I believe consumers will demand it. Brands that don't continue to connect all of their customers' touch points will struggle. Email will also become more and more interactive and engaging. Those that can keep up will see large amounts of success and customer retention.

LEARN MORE ABOUT BRETT

I've been in marketing for over ten years. I love getting my hands dirty and building out and implementing automated marketing strategies. I'm a data nerd and a highly analytical marketer. I consult part-time and would love to chat about helping your business grow.

✉ BRETTSWENSEN1@GMAIL.COM
in WWW.LINKEDIN.COM/IN/BRETTSWENSEN

MEGAN ROBINSON

VP MARKETING, @REVENUE

HOW DO YOU DETERMINE THE EFFECTIVENESS OF AN EMAIL MARKETING CAMPAIGN?

For any marketing campaign, the first level is reach (how many eyeballs you are getting). For email, this will be determined by your list size. The second measure of effectiveness is how and when your audience is engaging in the communication. For Email Marketing, I look at this as two levels of engagement: the first is your open rate (what percentage of the audience opens the email), and the second is your click-through rates (the percentage of your audience that is clicking on an opened email). If your audience is opening your message, great. If they are clicking through, even better! A click-through shows that your message is relevant, interesting, and important to the reader. True campaign effectiveness depends on your campaign goals. What exactly are your primary and secondary goals of the email campaign? The reason for sending the email will determine what and how you measure campaign success. An effective email campaign is measured by the ability of your company to see those desired outcomes.

WHAT IS THE SINGLE MOST EFFECTIVE EMAIL MARKETING TACTIC YOU'VE LEARNED?

A/B subject line testing is the best way to immediately improve your campaign. This is when you send a percentage of your audience two different subject lines. After a predetermined time (around four hours), the subject line that received the highest open rate within the test group will be sent to the remaining audience. For example, let's say you have ten thousand people on your list. You want to do a subject line test to 30 percent of the audience. This means that your email will go out at 10:00 a.m. to three thousand people; fifteen hundred of them will receive subject line A and fifteen hundred will receive subject line B. At around 2:00 p.m., subject line A has an open rate of 25 percent, and subject line B has an open rate of 20 percent. The remaining seven thousand emails will go out with subject line A. Subject line testing is great to quickly and efficiently optimize your email.

IF YOU COULD CARRY ONLY FIVE TOOLS IN YOUR EMAIL MARKETING TOOLKIT, WHAT WOULD THEY BE?

An Email Marketing platform—I love MailChimp because it is compatible with many of the other tools you choose and their A/B testing is fantastic. Beyond MailChimp, there are a ton of other email service providers to choose from. Just make sure that it works with your other digital tools. A good Customer Relationship Management (CRM) tool)—a proper CRM is not an Excel document or the contacts in your inbox; it is a platform that you can use to take robust notes, monitor follow up, and set clear next steps and reminders for yourself. A strong website lead capture form—if you have prospects visiting your site, it is important to do what you can to capture that interest and lead. Zapier—connecting your digital tools seamlessly removes many headaches and adds time to your day. Google Analytics—since email is an engagement catalyst directing traffic to the website, the more you know about the actions that take place on the website, the better you can understand your ROI. This is true for all digital tools that drive traffic to your website since that is where most of the action takes place.

WHAT'S THE SINGLE BIGGEST MISTAKE YOU SEE PEOPLE MAKE IN EMAIL MARKETING?

If you want to see email engagement increase, you have to have a strong call-to-action to encourage and measure that engagement. For those starting out with Email Marketing, they fail to think about the reader's journey and connect the immediate message with the next steps. Give people a reason to take the next step and make it clear what the next step is. The whole point of the email is to trigger an action, so make sure they take it. Most people are busy, they aren't paying attention, and they don't particularly care about you and your business. For marketing to be effective, you have to meet your audience where they are. Give them the information that is important to them and spell out exactly what to do.

WHAT ADVICE WOULD YOU GIVE TO PEOPLE WHO ARE LOOKING TO RUN SUCCESSFUL EMAIL MARKETING CAMPAIGNS?

Know your audience and what they care about. Email is a one-to-one communication, so you need to be able to connect with the individual. Why should they care about what you have to say? What makes your message important and therefore stand out? Often businesses want to shout at their audience and tell them why they are so cool/hip/helpful/awesome. When in reality, everyone is so focused on themselves, they don't care. If you aren't careful, your message will get lost in a crowded inbox.

HOW DO YOU THINK EMAIL MARKETING WILL CHANGE OVER THE NEXT FEW YEARS?

Increased automation—triggered emails are automated because of a specific action or event. These messages are more relevant because of the trigger and therefore more effective. What and how these are triggered will continue to evolve and get more specific and robust. Sophisticated functionality—GIFs, videos, and even microsites within the inbox will continue to grow and develop. Hyper targeting—similar to increased automation, the more relevant you can become with your audience, the better chance you have of connecting with them. Make sure to keep your targeting in balance and don't target ten people for the sake of it.

LEARN MORE ABOUT MEGAN

I am the VP of Marketing for @revenue, a sales and marketing collaborative. We create systems, strategies, and tools that drive leads, sales, and growth. I lead a team of marketing thought leaders and experts to create the messages that stick where your target audience is looking. We also offer sales coaching and training so your business can close on all their new leads.

🌐 WWW.ATREVENUE.COM
✉ MEGAN@ATREVENUE.COM

LEAH MIRANDA

EMAIL DEVELOPER AND DESIGNER

HOW DO YOU DETERMINE THE EFFECTIVENESS OF AN EMAIL MARKETING CAMPAIGN?

The effectiveness of any email campaign always starts with setting clear KPIs. Each campaign should have its own unique goals; the more complex the campaign, the more detailed your goals should be. Common key performance indicators are open rates, click-through rates, and unsubscribes. Each should be tracked and reviewed for all emails, big and small. For larger email nurturing campaigns, one of the most important KPIs is long-term engagement. A campaign is successful if your customers move through the email series, engage with your content, and ultimately convert.

WHAT IS THE SINGLE MOST EFFECTIVE EMAIL MARKETING TACTIC YOU'VE LEARNED?

One of the best tactics, and frankly least utilized, is preview text. All email marketers are chasing that white whale—that elusive subject line that will provoke their customers to open, read, and engage with every bit of content in their email. So they spend hours going through data, articles, and copy, but fail to utilize the 35 to 140 characters in the preview text. Take a moment and look at your inbox. How many emails do you see that read "View email in browser"? Take advantage of this area to further encourage and inform your clients as to why they should open your email.

To utilize preview text you'll need to create and insert a <div style="display: none; max-height: 0px; overflow: hidden;">Preview Text here</div>. Depending on your preview text character length and ESP, it's best to insert whitespace with a zero-width non-joining (‌) and a non-breaking space ( ) div, that looks like this: <div style="display: none; max-height: 0px; overflow: hidden;"> ‌ ‌ ‌ ‌ &zwn-

j; ‌ ‌ ‌ ‌ &zwn-j; ‌ ‌ ‌ ‌ &zwn-j; ‌ ‌ ‌ ‌ &zwn-j; ‌ ‌ ‌ ‌ </div>. This added whitespace ensures that your carefully crafted preview text is the only thing your customers will see.

IF YOU COULD CARRY ONLY FIVE TOOLS IN YOUR EMAIL MARKETING TOOLKIT, WHAT WOULD THEY BE?

The five most important items in my Email Marketing toolkit are:

1. ReallyGoodEmails.com. Creating emails everyday is awesome, but falling into a design or coding rut is a real danger. Really Good Emails is one of the best places to find beautifully designed and coded emails from all industries. As a bonus, many emails have live preview or CodePen links.

2. Brackets.io. There are many text editors, and every day it seems like a new shiny one comes out. I highly recommend finding one and sticking with it. Brackets is a free, simple, and powerful text editor. There are tons of great extensions; the must-haves are Emmet, an HTML and CSS extension to cut down on your typing and increase your workflow, and Beautify, a quick way to format your tables.

3. Litmus. Litmus is a must-have for all email marketers. It provides a myriad of services from text editor, spam tester, analytics and so much more. This online tool was built for and by seasoned email developers and marketers.

4. Email Geeks Slack channel. Email Geeks Slack community is where over twelve hundred email developers, designers, and marketers share code and talk about the wonders (and frustrations) of email.

5. Check-before-sending list. Being an email marketer means you'll make beautiful emails and some really cringeworthy mistakes. Keep a list of things that go wrong and add them to your "check-before-sending" list. As your list grows, it means you're becoming a better email marketer.

WHAT'S THE SINGLE BIGGEST MISTAKE YOU SEE PEOPLE MAKE IN EMAIL MARKETING?

A big mistake that many email teams make is designing only for the ESP they're currently using. For example, if you're coding only for Outlook and your customers are all using Apple Mail, Gmail, or another provider, then you are missing out on utilizing advanced coding and design tactics (e.g., interactive email and animated gifs). If you're not coding emails to look good on all email clients, you're providing a poor user experience for your customers. This could be the difference between a sale and an unsubscribe.

WHAT ADVICE WOULD YOU GIVE TO PEOPLE WHO ARE LOOKING TO RUN SUCCESSFUL EMAIL MARKETING CAMPAIGNS?

To run a truly successful campaign, you need to start with the data. Dirty data will result in sending inappropriate content to clients or customers. Ensure that your email lists are clean and properly segmented; this is especially important when you are inheriting lists. Never make assumptions about your data. Once your lists are clean and properly segmented, ensure you have all your tracking and analytic tools set up properly. Running a successful campaign means you're able to show the efficacy of your efforts. Create your campaign parameters using Campaign URL Builder and ensure any analytic tracking codes are added to your HTML templates.

HOW DO YOU THINK EMAIL MARKETING WILL CHANGE OVER THE NEXT FEW YEARS?

As an email developer, you often hear, "Your code is stuck in the 90s" or "No one uses email; it's dead." And lucky for us, it's just not true. While yes, we are still using <tables> to build emails, that's only one part of our coding and possibilities. As the big ESPs (Outlook, Gmail, Apple Mail, and others) continue to update, we will create new and better ways to communicate with our customers.

One of the biggest areas for growth and development is personalization. Many companies are personalizing emails with first names; it's just the tip of the iceberg. More and more companies will start introducing and using dynamic content to take personalization from "Hello, Leah," to delivering dynamic content specially designed to their customers' interests in real time.

LEARN MORE ABOUT LEAH

I'm a Nashville-based email developer and designer, by way of Hawaii and Minnesota (yes, I know, not a combination I'd put together, either, but it worked). I fell in love with coding when an in-house web developer showed me how to code an unordered list. Over a decade later and more cups of coffee than I can count, I still love coding emails. Have a question or just want to talk about email? Let me know.

in WWW.LINKEDIN.COM/IN/LEAHMIRANDA

@FIDGETCODER

ROBERT LEE MULLOWNEY III

EMAIL MARKETING AND AUTOMATION

HOW DO YOU DETERMINE THE EFFECTIVENESS OF A EMAIL MARKETING CAMPAIGN?

By setting well defined goals prior to starting work on a campaign. If you reach or come close to those goals, we have an idea on the effectiveness and success of the campaign.

WHAT IS THE SINGLE MOST EFFECTIVE EMAIL MARKETING TACTIC YOU'VE LEARNED?

Daily scrum-type meetings to ensure all team members are on the same page for progress in each campaign we are working on.

IF YOU COULD CARRY ONLY FIVE TOOLS IN YOUR EMAIL MARKETING TOOLKIT, WHAT WOULD THEY BE?

A/B testing, Scrum meetings, Litmus to confirm template look and feel in majority of browsers and clients, some type of project management tool, responsive design coding, and the ability to diplomatically say "no" more often.

WHAT'S THE SINGLE BIGGEST MISTAKE YOU SEE PEOPLE MAKE IN EMAIL MARKETING?

Ineffective and unclear communication on a project or campaigns goals.

WHAT ADVICE WOULD YOU GIVE TO PEOPLE WHO ARE LOOKING TO RUN SUCCESSFUL EMAIL MARKETING CAMPAIGNS?

To me, a successful campaign does not hinge on one person, but a village. Communication with all members is key so that the team knows why we are doing this, where we stand right now, and what our success was in reaching our goals.

HOW DO YOU THINK EMAIL MARKETING WILL CHANGE OVER THE NEXT FEW YEARS?

Deeper personalization and timing to each individual. With mobile technology becoming more sophisticated year over year, I see personalized communication with marketing getting to the point of walking into a store or an office and being marketed for that site right there and then.

LEARN MORE ABOUT ROBERT

I started out as an executive chef/food scientist but have been involved in Email Marketing since 2003, so I have seen it all. I have worked with and for major enterprise companies and smaller start-ups. It never gets old.

in WWW.LINKEDIN.COM/IN/ROBERTMULLOWNEYIII

JEFF HOGARD

WEB DEVELOPER, DIGITAL MARKETING SPECIALIST

HOW DO YOU DETERMINE THE EFFECTIVENESS OF AN EMAIL MARKETING CAMPAIGN?

By tracking email opens, link click-throughs, and site visits.

WHAT IS THE SINGLE MOST EFFECTIVE EMAIL MARKETING TACTIC YOU'VE LEARNED?

Targeted Relevance. Seriously, keeping track of customer data and targeting them with offers and events that are tied to what they are shown to be interested in is a VERY effective way to market products and services. Learn about what your customers want!

IF YOU COULD CARRY ONLY FIVE TOOLS IN YOUR EMAIL MARKETING TOOLKIT, WHAT WOULD THEY BE?

A good email service platform: GetResponse, Oracle/Responsys, ActiveCampaign, and the like. A robust customer database. Notepad++ or TextMate (any good text editing program with highlight and search features for quick fixing code issues). Activity tracking software (SaaS) and a laptop.

WHAT'S THE SINGLE BIGGEST MISTAKE YOU SEE PEOPLE MAKE IN EMAIL MARKETING?

Too much touching. You should gather data on activity of your site or service before sending out campaigns. Too many times, there are blanket promotions that just aren't general enough to be appealing or relevant to everyone. Rather than touching all your customers and potential customers with unwanted or useless contacts and communications, target them more specifically or concentrate on more generally appealing offers. Don't try to turn an ordering error from your supplier into a fake, hyped-up promotion. If you didn't want four thousand umbrellas during a drought, neither will your customers, and it makes you look stupid.

WHAT ADVICE WOULD YOU GIVE TO PEOPLE WHO ARE LOOKING TO RUN SUCCESSFUL EMAIL MARKETING CAMPAIGNS?

Target your customers. Offer solutions to their problems, not sales. People who buy drills don't want a drill; they need to put a hole in something. Make their life easier, and they'll make your job easier. Too many businesses and business people forget that the customer IS the business.

HOW DO YOU THINK EMAIL MARKETING WILL CHANGE OVER THE NEXT FEW YEARS?

I think we'll see much more targeted and relevant advertising and (hopefully) less spam and fewer unsolicited ads. I also see more and more successes in branching out into other areas (e.g., social, mobile, in-app ads) I think this will continue, and I foresee an expanding library of SaaS programs for collecting and acting on real-time consumer data.

LEARN MORE ABOUT JEFF

I have been an active freelance web designer, web developer, and marketing enthusiast for almost two decades. I am obsessed with making the online experience more enjoyable and useful wherever I can.

PHOEBE KING

COPYWRITING PRO

HOW DO YOU DETERMINE THE EFFECTIVENESS OF AN EMAIL MARKETING CAMPAIGN?

Metrics are an important indicator of Email Marketing campaign effectiveness (e.g., open rate, click-through rate, conversion rate, bounce rate, A/B testing, engagement rate). Most Email Marketing software, such as MailChimp and AWeber, have these analytics built in and will interface with Google Analytics, another important tool. You should always measure new campaigns against a control.

WHAT IS THE SINGLE MOST EFFECTIVE EMAIL MARKETING TACTIC YOU'VE LEARNED?

There are so many tactics that go into creating an effective Email Marketing campaign, such as a strong landing page, compelling calls-to-action, and the maintenance of the subscription list, that it's difficult to choose just one. Overall, I'd say subject lines are critical. If you can't get your prospect to open the email, what's the point of all the work you put into everything else?

IF YOU COULD CARRY ONLY FIVE TOOLS IN YOUR EMAIL MARKETING TOOLKIT, WHAT WOULD THEY BE?

1. MailChimp for the small to medium-sized business as my Email Marketing software.
2. Pardot for the large enterprise, which interfaces with Salesforce.
3. Google Analytics is a crucial metrics tool.
4. I use Google as my primary search engine every day.
5. Microsoft Excel is still the best tool I know of for tracking results over time. HubSpot also provides a useful template to keep track of campaigns over time.

WHAT'S THE SINGLE BIGGEST MISTAKE YOU SEE PEOPLE MAKE IN EMAIL MARKETING?

Crappy or misleading subject lines will kill a campaign faster than anything. For example, I received an email recently from a huge inbound marketing brand. The subject line, "3 emails that work on the c-suite," did not match the content. I actually searched through the email for anything that fit the description of the subject line. Nothing. It affected their credibility.

WHAT ADVICE WOULD YOU GIVE TO PEOPLE WHO ARE LOOKING TO RUN SUCCESSFUL EMAIL MARKETING CAMPAIGNS?

Know your audience and segment your list based on metrics. Make sure your content is impeccable and that you update your lists regularly. Spend a lot of time on your subject lines and measure results regularly.

HOW DO YOU THINK EMAIL MARKETING WILL CHANGE OVER THE NEXT FEW YEARS?

Video is encroaching on Email Marketing, but I believe well-written/designed campaigns that include graphics will continue to tantalize prospects.

LEARN MORE ABOUT PHOEBE

I help my clients, primarily in the B2B space, generate leads/revenue by delivering expert copywriting, content marketing, and other digital marketing services, including SEO, with proven quantitative expertise using standard digital metrics (e.g., Google Analytics, WordPress). I produce outstanding content (e.g., blog posts, white papers, case studies, feature profiles) and design effective Email Marketing campaigns. I have won clients' praise for my collaborative attitude, attention to detail, and adherence to deadlines.

🌐 PHOEBEKING.NET
✉ PHOEBEKING@ATT.NET
in WWW.LINKEDIN.COM/IN/PHOEBEKING
🐦 @ISTWRITECHOICE

MARISA AMORASAK

EMAIL PRODUCT MANAGER, SHOPRUNNER

HOW DO YOU DETERMINE THE EFFECTIVENESS OF AN EMAIL MARKETING CAMPAIGN?

I think it's important to build emails with a success metric in mind—it will act as a guiding light for a lot of decisions that you'll need to make on audience criteria, creative, etc. When I started out in Email Marketing, I worked at a couple of small companies and start-ups that just didn't have the data power to attribute dollars to emails, and so the success metric was often open rate or click rate. That makes sense when you've got no other options, but now I know that high opens or clicks don't necessarily correlate with conversions. Testing with a holdout group is also key to measuring the success of an email campaign. Make sure you've got large enough populations for statistical significance and send your campaign to one group and not another. I like to use 50 percent holdouts when running a campaign that's way outside the norm and a 3 percent holdout on all campaigns to measure long-term impact. And don't forget to randomize your test groups!

WHAT IS THE SINGLE MOST EFFECTIVE EMAIL MARKETING TACTIC YOU'VE LEARNED?

Launching high-impact journeys that leverage data about your audience is a way better use of your time than cranking out frequent, mediocre emails. The workload of an email manager is large; when you're frazzled, it's easy to get caught up in the day-to-day deadlines of a campaign calendar. It's so important to make time to think big-picture about what will really move the needle. And in my experience, that's using data to speak to people in a way that's relevant and personalized to them over a long period of time.

IF YOU COULD CARRY ONLY FIVE TOOLS IN YOUR EMAIL MARKETING TOOLKIT, WHAT WOULD THEY BE?

Some knowledge of all of these: HTML/CSS, data structures, copywriting, user testing, and Photoshop. Wear all of the hats and you can create an email program from start to finish.

WHAT'S THE SINGLE BIGGEST MISTAKE YOU SEE PEOPLE MAKE IN EMAIL MARKETING?

The biggest mistake that I see people making about email is the idea that the more emails you send, the better. You should treat your database like a prized possession—these are people who are (hopefully) opted in with their eyes and ears open for your messaging. So don't barrage them with irrelevancies. They'll just end up unsubscribing—or worse, ignoring you while subscribed.

WHAT ADVICE WOULD YOU GIVE TO PEOPLE WHO ARE LOOKING TO RUN SUCCESSFUL EMAIL MARKETING CAMPAIGNS?

QA like crazy, but never by yourself.

HOW DO YOU THINK EMAIL MARKETING WILL CHANGE OVER THE NEXT FEW YEARS?

I think the term "personalization" makes some email marketers cringe at this point, since it's such a vague buzzword. That said . . . if you're not using personalization in your email program, you're not setting it up for success. Use dynamic content, drip campaigns, journeys, and trigger emails; use every bit of personalization ability that your team and your email platform can do.

Secondly, we know that companies are becoming more socially integrated with their customers. As that happens, I expect these companies to better position their products around solving customer problems and addressing recurring customer themes. And with that, I look forward to user research playing a bigger role in email. In most of my past roles, the user research team was either nonexistent or very siloed from email. That doesn't make sense. At ShopRunner, we put email prototypes in front of real people and basically ask them to give us the real deal. Their qualitative feedback is priceless.

LEARN MORE ABOUT MARISA

I've worked in marketing for about seven years, and most of those years I've specialized in Email Marketing and automation. At ShopRunner, I'm doing email through a product lens, which has been equal parts challenging and invigorating. I know best practices, but I also like to challenge and refine them through testing. I like doing the platform work and getting my hands dirty and also attending trainings and conferences to stay current. I can code—HTML, CSS, R, simple ESP languages—which makes me a little more technical than the average email marketer. Essentially, I make emails happen end to end. Also, pressing "send" still terrifies me.

✉ MARISA.AMORASAK@GMAIL.COM
🔗 WWW.LINKEDIN.COM/IN/MARISA-AMORASAK-9835A3IA

CONCLUSION

You've made it to the end of *Digital Marketers Sound Off*!

My hope is that your head is swimming with new digital marketing tactics, tools you want to try, and ideas for optimizations for your own campaigns.

Chances are there were a few contributors' insights that really stood out to you. Wouldn't it be cool if you could get in touch with them and pick their brain? Wait, you can!

One of the reasons I had the contributors include a bio, contact info, and social media links in this book is that I hope you, the reader, connect with them directly.

Drop your favorite contributors a tweet or LinkedIn message or email them and start a conversation. You'll be surprised how open and helpful people can be if you're genuinely looking for guidance or recommendations.

Feel free to connect with me on social media and ask me questions about the book. Or let me know if you're interested in contributing to future editions of this book.

Lastly, if you're running digital marketing campaigns and need a little extra help, reach out to the contributors to this book! These people know what they're doing, and many of the contributors either own or work for digital marketing agencies. Many take on freelance work.

Finally, I hope this book inspires you to think differently about digital marketing. Our industry is constantly shifting and evolving. Stay curious, keep testing, and never stop questioning and improving.

Happy marketing!

MATT CHIERA

ABOUT THE AUTHOR

Matt Chiera is Founder of Ice Nine Online, a Chicago-based digital agency by day and market research lab by night. Over the past ten years, Matt has worked on diverse, highly technical digital projects like PPC account restructures for Fortune 500 companies, building custom company Intranets, manual SEO audits on websites with more than fifteen thousand pages, and building an effective online presence for a brand in under a week.

Some of the most rewarding work Matt has done is related to training people about digital marketing. He enjoys sharing his experiences with clients, students, and colleagues so that they have a better understanding of digital marketing and the digital ecosystem for their business.

Matt is a Chicago native, residing in Chicago's north side with his wife, and is an avid runner and traveler. If you're planning a trip—especially to Japan—reach out to him for recommendations. Matt also blogs about restaurants and food at MattsTaste.com.

Matt welcomes new connections and would be thrilled if you connected with him on social media.

⊕ WWW.ICENINEONLINE.COM
🔗 WWW.LINKEDIN.COM/IN/MATTCHIERA
🐦 @MATTHEWCHIERA

Made in the
USA
Monee, IL